Paul Cézanne

About the Author

JEANNETTE ANGELL grew up in Angers, France. She earned academic degrees at the Université Catholique de l'Ouest and Lesley College for undergraduate work, and Yale University and Boston University for her master's and doctorate-level studies. For three years she led a dual life as a lecturer by day, callgirl by night. She eventually left both academia and the escort business, and since that time has worked exclusively as a writer. Her novels include *Légende, Wings, Flight,* and *The Illusionist*. She lives in Boston with her husband and two cats, and is working on a mystery series.

CALLGIRL

Confessions of an Ivy League Lady of Pleasure

JEANNETTE ANGELL

Perennial Currents
An Imprint of HarperCollins*Publishers*

A hardcover edition of this book was published in 2004 by the Permanent Press. It is reprinted here by arrangement with the Permanent Press.

HarperCollins books may be purchased for educational, business, or sales promotional use. For information please write: Special Markets Department, HarperCollins Publishers Inc., 10 East 53rd Street, New York, NY 10022.

First Perennial Currents edition published 2005.

Library of Congress Cataloging-in-Publication Data

Angell, Jeannette L.
    Callgirl / Jeannette Angell.
        p. cm.
    Originally published: Sag Harbor, N.Y. : Permanent Press, 2004.
    ISBN 0-06-073605-4
    1. Angell, Jeannette L.   2. Novelists, American—20th century—Biography.   3. Women college teachers—United States—Biography.   4. Prostitutes—United States—Biography.   5. Prostitution—Massachusetts—Boston.   6. Boston (Mass.)—Social conditions. I. Title: Callgirl.   II. Title

    PS3551.N4595Z464 2005
    813'.54—dc22
    [B]   2004060073

05 06 07 08 09 RRD 10 9 8 7 6 5 4 3 2

The author would like to thank many people who cannot be named here, mostly and especially Peach, as well as the women she employed, for providing so much help in writing this book.

I'd also like to thank my husband, who is my first editor and who lifted this book (and all my books) far above the level at which it started. He is smarter than I'll ever hope to be and far more creative than he thinks he is.

Many thanks to my agent, Philip Spitzer, who really did make this book better (sending it back to me for revision after revision after revision!), and who patiently submitted it to a lot of publishers before finding it a home. Thanks also to Lukas Ortiz for doing a lot of hand-holding throughout the process. And, finally, thanks to Martin and Judith Shepard of *The Permanent Press,* for believing in *Callgirl* when others wouldn't.

Introduction

People ask so many questions about it. You did that? You're kidding, right? How did you start? What's it really like? What kinds of people use the service? What kind of girls work for it?

Men, especially, are utterly fascinated by the subject. They want to talk about it, they ask the same questions over and over, they can't get enough information. It's like getting a glimpse into some mysterious semi-forbidden world, a world caricatured by pornography and attacked by conservatives and speculated about by just about everybody. Men get a vicarious sexual *frisson* thinking about it. Women wonder what it would be like to have someone pay – and pay well – for something they routinely give away for another kind of currency.

And, inescapably, people look at me and get a little scared. I could be – I am – one of them. I am their sister, their neighbor, their girlfriend. I'm nobody's idea of what a whore looks like. Maybe that's why I'm scary.

They want callgirls to be different, identifiable. That keeps them safe.

But the reality, of course, is that usually we're not. Oh, the girls on the streets at night, yeah, with them, you know. But to be honest, those girls scare the shit out of me. I was out one night with Peach and we locked the car doors when we drove past them, and we're *supposedly* in the same business. The truth is, we have nothing in common.

But callgirls – women who work for escort services, especially expensive ones, especially those run by other women – we don't look any different than anyone else. Not even always prettier. So we're scary: because, you know, we could be you, too.

Maybe we are.

* * * * * *

I hate using literature to refer to television, but I have to here. These days I regularly watch a program called *The West Wing*, an intelligent, witty, politically-aware and humanely sensitive weekly

5

drama. I'm impressed with the characters, with their thoughtfulness and their dedication.

Yet in an early episode, a character articulates to a callgirl the same assumptions that appear to be virtually universal: that she has no ethics to speak of, that she would do anything for money, that she, essentially, *is* her profession. And that her profession is nothing to be proud of.

Who else among us would tolerate such an assumption?

Please hear this. Callgirls have ethics. We make decisions like everybody else does, based on our own religious and/or moral convictions. We are Democrats, Republicans, Independents, Socialists, and Libertarians. Some of us are kind to small animals. We are neither sex-obsessed nor nymphomaniacal. We have relationships, we build trust, and we keep secrets. We are daughters, sisters, and mothers; we are wives.

The reality is that men need us. And they don't want to need us. So they blame us for it. It's why Muslim women have to be hidden from men – it's their fault, apparently, that the men feel tempted by them. It's why "hookers" are amoral – because their job is to cater to that which is amoral in all of us.

So – try to put all of that aside. All your assumptions, all your conditioning. For just a little while, free yourself of your guilt, your prejudices, your judgments. Then you can hear my story.

* * * * * *

In 1995 I had just received my doctorate in social anthropology and was anticipating full-time, tenure-track employment at some recognized institution of higher learning. What I got, instead, was a series of lecturer positions, because most universities were no longer offering professorships, or offering very few. It was, after all, the nineties, and grants and other resources weren't stretching as far as they once had. I was willing to keep at it, however, because it was my chosen profession. It was my vocation.

When I started working for an escort service I was teaching classes on a semester-by-semester basis, being paid – at the end of the semester – the less-than-princely sum (before taxes) of thirteen hundred dollars per class.

The woman I have called Peach ran an agency that could be considered a mid-level escort service. Let's see: how can I explain it?

She didn't get the rock stars when they came to town, but she did get their entourages. She got people who owned companies, but not necessarily companies anyone had ever heard of. She got people with condos at the Four Seasons, but not at the old Custom House. She never got clients who wanted a quick blowjob in the car; but she also rarely got the clients who wanted to take the girl to the Bahamas with them for a week, either.

Peach ran ads looking for employees, and hers stood out from others in that she required a minimum of some college education. The fact is that she helped pay off a whole lot of graduate student loans. She had a specialty niche: she did well with clients who wanted intelligent conversation along with their sex. She inspired loyalty in both her callgirls and her clients, and she tried to be fair to everyone.

Her clients were university faculty, stockbrokers, and lawyers. They were underworld characters who offered to "fix" problems for her and computer geeks who couldn't tell a C-cup from a C-drive. They owned restaurants, nightclubs, and health spas. They were handicapped, busy, socially inept, about to be married. They saw girls in offices, restaurants, boats, and their own marriage beds, in seedy motels in strip malls and at suites in the Park Plaza Hotel. They were the most invisible, unremarkable group of men in Boston, having in common only that they could afford to spend two hundred dollars for an hour of company.

They used the time for which they paid in a variety of ways, and that is my usual response when someone – and someone *will*, inevitably, in any conversation about the profession – says something judgmental about the perceived degradation of exchanging sex for money. Because, in my experience, that doesn't make sense.

You think I'm just manipulating semantics here, don't you? I'm not: hear me out, and you'll see that it's not mere spin. Many people in a number of professions are paid by the hour, right? Employers hire consultants, for example, on the basis of certain areas of expertise that the consultant can offer, and that the employer wants to have, use, leverage, whatever. The employer – or client – pays for the consultant's time by the hour. The consultant performs certain pre-arranged and mutually agreed-upon tasks for the client during that time.

The consultant is using his expertise and experience to create something for the client; he is not "selling" his expertise. He is a

7

skilled professional possessing an area of knowledge for which there is a demand and for which the client is willing to pay a pre-determined rate per hour. What he is selling, in point of fact, is his time. He keeps the expertise; the client keeps the product; but the hours put into the project are gone.

A callgirl is a consultant, using her expertise and experience in seduction and giving pleasure to fulfill a verbal contract with a client who is paying her by the hour to complete an agreed-upon project. She is a skilled professional possessing an area of knowledge for which there is a demand, and for which the client is willing to pay her a pre-determined rate per hour. She is using her expertise and experience to create something for the client; she is not "selling" her expertise, or the tools that she uses to implement her work.

If there's such a gulf between these two people, if there is more degradation in one than in the other, I'd like to have you explain it to me, because frankly I don't see it.

I have women friends who are waitstaff, waitstaff in so-called sophisticated restaurants on Newbury Street and Columbus Avenue and on the waterfront, and I'm sorry, but I would *never* put up with what they have to endure every night. Not for any amount of money.

Speaking of the money, it's a pretty good hourly rate. Remember that what we get, we don't have to share with anybody – no state or federal tax, no social security. I take that back: it's a damned good hourly rate.

Occasionally there is no sex. Lonely men sometimes are just looking for company, for someone to listen to them: that's worth the fee. I remember an early scene in *Frankie and Johnny*, when Al Pacino, newly released from prison, hires a woman to "spoon" with him – allow him to fall asleep curled into the curve of her body, her arms around him. I always found that scene incredibly touching.

Some clients use the time for public appearances at restaurants or concerts, either because they genuinely want company for these activities, or because they want to show off their ability to date a pretty girl. Some clients mistake us for therapists and use the time to talk, to have someone listen to them, to their problems, to their emptiness.

However, the reality is that most clients do want sex. Some want it quickly and efficiently, after which the girl is free to go; others want it as part of a date-like interlude and argue if they think they've received a minute less than they paid for. And there's every imaginable situation in between.

* * * * * *

I've changed all the names in this book, except my own, for a number of reasons that I'm sure you can appreciate. But it's not-make-believe. These people are real. I am real. This all happened, in Boston, in the mid to late nineties. Promise.

So . . . are you one of the curious, the inquiring minds who want to know? Do you want to know what we think, how we feel, who we are?

Then welcome to my world.

Chapter One

"Mind the gap . . . Mind the gap!" I was standing on a subway platform in London, in the Underground, listening to a disembodied voice telling me in the tones of a not-too-friendly nanny to watch my step. I appreciated the concern, if not its delivery.

So I stood there dutifully minding the gap, and I thought about the newspaper advertisement folded into the shoulder bag I carried. It felt conspicuous, as though everyone else on the train platform could tell exactly what was in there, and what it said.

I had picked up the *Phoenix* just before leaving Boston, on an impulse that wasn't really an impulse but was disguised as one anyway. My impulses usually are. I was in London for a week, lecturing at the London School of Economics, and my mind wasn't exactly on my work.

It should have been, of course. It was an honor and a privilege to be here, and my professional life shouldn't be impacted just because I was having problems in my personal life. But that's the way that it always works, isn't it? You think you can separate it all out, put your life into neat little compartments where nothing overlaps with anything else. You think that, and you're wrong.

My personal life was screaming for attention. Loudly. I needed money. I needed a lot of money, and I needed it quickly.

I needed the money because Peter, my most recent boyfriend, had not only decided to fly to San Francisco to meet up with some ex (whom he had been fucking behind my back the whole time we were together, as it turned out), but had also emptied my checking account before leaving. A prince among men.

Rent was due. The decimated bank account had held all the money I had to live on until the end of the semester. That was when the two community colleges where I taught sociology elective classes would be paying me. I had to live within those parameters, with budgets planned well in advance and no extra or surprise expenses allowed.

Peter's desertion decidedly qualified as a surprise expense.

In any case, the end of the semester was two months off. Which was why I needed a lot of cash.

I dealt with the crisis in my usual way. I spent one night getting very drunk and feeling very sorry for myself, and I got up the next morning, did what I could to deal with my hangover, and made a list. I love lists, I always have. Lists give me the illusion of being in control. I listed every possible way I could get the money I needed.

It was a depressingly short list.

The one thing I was not going to do was ask for assistance in any way. Not from my family and not from the Commonwealth of Massachusetts. I had been the one to make the bad judgment call, it made no sense to ask anyone else to pay for my mistakes. So even though I had written down the words "government assistance" on my list, I ignored them and moved on.

I frowned at the remaining items, crossed off "childcare," both since I'm really incompetent with children and also the pay was too low to make much of a difference, and frowned again at what was left.

I was going to have to try *one* of these options. I didn't have a lot of choices left. I took a deep breath, and I went to work.

I called a number I had found in some campus newspaper, BU or Northeastern or something, the ubiquitous one we've all seen, the one that is looking for people to sit in cubicles and respond to 900 calls. Talk sex, convince them that you're hot for them, that sort of thing.

Well, the rat bastard boyfriend *had* told me that I had a sexy voice, so I figured it was worth a try. I'd only do it this once, of course.

I clearly hadn't given the idea enough thought, because I was totally unprepared for the sleaziness of my interview. I hadn't imagined ahead of time the really scary visuals: the rows of tiny cubicles, with women sitting in them wearing headsets and talking; they never stopped talking. Lights were flashing on their phones. Mostly they were middle-aged, with sagging flesh and garish makeup and an air of indifference that might have been cruel if it hadn't felt so hopeless.

And I hadn't visualized the way-too-young greasy guy with way too many piercings who never even looked at me as he squeezed words out past a toothpick sticking to his lower lip. His eyes didn't leave the skin magazine he was thumbing through. "Okay, honey. Eight bucks an hour, two calls minimum."

"What does that mean, two calls minimum? Two calls an hour?"

That earned me a glance. I couldn't tell if it was amusement or pity. "Two calls minimum at a *time*."

I stared at him. "You mean keep two different people on the phone . . .?"

"Yeah, that's right." He sounded bored beyond belief. "If one of 'em wants you to be a Ukrainian gymnast and the other wants you to be a tattooed lesbian, you go with it. Time's money. Want the job?"

I was still stuck imagining the reactions of the clients when you got them mixed up. It was indescribable. Sure. For eight dollars an hour. This could happen.

So I gave up, tore up the list, and panicked again for a while about the money thing. The bills kept coming in, as they have a habit of doing: time stops for no bankruptcy. I could read the official-looking print through the rusted gap in my mailbox: computer-generated, thin envelopes. Some had a strip of red around the edges. No need to open them. I knew what they said.

Suitably enough, one of the classes I was teaching was a sociology elective called *On Death and Dying*. Suitably, of course, because I was accompanying it with such dark thoughts. I would break the class into discussion groups and stare over their heads out the window and feel that cold claw of fear somewhere in my stomach. One of those weeks we talked about suicide.

It didn't sound like such an impossible option.

And then, slowly at first, my thoughts kept going back to the newspaper. I sometimes looked in the *After Dark* section of the

Phoenix, even after I decided that I couldn't possibly be both a Ukrainian gymnast and a tattooed lesbian, and I wasn't stopping anymore at the 900 number ads.

The next pages, the ones after the telephone lines, were for the escort services.

I'd look, and then I'd shut the paper and let my cat Scuzzy sleep on it while I pretended that it wasn't there, and corrected student essays instead. And yet . . . and yet.

Why not?

Was it such an impossible idea? Did I really want to add an extra fifty hours a week to my schedule, working at a Borders bookstore or a Starbucks coffeehouse for just over minimum wage? Those were the next options on the list, after all. I'd even interviewed. Borders said I could start any time.

It was around then that a voice in my head started speaking up. It sounded suspiciously like my mother's voice, and the voice was not happy at all about the direction my thoughts were taking. It was interesting that the voice hadn't spoken up when I looked into the 900 number sex-on-the-phone idea, but that was another issue altogether. The voice was certainly going into overtime now.

Just wait, I said to the voice. Hold on a moment. Let's think about this. You can sit in a cubicle and pretend to be having sex with two (or more, as seemed to be the assumption) men at once, keeping them on the phone for as long as you can, and having the same conversations twenty or thirty or forty times a night. Or you can do the real thing. Once a night. For a hell of a lot more than eight dollars.

And what's the difference? Honestly?

There's a *huge* difference, the voice responded. It sounded exasperated, as my mother's had when I was disagreeing with her on a moral question. Okay, I said, trying to be open: but why? Where *do* you draw the line? Why is one thing semi-acceptable and the other not at all? You wouldn't exchange sex for five dollars; I'll accept that. But, let's see: would you for five hundred? For five thousand? For five million? Ah, yes, that's a different question, isn't it? So, as Churchill once said, now we know what you are, we just have to determine your price.

The voice had fallen oddly silent. I couldn't blame it: it's hard to talk back to Churchill.

Later on, when I got to know some of the other callgirls, I asked

12

them the same question. Why is having casual sex with a man you pick up in a singles bar considered acceptable, but having sex as a business proposition is not? Which is more ethical? Marie said that what decided her to start working for the service was the moment she stopped and really thought about how many men she had allowed to put their penises inside her, men who later made her skin crawl with disgust – and that for no money at all.

It gives you pause, it really does.

I had let the rat bastard boyfriend touch me, kiss me, fuck me. Now the mere thought of his dick, his hands, his tongue made me feel queasy, dirty somehow.

And in the end, as it turned out, *I* had paid *him*.

So I picked up the *Phoenix* on my way to Logan and England, and I sat in the student dormitory that was all I could afford for the week I was lecturing there, and I opened the *After Dark* section and read the ads.

I circled one.

* * * * * *

Peach was brisk when we spoke on the telephone. "You can refuse any call if you don't like the sound of the guy, or how it feels," she said. "You can say no to anything that he asks for that you don't want to do, and I'll back you up. The only thing you can't do is steal clients."

"Steal clients?" I must have sounded blank.

"Yeah, slip them your phone number, make a deal with them. Arrange to see them without going through the service. They try it all the time. I've got the regulars pretty much whipped, but they'll always try it with a new girl."

It had never occurred to me to steal clients. The whole point of going through an agency, I had thought, was so that I would be protected by that agency. Okay, so I was still pretty naïve at that point.

She had a little canned, obviously well-rehearsed speech. I tried to take it all in. This business is a crapshoot, sometimes it's okay, sometimes less so. You've never done this before? That's good: they like that. They like to think that they're the first. Remember: you can say no to anything. One hour exactly. I get sixty dollars, you get the rest. Tips are all yours, but don't get too excited; the eighties are over. No one tips anymore. So why don't you try it out, just one call? Just give me your description and I'll send you out, after that you can decide whether it's something that you want to do again or not.

I could have sworn that somewhere in the narrative she stifled a yawn.

I was far from yawning, myself. I answered with some trepidation, but apparently they were the right answers; apparently I passed whatever internal test to which I was being subjected. There was the briefest of pauses when I had finished. "Hmm. All right. I'll have you see Bruce tonight. I know he'll like you."

"Tonight?" For all my eagerness, that seemed very soon. Too real, too fast. Panic set in. "Peach, I'm not dressed up –" I was wearing jeans and a t-shirt, with a black vest and an olive linen jacket over it. Not my image of how a callgirl should dress. (Like I knew anything: I had seen *Half Moon Street* and *Pretty Woman* and that was about it. What you might call a limited frame of reference.)

Besides, how I was dressed was not the only issue here. "You see, I had hoped to meet you in person before I started," I said. You know, like a real interview.

"That's not necessary," she said, her voice brisk. "You can't lie about your description, the guy you see will tell me the truth. I don't need to see you first."

"I want you to," I said, thinking that I was sounding petulant and not knowing what to do about it. I had wanted to come across as – oh, say, at least marginally sophisticated. "I mean, there's no problem, I look young, I look good, but . . ." My voice trailed off. Now I was definitely sounding lame. Great interview. Articulate as hell. Try that on one of your classes someday.

Her voice changed subtly. Later, when I got to know Peach, I recognized the slight shift in manner and attitude: the nursery nanny whose charges aren't following directions. Obedience and agreement are expected. Don't tell me you're going to be difficult. "A lot of different women work here," she said. "Our clients have all sorts of tastes. I'm already thinking of one or two who I think you'd enjoy; one's a surgeon, the other is a musician. They're guys who want to talk, guys who'll appreciate you, who don't just want a quick visit." She was being careful, I realized, not to use the s-word, not to be any more specific than she had to be. "I think you'll enjoy spending time with them." Come on, now, children, playtime is over, listen to Nanny.

I said, trying not to sound stubborn or defensive, "I still want to meet you first. I want you to see me. I want to be sure."

Peach was dismissive. "There's no sense in meeting unless you find you like the work, unless you want to keep doing it. And don't worry – you're dressed perfectly. A lot of the clients go for casual. So do it, or not. You decide. Call me at seven, if you want, and I'll set it up."

And that was that. Do it, or not.

I decided to do it.

She was as good as her word. When I called her back she was full of information, delivered at the staccato speed of a submachine gun, and I found myself scribbling on the back of an envelope from my jacket pocket. "His name is Bruce, his number is 555-4629. Your name is Tia – isn't that what you said you wanted to be called? Anyway, you're twenty-six, you weigh 125 pounds, thirty-six, twenty-six, thirty-five. C-cup bra. You're a student. Call him, and then call me back after you've talked to him."

Did she always tell her employees what they were supposed to look like? I wondered. I didn't ask, though, and later found out that, indeed, Peach tailored the precise description to what the client was looking for. Within reasonable bounds, of course. Now, however, I was just reacting to the speed of it all. I said, slowly, "Peach, I called you to say that I want to try it. How did you get me a client so quickly?"

She laughed. "I had a feeling that you'd say yes. And I always call Bruce when I have a new girl on. Now call him. Do you remember everything I told you?"

Barely. That was a lot of data, I thought, staring at the envelope. A lot of data that I had never thought about actually articulating to anybody. I remembered a line from *Half Moon Street*: "Don't worry, I'm naked underneath!"

Apparently these were guys who didn't want to take that on faith.

Well, okay. I didn't have any idea what my real measurements were, but those sounded as good as any. I took a deep breath. This was it. I was really doing this.

Bruce asked me to go through the statistics again, but he seemed pleasant enough (I had been expecting stuttering, maybe?) and gave me directions to Revere. To a marina. He lived, it transpired, on a boat.

He was a bear of a man, bearded, with eyes that twinkled behind his glasses. We sat on a small sofa in the cabin of his sailboat, drank a very nice chilled Montrachet, and talked about music, our conversation interspersed with clumsy silences. It felt oddly familiar, as if . . . well, to tell you the truth, what it felt like was a date. A first date. A blind date.

An extremely awkward one.

He got up to refill our wineglasses and when he came back he did the little classic pretend yawn and stretch that is a favorite move from everybody's first junior high romance; but at that moment I leaned forward to pick up my glass and so he missed. Oops.

I hadn't done it all that well in junior high, either, come to think of it.

He cleared his throat. "Do you mind if I put my arm around you?"

I was bemused. Did I mind? Um – well, no. I came here for you to fuck me, you're paying two hundred dollars an hour to fuck me, I don't expect I should balk at you putting your arm around me . . . I looked at him, unable for a moment to respond. He really meant it. It was endearing beyond belief.

I'd imagined a lot of things, back in London. I'd imagined even more since then, sitting alone in the whirlpool at my gym and thinking about what I was about to do. I'd imagined a lot of pretty unimaginable things, to tell the truth. What I could never have imagined was this polite awkward guy asking my permission to put his arm around me.

"That would be nice," I managed to say, and a moment later he kissed me.

Definitely a first date kiss.

I returned it with some enthusiasm, moving my arms up his shoulders and around his neck and drawing him deeper, closer to me, opening my mouth to his and gently sliding my tongue against his teeth.

And it was at that precise moment that I knew it was going to be all right. This wasn't anything esoteric or bizarre or dangerous: this was something I had done before, something I did well, and – best of all – something I enjoyed doing.

He slid his hand up under my t-shirt, raising my bra, and then he was touching my breasts, playing with the nipples as they hardened in response, still with his mouth crushed against mine. I moaned slightly and pressed my body closer to his, and I could feel his heartbeat accelerating, hear his breath coming faster. We pulled away from each other, slightly, responding to some inner common impulse, and his eyes met mine. "You're beautiful," he said.

"Thank you," I whispered, tracing the shape of his lips with my fingertip.

He cleared his throat. "Would you – can we go in the bedroom?"

I knew just what to say; this was easy, after all. I could do this in my sleep, on automatic pilot. I didn't even have to think about anything. It couldn't have felt more natural. "Yes, please," I said, keeping a sense of controlled eagerness in my voice.

The bedroom wasn't far. We were, after all, on a boat.

I had taken the precaution of buying condoms on my way over. Now I hesitated before following him, ostensibly finishing the wine in my glass, and I slipped one from my handbag into my jeans pocket. Nice work. Unobtrusive as hell. Hey, what do you want, I'm new at this.

And it was still feeling like a first date.

The room was illuminated only by the open door to the living space. I could see a bed and little else. It didn't matter; the bed was really all that we needed. I slid out of my jacket and vest, pulled off my t-shirt and bra. I did it slowly, as seductively as I could manage, unhooking the bra behind me and letting it drop to the floor. Bruce was watching me. "You're beautiful," he breathed again, and I smiled and extended a hand to him, suddenly confident of my power, of my attraction. "Come here," I said, my voice as low and husky as I could make it.

Marlene Dietrich, eat your heart out.

We ended up sitting on the bed, next to each other, kissing deeply. Later, I learned that some callgirls won't kiss, that they consider their lips the only part of themselves that they can withhold. Even now, I disagree. Maybe the pretense of romance is better than no romance at all. Or maybe I just like to kiss.

He pushed me back on the bed, gently, his head going down to my breast, his mouth on my nipples. I leaned my head back and closed my eyes.

I had thought it was going to be terrible. I was still dealing with the confusion of it being – if anything – pleasant.

I was struggling with the buttons on his flannel shirt, pulling at them, my own breath sounding ragged. I pulled the sides of the shirt apart, ran my hands against his chest, up to his neck, pulling him up to kiss me again, more demanding this time, murmuring something as I did.

There was a moment of awkwardness with the jeans, both his and mine, and then they were off and we were lying next to each other, our hands groping, our bodies pressing together. I could feel his cock hard against my leg, and I sighed again as my fingers crept down and touched it; I could feel the excitement pulsing through it, through him.

He was kissing my neck, running his tongue along my collarbone, his hand holding my breast. I stroked his cock, gently, firmly, feeling all of his body straining against me. I moaned softly, my fingertips light on him, his inner thighs, his curly hair, his cock, his balls. I felt myself getting wet, felt my pelvis straining to be closer to him, and it was he who, to my surprise, pulled himself up on an elbow. "Do you have any protection with you?"

Wow. Either this was the nicest man in Boston, or else Peach really did have him trained. "In my pocket," I said, gesturing at the clothes on the floor.

"Do you mind?" He picked my jeans out of the pile and handed them to me, immediately going back to kissing my neck. I fumbled for the condom package, and he took it from me.

I sat up then and leaned down to touch his cock with my lips. Yeah, I know, I know, you shouldn't do anything without protection, what can I say, he wasn't all that close to coming, and I was trying to show him that I liked him. Even then, I was thinking about repeat business.

I was already understanding, if only at an intuitive level, the credo of every callgirl. Regular clients are our bread and butter, the reason that we can keep doing what we do. Finding someone like Bruce and making sure that he asks for us, over and over again.

I hadn't thought about how Peach had gotten him so easily for me, for my first night. Later, I found out that she had an arrangement with Bruce, that he saw new callgirls. Instead of him calling her, she called him. Everybody won: Bruce got the thrill of initiating a first-timer, the girl got an easy call. At the time, however, I was just feeling lucky, feeling like this wasn't going to be so awful and tedious a job, after all.

All the questions – is it wrong to like my work? Am I supposed to hate working for a service? – came later. At that moment, I was just glad that I could do it, that it wasn't unpleasant, and that I was good at it.

I licked up and down his cock while he opened the condom package. He paused from time to time to pull my hair back from my face so that he could watch me, watch his cock sliding in and out of my mouth, between my lips, and he sighed. "God, you're good."

I moved back so that he could slip on the condom. He kissed me while he was doing it, our tongues touching; he was still sighing with pleasure. And then I was leaning back on the bed and he was on top of me, his big body over mine, his hardness sliding inside me, and I opened my legs to him, wrapped my legs around him to pull him in deeper, and he sighed again, even louder.

I kissed his neck as he started to thrust inside me, and then I gripped his shoulders and took his thrusts, his cock big and hard inside me, his beard rough against my cheek. At one point I thought I heard him say "Tia." I wasn't quite sure, but I said "Bruce," and that seemed to please him. He moaned again and thrust even harder.

I could feel us both sweating, even though it was only March, and I had been chilly when I got there. The portholes were open, but it wasn't the lack of air that was making me so hot, making us so hot together. I slid my hands up over the hair on his chest as he continued to move inside me, and tightened my hands around his shoulders again – they almost slipped off from his sweat.

He came suddenly, just as I was grabbing his hair and pulling his face down to kiss me again. He groaned and his whole body shuddered; I pulled him against me and held him tightly. "I'm here, baby," I whispered. "I'm here."

Can I tell you this now? It was better sex than I'd had with the rat bastard boyfriend. Ever. And – best of all – I was getting paid for it.

And it got better. There was none of the postcoital abruptness I usually associate with one-night stands. He rolled off me and pulled me over to him, my head on his chest, listening to the thudding of his heart. I continued to caress him, gently, my fingertips playing lightly over his chest. I blew gently on the sweat, and he shivered and tightened his arm around me. Better, on the whole, than any other one-night encounter I'd ever had.

Bruce disappeared into the bathroom and was dressed first, but had wine waiting when I emerged from the bedroom, and he kissed my cheek as he handed it to me.

The telephone rang. He picked it up, said, "Yeah, Tia's here, hang on a minute," and passed the receiver over to me. "For you."

I was puzzled. "Hello?"

It was Peach. "All set?"

"Yes." I had no idea what she meant.

"Okay, good, call me when you get out." She must have sensed that I didn't understand. She sighed. "I always call when the hour's up. Some guys play games. Sometimes they try to make you stay longer. He pays for your time, and I make sure that he gets what he paid for. And that you get out safely, that you're not stuck or stranded or anything like that. So leave now, and call me from a pay phone."

"Okay." I handed the telephone back to Bruce. He obviously knew the drill: he had the money in his hand already. Say goodnight, Gracie. "I really liked meeting you, Tia."

I smiled as I slid the bills into my jacket pocket. "It was nice meeting you, too, Bruce. I hope I can see you again."

"I'd like that a lot." He even sounded like he meant it.

He escorted me off the gangway, kissed me again on the cheek, gave me a brief hug. "Good-night."

"Good-night, Bruce." And I walked away toward my car; I felt like singing, or skipping, something joyous and happy. I had just spent a pleasant evening. After I took out the sixty dollars that was Peach's fee, I had made one hundred and forty dollars. In one hour.

Anybody else out there making that kind of money?

I called her from the first pay phone I spotted; she asked politely how it had gone, and wished me a good night.

I hung up the telephone and was struck by an incongruous thought. I remembered sitting in that whirlpool at the health club, and feeling grateful that I had the lifetime membership (a gift, ironically enough, from my mother), so that I would always be able to go

20

there. I was grateful that they were open late at night. I remembered sitting there and thinking, when I start working, I'll come and sit here and let all the bad feelings soak away with these bubbles. I'll use this place to feel clean again.

I was smiling broadly as I got back in my car to drive home. There was nothing that I needed to cleanse myself from. What bad feelings?

I slept really well that night. No nightmares, no waking up sweating with the panic pressing in on me, no knots in my stomach. I was gainfully employed. I even wrote a check to the electric company.

This was going to work. And I wasn't even shocked that there weren't any bad feelings at all.

Chapter Two

The next day dawned, as next days inevitably–and depressingly–do. I had showered when I got home, and did it again out of habit before getting dressed and heading out for class. I dressed in community college attire, which (per my definition, anyway) means professional enough to be able to be distinguished from the students and not so formal as to make people think that one is taking oneself too seriously. In the world of academia, community colleges are certainly not to be taken too seriously. That's unfortunate and not even very accurate; but wasn't it Lenin who said that perception is reality? It's where a lot of people start – and where a lot of people finish up, too.

I didn't want to think about that.

I was fortunate in my *Death and Dying* class. It was being offered as a partnership agreement between the college and a local hospital, and was largely populated by registered nurses going back to school to acquire a B.S.N. So there was not only a lot of motivation among the students, there was also a lot of expertise. I was talking about death: my students were people who dealt with it every time they went to work. It was more than a little humbling.

That first morning after working for Peach, though, I have to admit that I wasn't feeling particularly humble. I was feeling high.

That day we were talking about death and war. It was one of my favorite classes on the syllabus, because there was so much material with which to challenge the students. I didn't want to tell them whether war was right or wrong; I wanted to challenge their perceptions and help them come to their own conclusions. Or their own confusion. Either was acceptable.

I read two poems aloud – Edna St. Vincent Millay's "The Conscientious Objector," and Randall Jarrell's "Losses," both of them highly emotional, exquisitely beautiful, and extremely challenging. I read the poems as I always did, not really reading but reciting them by heart. I was watching the class, looking for reactions that I could use in the discussion that was going to follow. And then, suddenly, for a scary split second – it honestly was no more than that – I was back on the boat, sitting and sipping wine after getting dressed, having a packet of money pressed into my hand.

And I liked it. As though seeing it all in fast-motion, I stepped back from where I was standing, stepped out of my body and looked at myself, and I liked what I saw. I liked my professional competence, the fact that I was teaching something important and teaching it well. And I also liked the secret knowledge that the night before I had been paid to be sexy, beautiful, desirable. I liked both sides of myself. I liked them a lot.

I came back fast. Randall Jarrell's last words were echoing in the room. *"But the night I died I dreamed that I was dead/ And the cities said to me: "Why are you dying?/ We are satisfied, if you are: but why did I die?"*

I waited. Silence is my friend. It makes people uncomfortable, and so they talk to end the silence, often saying things that they might not say otherwise. Edna St. Vincent Millay's words echoed in the silence: *"I shall die; but that is all I shall do for death./ I am not on his payroll."* And I hadn't even given them the worst, this time around. Jarrell's "Death of the Ball-Turret Gunner" could empty the room. I'd done that one the first year I'd taught the class, and I think that a third of the students got sick. They looked it, anyway.

I waited. And in the silence, my own thoughts intruded.

These people, my students, listened to poetry that they fiercely believed had no place in their lives, simply because I had asked them to. I had built up a measure of trust with them over the weeks and months of this course so that I could ask them to listen to archaic words and find the truths spoken through them. They trusted me. I was an authority figure.

In fact, half of the class called me "Doctor." The authority figure to the fore. It was a little scary. What if I was too much of an authority figure to be sexy? What if I couldn't do another call for Peach? What if I went on a call and got rejected? What if Bruce had been an exception? What if I really was too old for all this? Would I end up remembering that first night and becoming bitter because I had glimpsed something that I wanted and couldn't have? Wouldn't it have been better, if that were to be the case, to never have started at all?

So when I called Peach later that afternoon, I told her once again – and somewhat more firmly – that I wanted to meet her in person.

She didn't like it. She fought it. As I would find out later, she never liked meeting any of the girls, not at first. Sometimes not ever. She always waited until she had already formed an opinion of them through the telephone, through reports from the clients. I never knew why. Maybe seeing them would make the whole endeavor too real to her. Maybe she could keep some distance as long as both her employees and her clients remained disembodied voices on the other end of a telephone line.

But the reality – the necessary reality of her job – was that she sent some girls, knowingly, into some pretty awful places, and some even more awful situations. She had to. As she said to me once, in a curiously unguarded moment, "Jen, if I ever really thought about it, I could never send anyone anywhere." I think that maybe her job was easier for her if she didn't have to visualize them, feel that she had really encountered them, acknowledged them as individuals. At the end of the phone, a girl could be a list of statistics and lies: her measurements, her height and weight, the color of her eyes, the length of her hair, her approximate age. Add an invented abbreviated history ("She's sweet, just moved here from Kansas to go to school,"), all the information adapted and re-adapted, tailored afresh for each client. And the clients were consistently (and, I thought at first, a little naïvely) surprised that Peach could meet their specifications so exactly.

A brief aside, a matter of mild interest: here's a fact: Men can't guess a woman's age. There has to be some brain cell in men that

23

doesn't activate, some deficit encoded in male DNA, this inability to look at a woman and make reasonable chronological conclusions about her. Or maybe it's just a result of intense sexual arousal, when, as we all know, only one head is fully functional. But in any case, they can't tell how old a woman is. Especially if she's already given them a number.

I was a few months away from turning thirty-four when I started working for the agency, but Peach's assistant Ellie immediately took care of that.

The day after my first call with Bruce, I spoke with Peach when I called to confirm that I was available that evening. As it turned out, Peach herself wasn't. "It's my night off, I'm going out," she said. "Don't worry, I told my assistant Ellie about you, she'll be talking to you shortly." It made me a little nervous, but I had psyched myself up – and my bank account was reminding me that it wasn't the moment yet to take a night off. Besides, if I chickened out now, I might never call again. I was on a roll. I had to take advantage of it.

Ellie was working the phones and called me around seven to take notes. She needed my general description, hopefully to connect it with a client's request; and she asked me my age. Her reaction was direct and no-nonsense. "No way. No one wants to see someone who's over thirty," she said. I tried to tell her the number didn't matter. I tried to explain that at work I was always mistaken for an undergraduate rather than a faculty member. I might have been thirty-three, but I didn't look it.

Apparently the number mattered to Ellie. "These guys have no idea what anything over thirty looks like, they're morons with only one thing in their little pea brains." Ellie, as I was to discover, had a cynical view of the clientele. And, come to think of it, of life, too. "Even twenty-eight, twenty-nine, that's pushing it, 'way old to them. I can't get you a call if I tell them you're thirty-three."

"Okay." I wasn't going to argue. She knew more about it than I did. New game, new rules, I was willing to learn. I later found out that Ellie, herself, had only just turned twenty.

She was still talking. "We'll say you're twenty-four, that way you can be in grad school, the intellectual thing is a turn-on for some of these guys. You'll be great with the smart ones; they're always asking for someone who's in school."

Worked for me. Got me a client that night, in fact, a soft-spoken engineer from New Delhi. And after that, Peach generally told clients that I was anything from twenty-two to twenty-nine, depending on who the guy was and what he wanted. I thought that twenty-two was a little over the top, but none of the men I saw ever questioned the veracity of what she said.

I have to say, though, that in spite of my confidence in my looks, I *was* a little spooked by the age issue. After all, the common perception of prostitutes is that they are young, even underage sometimes, the cheerleader sort. If they were of the *femme fatale* type, it was always on the Lolita end of the spectrum. I had seen *Pretty Woman*, okay? She was young, young enough to still be idealistic, as the movie was quick to point out. I'd also seen *Half Moon Street,* but it was careful to indicate that Sigourney Weaver's age and intelligence were the exception, that even her clients weren't initially sure she was what they wanted. Julia Roberts' character – young, hip, fast-talking, and sweet – was the conventional norm. The hooker with the heart of gold.

I was not young, hip, fast-talking, or sweet, and I had no illusions about the state of my heart. I wasn't going to fit into the mold. That made me uneasy. After Peter the Rat Bastard, I really didn't need another rejection.

The funny thing is that when I think about all the processing, all the thinking, all the planning that I did when I was starting out, there was never a moment when I doubted that I could do this. I sat in the dormitory in London staring at my notes for the following morning's lecture, and I felt nervous about how the lecture would go over in another culture, what sort of questions people would be asking me, that sort of thing. I sat there feeling nervous, and even then half of my brain was rehearsing the lecture and the other half was considering whether or not to become a prostitute. It was an odd juxtaposition, and yet I never for one moment wondered whether I *could*.

I just knew. I knew that I was pretty, but my confidence really didn't have a lot to do with that. It was more along the lines of knowing that I was powerful. I had had a succession of boyfriends – and, let's be honest here, girlfriends too – before the rat bastard, and they all claimed that I was the best lover they'd ever had. Well, okay, maybe you've heard that too, perhaps they were just saying what they thought I wanted to hear. I'm willing to consider the possibility. I'll grant you that they didn't all mean it.

But you *know* it when you're good at something, really good, you know it viscerally, in your muscles and your cells and your blood, at some non-rational and yet absolutely certain level. I knew I was good at sex, at romance, at seduction. It was something innate, something I didn't think about. When I was flirting with a man I went into automatic pilot. I just did. I didn't think. I flirted. And I always got him. Whomever I wanted, I got.

It was just my bad judgment that I had once wanted the rat bastard.

Once preliminaries were aside, I was confident of my power. I knew that once I had a man – any man – alone in a room with our clothes off, I would please him. I could make him crazy, make him ecstatic, make him want more and more and more. I knew that there is a certain sexiness about experience and education, that I had something to offer that the twenty-year-olds did not.

That was why I had circled Peach's ad in the first place. I had been dazed by the array of pictures of silicone-enhanced breasts and blonde women with pouting lips claiming, "I want you in my hot cunt now!" But there among them were the two advertisements that Peach ran. One was for the clients, and it was simple: "Avanti," it declared, in a medium-sized box with a lace border. "When you want more than just the ordinary."

Well, okay, so that could mean anything. But there wasn't any silicone, either, which had to be a good sign.

The other ad, presented on another page in the same typeface, was looking for help: "Part-time work available to complement your real life," it said; "Some college required." That was what got me. No one else mentioned college. This agency had clients who wanted education, clients who presumably wanted to talk intelligently with their escorts, who were looking for something beyond firm breasts and empty thoughts.

These were the clients I wanted to see, men who would view my graduate degrees as enhancing my sexuality rather than detracting from it. This was a possibility.

It was the only one I circled. I sometimes wonder what I would have done if it hadn't worked out. Would I have returned to the ads, found another one to try, one that was less offensive than the others? I don't know.

I took the paper with me to London and the name Avanti sat in the back of my brain while I talked to lecture-halls of students for four days.

I got home, and before I even unpacked I called Peach. And that was the day she sent me to see Bruce.

And so I found that there were people willing to see me – Bruce, the Indian engineer, a legislative aide from the state house; but I was still intensely unsure of my place in a youth-dominated profession. I pressed her again. Just to be sure that "the professor" could fit into her world, that Bruce and the others hadn't been total aberrations.

I guess that by then she figured I was worth the investment of her time. A few days after I saw the legislative aide, she agreed to meet. "All right. What about lunch on Thursday, Legal Seafoods at Copley, one o'clock?" Rapid decision, rapid planning; it was all so typical Peach.

My palms were sweating. "Okay, great, I'll be there."

I was there. She wasn't. She managed, in point of fact, to avoid me for a week. She didn't go to Legal Seafoods; when I called her at two she had some excuse about a sprained ankle. I, in the meantime, was overdressed even for a downtown mall in a short business suit, had been on my feet in uncomfortable heels for the past hour, and had spent that time nervously scrutinizing every woman who walked in the door in case it was Peach. I was exhausted.

She cancelled two more appointments with me, fortunately with somewhat more notice. I had already paid a teaching assistant I knew from graduate school to cover my class for one of the appointments. I really couldn't keep doing this, letting a potential job screw up what was, after all, my real career. And her choices of venue were never convenient: it was a fair commute to get downtown from my studio apartment in Allston, and then I needed time to find a place in the parking garage and time to locate the restaurant and start guessing which person could be her.

I was beginning to seriously think it wasn't going to happen. It was as though the time spent on the boat with Bruce had been nothing but an image, a snapshot, something so fleeting that it was hardly worthy of the memory. The Indian engineer that Ellie had sent me to see hadn't counted, not really: I had been with him for twenty minutes, tops, and I don't think that he looked at my face once. The guy at the State House had been more interested in the daring aspect of his act than in whom he was doing it with. So I didn't have a lot of experience to draw from.

At the same time, I was also slowly becoming obsessed with the concept of prostitution. My brief brush with it seemed to have sucked me into a well of curiosity – or was it just the researcher in me, the academic? I had started reading about prostitution and was constantly thinking about it.

But I couldn't even manage to meet with my own madam.

I finally was instructed to go to another Legal Seafoods, this one in the Prudential Mall, and I went, resigned to being blown off again. I didn't even bother dressing up; there seemed to be no point to it. I was wearing my usual at-home uniform of jeans, a sweatshirt, my Ryka sneakers.

I had a plan this time: I was going to wait fruitlessly for her, call her number and collect yet another improbable excuse, and then I was going to spend the afternoon at the Boston College library. I was dressed for it, rather than for her. This time I was prepared, and I had at least brought work to do while I was in town. I wasn't going to waste precious time that could be spent constructively. I had gotten a little jaded by then. I didn't believe for a moment that Peach would keep the appointment.

She did.

She was anything but what I expected. I had been eyeing the brittle, mannequin-like women one sees downtown in Boston, the products of hours spent in the spas and shops of Newbury Street. I assumed she would look like one of them, those women who wear clothes like a challenge, like an armor.

My friend Irene and I had sat once and giggled about them, feeling quite complacent in our assumed superiority. They fell into two categories, we'd decided. Some of them were wealthy non-working wives in from the suburbs for their weekly dosage of collagen, hairspray, and gossip, trying to convince themselves by this contact with the city that their lives in Andover or Acton or southern New Hampshire had meaning and beauty. The others were middle-management professionals, women from the banks and high-rise offices surrounding the Prudential. These women looked perfect because they had to; it was the unwritten agreement in their job descriptions. (Well, maybe it was the unwritten agreement in the suburban wives' job descriptions, too, for all I know.) They had less leisure, less time: they hurried into the mall at lunchtime to buy a birthday gift or a necklace to wear on their power-date after work.

We giggled about it, Irene and I; but there was truth in our observations. These were the women who *were* downtown Boston. And so of course I thought that Peach would look like them. You don't get any more "downtown" than a madam, after all.

God knows I had tried to imagine her. Peach's voice was light, but intense: she was a woman who made quick decisions and usually stood by them – until somebody like me made her change her mind. She had started her own business, and had run it for the past eight years; so perhaps the suits weren't so far off. But her business was seduction and pleasure: the softer fabrics of the women from North Andover and Manchester-by-the-Sea might be more her style. Which way would she go?

There was a voice at my elbow. "Jen? Are you Jen?"

I hadn't even seen her coming. She was my age, give or take a few years – she had to be, to have been in business that long, and have gone to school; it seemed obvious that anyone who required an education from her employees certainly had one herself. She had long thick red hair, a pale face, and tremendous green eyes. She would have looked as though she had just stepped out of a Burne-Jones painting were it not for her khakis and leather jacket. The pre-Raphaelites, if I remember correctly, favored ethereal white gauzy dresses instead.

I offered my hand, and she hesitated before shaking it. "Hi, yeah, I'm Jen, you must be Peach." Another scintillating remark brought to you by the professor.

"Let's go sit outside," Peach suggested. So much for lunch.

We sat on a concrete wall in the sun and wind, and she came right to the point. "Are you a police officer?"

I stared at her. "Um – no. That was why I called you . . ."

She was calm. "I just have to make sure. You are not a police officer?"

"No. Do I look like one?"

"Fine, then," she said, and we went on from there.

I wish that all of life could be that simple.

* * * * * *

Okay, so here is what you learn. The Gospel According to Peach. I don't know whether it's true or whether it's one of those cherished urban legends, one specific to activities outside the law. In any case, the common understanding is that if you ask a person if he or she is a police officer, and he or she answers "no," but in fact *is* a police officer, then any subsequent arrest won't stand up in court. It still sounds odd to me; but Peach knew her stuff, so I assume that she knew about that, too.

She wasn't one for small talk. She even had a canned speech for this part, too. "If you ever, ever have any suspicions or bad feelings about a client, don't do the call. There are a couple of ways out of it. If you think it might be a setup, ask if he's a police officer. If you really are suspicious, then say you think you left your keys in the car, you'll be right back, and just get out. If it can wait a few minutes, then when you call me to check in, ask me if your sister called."

I was bemused. "My sister wouldn't call you."

"Doesn't matter," she said impatiently. "It's a code. Hang up and tell the client that I heard from your sister whose husband is much worse, he's in the hospital, and you have to go. Say you're sorry, tell him to call me back, that I'll take care of him. And then leave. I'll talk with you before I take his call so I know what's going on. Never, ever do a call that doesn't feel right. Trust your instincts."

Think what you will, her system worked. No one from her agency ever was arrested, the whole time that I worked for her.

So we met, and she reassured me that I was attractive enough and young enough (at least in appearance) to make it in her profession, and I went home a little bemused and oddly self-confident. Months later, she would tell me that she had felt intimidated by me at that first meeting, that she saw me as clever, sophisticated, and educated and that scared her; but of course at that time I didn't know that. All that I was aware of then – blissfully – was that I had passed muster.

The reality, like it or not, is that we are all governed by the dictates of Madison Avenue, by the excesses of Hollywood. No matter how much we want to say that it isn't true, it is. If you say that you aren't influenced by Gap posters or twenty-something television programs, if you say that you never compare yourself to them and wonder in your heart of hearts whether you measure up, then I'm sorry: you're simply not telling the truth. *Newsweek* talks about youth culture as though it were a distant phenomenon, to be studied anthropologically; but I guarantee you that the reporters working on the study are concerned about belonging to the very group that they write about.

Take me. I had earned two master's degrees and a difficult doctorate. I was living independently and reasonably happily. I was embarking on a career that I had wanted desperately for all of my life. And yet, that afternoon, I got more pleasure out of the assurance that I was young enough, thin enough, pretty enough, seductive enough to be able to work for an escort service, to hold my own along with twenty-year olds, than I did out of all of my real, important accomplishments.

So maybe I'm not so smart after all.

* * * * * *

I didn't work that night after meeting Peach. I gave myself permission, instead, to invest in my new job, to fashion and create and slip into my new persona.

I went to my health club and stayed there for three hours, sweating and straining on the Stairmaster and in the weight room, then rewarding myself with twenty minutes in the whirlpool. I chose a Stairmaster machine next to a woman I knew casually from the gym. She worked for one of the software companies out on Route 128. We saw each other once in a great while outside of the club, but mostly our conversations took place as we were panting and watching our heart rates. We told each other about our love lives, or that lack thereof, depending on what was happening at the time. "Want to come to a cook-out tomorrow night?" Susan asked, her eyes on the glowing red dots of the program monitor in front of her.

I hesitated, then replied. "I can't."

That piqued her interest. "Oh, my God, you didn't tell me, that's so cool, Jen, are you *seeing* someone? See, I told you! I knew you'd get over that loser Peter."

"Nothing like that." I paused to swallow some water from my bottle. I couldn't help my thought, I couldn't help but imagine what she would say if I told her the truth. No, Susan, it's not really a date; only sort of. How shocked would you be if I told you what I was really going to be doing? That my date will end with him paying me two hundred dollars? I stifled the laughter that bubbled up with the thought.

I couldn't even imagine what she'd think. *If* she believed me. That was a big if. "I just need money, I'm doing some tutoring."

"That's cool." She was focused again on her hill-climbing pattern. "I need to do something like that."

I smiled my Inner Secret Smile and asked, innocently if a little breathlessly (well, I *was* on a Stairmaster), "Why? I thought you high-tech geeks made all the money."

"Yeah, but tutoring, at least you meet someone who's not a cubicle rat. I'd just like to occasionally have a conversation with someone who has some social skills."

Well, yeah, I thought, the ones I'm seeing aren't all geeks. The social skills part, I wasn't so sure about yet.

After showering and drinking some fruit juice at the club bar, I headed out to make some additions to my wardrobe. Nothing fancy, just as far as the Citibank card would allow me to go. New job, new clothes, my mother always used to say. I had a picture of her, the first day at the bank where she was an assistant vice-president, her hat just so and her gloves matching her shoes and . . . well, different times, different wardrobe.

I went to Cacique and bought matching sets of underwear. Not knowing what might lie ahead, I added a few loose camisoles, lacy tops that could work as either lingerie or real clothes. And then of course there were the dreaded and *de rigeur* garter belt and stockings; I was hoping that I'd not have to use them too frequently.

Why, you ask? Here's an insight for the gentlemen in the audience: if a woman ever says that she's comfortable in those things, she's lying. She may be lying to be nice to you, because she knows how much that whole outfit turns you on: but she is lying nevertheless. So appreciate her. A lot.

I, on the other hand, was being paid for it. That makes a little discomfort a lot more comfortable.

I went to a couple more shops, buying clothes that were only slightly more risqué than those I normally wore: slightly shorter skirts, slightly more revealing shirts, that sort of thing. Lots of black. A small black beaded handbag. Clothing in layers, easy to take off, easy to put on – the cramped quarters in the bow of Bruce's boat/bedroom had taught me something about that.

And then I went to a salon and had my hair shaped and blown dry, over-tipped the stylist, and went home. It was ten o'clock. I had a class at two the next day, and was prepared to start my new job in earnest immediately after.

A tale of two careers. I grinned to myself. It doesn't get much better than this.

Chapter Three

The fact is, it was prostitution. You can dress it up however you'd like; but for me to tell myself that earning my living as a prostitute was a situation that couldn't get any better was at best a little naïve. At worst, a little delusional.

After meeting Peach, I had a week and a half of a remarkably ordinary life. Ordinary classes, ordinary calls through Avanti with remarkably ordinary sex.

I'm not sure what I had been expecting – whips and chains, perhaps? Or nun's habits, or something? What I got instead was the sort of unmemorable sex that invariably characterizes first encounters. A little clumsy, a little awkward, and the thought occurring midway through that perhaps you don't really like this person all that much after all.

It happens in real life all the time.

Of course, my situation had a certain advantage over real life. I could leave after an hour. In real life, you're stuck with him for somewhat longer.

A lot of the clients told me what to do, which I found a little off-putting. I'm pretty creative, after all, and can probably find my rhythm a little easier than I can follow yours. I've never dealt too well with being told what to do. Not in real life, anyway. It didn't matter: in this context it was acceptable. They got off on it. Sit here, do this, take that off. Do that again. Do it harder. Do it some more. Stand up, kiss me here, turn around, bend over.

Maybe nobody listened to them in real life. Maybe this was the only power they ever felt.

There was a guy out in the suburbs, up in North Andover, a handsome middle-aged African-American who I saw from time to time. After a semi-successful three quarters of an hour spent on his bed, he would make out a check (previously cleared with Peach, of course; this tends to be a cash-only business), always with something of a flourish. He winked at me as he added on the comment line that it was for "purchase of art work." I guess that I qualified.

There was a ridiculously young man in South Boston, nice, who offered me a light beer and then never gave me a chance to drink it.

There was my first hotel client, a regular who visited Boston once a month on business. He was very busy, he informed me, gesturing toward the open laptop on the coffee table with papers scattered all around it. He was as good as his word, too, loudly encouraging me through an energetic blowjob, offering a ten-dollar tip on top of the agency fee after I'd finished. I was out of there in just under twenty minutes. It was eight-thirty at night, I was well-dressed and feeling attractive, walking down a hotel corridor, with one hundred and fifty dollars that I had made in less time than it had taken me to get dressed.

I had been firm with Peach when she called me with the hotel job. I had this idea of guys just passing though Boston, sitting in a hotel, looking up an escort service, maybe not being as careful as they should be. The one thing, I knew, that would bring me back down to earth with a resounding thud would be for me to get arrested. I was willing to have sex so that I could make a living. I wasn't willing to give up my real career, however, and an arrest would do that in a heartbeat. "I only want regulars," I told her. "I only want to see guys that you know."

"It's okay, Matt's a regular," she said, her voice comforting. "He's fine, he's been with us for over a year."

"Okay." I hesitated. "But, Peach, just for the record – I never want to see a new client. Ever. I just can't take that chance."

"Oh, honey," she said. "I understand."

There was the client in Brookline Village who extended his time to a second hour, and used the extra time to take me out for Chinese food after we'd had sex. Very sweet. Double the money, and an expensive dinner with someone I probably would not have chosen to date under different circumstances – but not altogether unpleasant.

Certainly not as unpleasant as some of the dates I'd been on in the past.

None of these men had a particularly scintillating personality. Most of them were, to be honest, incredibly unmemorable. One of them was gruff and pushy. Another kept following up his remarks with, "Oh, you probably don't understand that. Like, who am I talking to here, Einstein or something?" I was new to the profession; I let that one get to me and couldn't suppress a response. "True," I agreed, the third time he said it. "Einstein's doctorate wasn't in anthropology; mine is." He was pretty much quiet, after that.

But the reality is that, all in all, they weren't bad people. Ordinary, marginally attractive, with questionable social skills, yes. Dull, predictable, full of insecurities that they projected onto me, sure. They weren't unfamiliar, or scary, or detestable. I had dated men just like them, in the past, and for no compensation.

One Thursday – about one month after I'd started working regularly for Peach, doing about three or four calls a week – I was nearing the end of the *On Death and Dying* semester. This was my favorite time of all, a time to see what issues I had raised, what ideas I had sparked, what creativity I had unleashed. From the beginning of the semester, students knew that part of their grade would come from a final project, to be done either individually or as part of a group, something that had gripped them, interested them, brought out their passion. I saw amazing things, when projects were presented.

I was not disappointed on this Thursday.

Karen, one of the few students in the class who was not in the nursing program, had done a project on her own. She had gone to a hospice and interviewed dying AIDS patients, recording the interviews on tape. While she talked with them, Karen – who was a professional artist – drew their portraits (all of which she later gave to the subjects, a generous gesture that was a whole story in itself).

I don't think that there was a person in that room who was not mesmerized by what was happening in front of them. The voices on the tape filled the space around us, strong and frightened, peaceful and angry . . . We listened to their words and stared at these achingly beautiful faces, these haunted eyes, these hollowed cheeks. I looked around the room, seeing tears, seeing entranced attention, seeing compassion, and my own heart swelled.

Then – how can I make sense of this? – in this wonderful, sacred moment, suddenly my mind flashed back to the night before, to the apartment in Chestnut Hill and the sleek Scandinavian furniture and the guy who was saying, "You teach a class about *death*? Man, that's hot! Death's the best aphrodisiac of all!"

I pushed the image away immediately and blocked it out fast, shocked by its intrusion into this moment. I listened to a man talk about losing his friends, about having his mother afraid to touch him, and my cheeks were flaming. In the midst of this important moment, while doing exactly what I knew that I had been born to do, I had left. I had left as surely as if I had opened the door and gone through it. I had betrayed Karen's beautiful work, and I had betrayed myself.

I didn't know what to do with that knowledge.

I didn't want to think about it.

I tried to forget it.

* * * * * *

That night, if you believe in direct punishment immediately after a misdeed, you would be vindicated. I was punished. I went on a call to Back Bay.

Boston's Back Bay is old brownstones, old families, old money. They are like the apartments of Paris and Budapest – inherited, not sold, and certainly never rented.

It is Commonwealth Avenue at its tree-lined, sweeping best, not the Comm. Ave. I lived near in Allston, with the sound of the creaky Green Line train and the Hispanic markets and the Russian pharmacies. This was Comm. Ave. down near the Public Gardens, where it was modeled on Haussman's boulevards in Paris and almost makes one believe that one is there.

It is Beacon Street, with twisted wrought iron fences and staircases and balconies; it is Marlborough Street, with fanlights over heavy oaken doorways.

It is gaslights on corners and the quiet swish of traffic sounds coming up from Storrow Drive.

You walk along those streets and you wonder about who lives behind the mullioned windows, behind the thick velvet draperies. You imagine that it must be people of culture, people who discuss Rimbaud and Verlaine – or Hofstadter and Minsky – over snifters of brandy on a winter's night.

And, to be honest, I did have some small margin of experience, at least with Beacon Street in the Back Bay. While I was still doing my doctoral coursework I had spent a couple of semesters as a teaching assistant for a professor who lived there, and it was to his apartment that I frequently delivered corrected term papers. The apartment was long and dark, the walls covered with huge dismal oil paintings framed in thick gold gilt frames, each frame nearly touching the next, so that you could barely discern the wallpaper behind them. The rugs were hand-made Orientals, the furniture heavy and mahogany, the books all bound in leather. He gave me tea sometimes, a delicate blend that I couldn't identify, and that I have never tasted since.

So when Peach sent me to Beacon Street, I felt nothing but a sense of mild anticipation. The guy wasn't particularly pleasant on the telephone when I called to set it up, but by then I was amassing my own wisdom about such things. That wisdom said that in general the clients who were the most obnoxious on the telephone were the least so in person, and vice-versa.

Well, so I was wrong about that, too.

But I was still operating from that framework when I talked to him, so I was taking the whole conversation with a grain of salt.

"So, what do you like?"

In my short time in the business, I had already developed an aversion to that question. The point was never what *I* liked, but rather what the client liked, and sometimes this opening felt like an exam, a trick question, a way to get me to say something that he could then pick apart. I was starting to understand clients' minds, you see.

I cleared my throat. "I like lots of things. I'm sure that I'll like you. Why don't I come over, and we'll see how it feels together?"

It was a fourth-floor apartment, one of the apartments that directly overlook the Charles River, and as soon as I got there I moved toward the window with an exclamation of delight. Most guys appreciate that, you complimenting their place. And this was truly magnificent.

All around me, below me, the darkness was punctuated by pinpoints of dazzling brightness, windows spilling out warm yellow light into the night, the flashing red lights on the roofs of the buildings across the river, sparkling unknown reflections in the dark water itself.

The client – Barry by name – wasn't paying me to enjoy the view. I know this to be true because he said so, even as he grasped my arm and pulled me away from the window and toward him, a grasp that was to leave clear deep imprints of his fingers on my bruised skin later.

That first kiss bruised my mouth, too.

He was pinning me against a brick wall and it was uneven, cutting into my back, and it hurt. And his hands hurt, too, pushing against me, squeezing my breasts – hard, too hard. I gasped and pulled away, as far as I could, told him to stop, and he laughed, he actually laughed. "You don't tell me to do anything," he said. "You're just a whore. You hear that? *You* do what *I* say."

I probably should have left then. I had that option; Peach wouldn't have been happy about it, although she would have supported me. I was still feeling my way in the profession, still in my heart of hearts wondering if I really could do it. I still had something to prove.

So I thought, okay, I can handle this. It's only an hour. I can do this for an hour.

He pushed me through an arched doorway into an extremely small bedroom, the bed unmade, a slight undefinable unpleasant odor in the air. There was track lighting, all of it pointing to the bed. A class act, all the way.

He hadn't taken his hands off me once – squeezing, pinching, mauling. He was taking my clothes off and ripped two of the buttons at the neckline to the dress. When I tried to get a modicum of control back, saying that I'd take off my clothes, he grabbed a handful of my hair and shoved his face to within a half-inch of mine. "Shut up, whore!"

Oddly enough, he took a moment to spread towels on the bed. With the mess that the room was already in, the gesture seemed a little ominous.

You probably won't believe this, but the truth is that I don't really remember exactly what happened next. Everything happened so fast, everything became such a blur of pain and fear, that I cannot fashion the experience into words, into a coherent narrative.

Here's what I remember. I remember being pushed down onto the bed, with him on top of me, pinning my hands up above my head, his weight pushing down on my lungs and making me struggle for breath. I remember his voice, over and over: "You're just a whore, aren't you? You're just a dirty little whore. Say it! Say you're a whore! Say you love it!"

I remember being terrified about having no control over what was happening, terrified he wouldn't use a condom and I wouldn't be able to stop him. I remember the moment of relief when he put one on and the immediate fear again as he started to tie my wrists together with a pillowcase. I screamed, then. I knew that once I was tied up, there would be no control at all, and I struggled and flailed until he gave up. After that, he was even nastier in what he had to say.

I remember him fucking me, hard, slamming into me with a force that had more to do with rage than anything else, ramming so hard that I thought I couldn't take another stroke, the pain was so intense. He was hitting my cervix, he was ramming it so hard that I was convinced he was ripping my flesh, ripping my insides. I remember him pulling back and pushing me onto my stomach, and I remember the horror I felt as I realized that he was trying to push his way into my ass.

I'm not a prude; far from it. I've had anal sex many times and have enjoyed it. I've role-played all sorts of things that involved submission and dominance, and, with the requisite safe words in place, felt free to explore all sorts of facets of my sexuality.

But there was nothing that felt safe or free about this transaction, and I reacted intensely.

Barry was not pleased. "Hookers take it in the ass," he snarled.

"Not this one," I said.

Most people would have left it there. Most people, even people with only a modicum of social skills, would have accepted that it wasn't going to happen and would have moved on as gracefully as possible. Some might even have apologized. Later, I learned that many of Peach's girls shared my fear of having anal sex with a stranger – and particularly one who has already inflicted pain – so Barry, who had a long history with Peach, might well have known that I would refuse. He might have requested it during our brief telephone conversation. It seemed clear, now, why he hadn't. If you don't ask, no one can say no. And he just might be able to trick or force me into doing it . . .

So, as I said, most people would have moved on.

Barry was not most people.

If I hadn't been so irritated, and so frightened, what ensued might have almost been comical. An adult man, hairy and naked, whining as though he were a five-year-old boy being denied an ice cream cone. "Oh, come on, do it, just this once."

"No, I don't want to." Okay, so I was sounding a little childish myself.

"Come on." His voice was wheedling, as though he might be able to wear me down through insistence alone. "Just for a minute. I promise when you say stop I'll stop. You'll like it, you'll see how much you'll like it. I'll listen to you. Whatever you want."

Yeah, I thought, like you've done so far. "No. Why don't we . . ."

"I don't want to do anything else!" He was explosive now, and really scaring me. "You bitch, this is what you're here for, and this is what you're gonna do!"

I struggled away from him and crouched, naked, next to the headboard. I think that I was shaking, and it was partly out of fear and partly out of anger. "Barry, I've said no. You should have told Peach that was what you wanted. I don't do it and I won't do it." And especially not with you.

He sat on the edge of the bed, considering his options. Apparently he decided to turn to Plan B, because he reached out and gently stroked my shoulder. "Okay, okay. It's okay. Come on over here. I won't make you do anything you don't want to."

Thinking that the hour had to be close to being up, please God, I crawled tentatively toward him. This sudden switch from aggression and insults to gentleness and sympathy was disconcerting. So what's the story here? I'm supposed to get in an affectionate mood now? And the other voice in my head answered, Yes, you are, it's what you're being paid to do.

In any event, I didn't need to. As soon as I was within comfortable reach, Barry grabbed me and threw me down on the bed again and got on top of me. My face was pressed down into the pillow and for a few terrifying seconds I thought that I was going to suffocate. To die. My world had disappeared. There was nothing but red, pulsing blood-red, beating rhythmically against my eyelids, and I struggled upward, backward – anything to be able to breathe again. That was all I wanted. Just to breathe again.

He wasn't concerned with my head; he was still trying to force his cock into my ass. And coming close to succeeding, despite the resistance that I was putting up. I gasped for air, my face up against his headboard, and I could hear him at it again. "You fucking whore, you fucking bitch, take it, fucking take it . . ."

No amount of money was worth this. I took another deep breath and screamed. And did it again.

Barry was suddenly struggling with me, trying to get me to stop. When he put his hand over my mouth, I bit it, hard, and he swore and pulled it away. I took advantage of his distraction to scramble out from under him, to get off the bed and stand in the beautiful arched doorway, my arms ineffectually covering my breasts. As though it were a moment for modesty. I guess that my mother taught me well, after all.

He was furious, that was clear. He was shaking, and there was a tiny globule of spit at the edge of his mouth. "You fucking cunt!" he yelled. "No whore does that to me!"

I didn't dare take my eyes off him. "If you hurt me, Peach will never send anyone to you again," I said, not knowing if it was true or not. I was thinking that I was really glad that I had gotten the money up front, because I was going to be doing well to get out of here with my clothes. Maybe the fact that Peach had said to collect the money right away should have told me something; with regulars, we usually got paid when the hour was over. "I'm leaving."

The threat, idle or not, worked. Later on, I learned how whipped Peach kept her regular clients, little boys who tried to push their luck with the callgirls, but who whimpered and apologized when confronted by Mummy on their bad behavior. Barry sat down on the bed, the fury draining from him, and said, merely, "Shit."

It seemed an apt commentary. I reached down to the floor and picked up my clothes, pulling the dress hurriedly over my head, not bothering to look for the missing buttons, stuffing underwear into my purse, not wanting to stay in that place a millisecond longer than I had to.

He walked past me as I was slipping into my shoes and stalked over to the bathroom. "Don't slam the door on your way out," he said, coldly. "I'm taking a shower. You made me feel dirty, you lousy motherfucker cunt."

I had made *him* feel dirty.

I called Peach immediately as soon as I hit the street. I had just bought a cell phone, and was grateful for the anonymity it provided as I unlocked my car and slipped inside. "It was pretty awful," I told her, a little angry, a little tearful.

"I know, honey," Peach said, and in her voice I heard such a depth of understanding and compassion and caring that it suddenly didn't matter anymore. "You don't ever have to see him again if you don't want to." And I felt a rush of gratitude toward her that was as deep as the ocean.

It wasn't until months later that I remembered that conversation, and realized that she had known exactly what she was sending me into, and she hadn't warned me. True, I probably wouldn't have gone. And the bottom line *was* to make the money. But, still . . . she should have told me. And all the compassion and understanding and kindness that followed was calculated, too. But by then I knew all that.

Later that year, I met a woman named Margot who also worked for the agency. We did a double together, then over drinks at Jillian's we began sharing client experiences. Barry, it transpired, was one of Margot's regulars. I stared at her, transfixed and a little shocked. "How can you *stand* him?" I wanted to know.

"Well, see, I have this theory." Margot took a liberal swallow of her Manhattan. I always thought I should be more creative in my choice of cocktails; she was inspiring me. Her breath was sweet, smelling of warm vermouth. "Guys like Barry, they have so much rage against women, you know?"

"No shit," I muttered. "So do about eighty percent of men." I was remembering my class on insanity, and the fears that made men lock women away for life.

"Granted. But with Barry, it's a lot closer to the surface."

"Granted," I echoed, fascinated at where this might be going.

"Okay. So he keeps pacing around that little apartment of his and muttering about women being whores. Maybe he watches them through his windows, pretty women down on the Esplanade or Memorial Drive, sunning themselves or doing inline skating or something, and all the while it's stoking up his feelings of insecurity and inadequacy – well, eventually there will be too much pressure, and it'll blow." She sipped her drink, demurely, before delivering the punch line. "And you probably know that I've just described a text-book rapist, by the way."

It *had* felt like rape, what had happened that night. I shivered at the flash of memory, my face in his pillow, suffocating, his weight on my spine, pushing my buttocks apart . . .

Margot didn't notice. "So if the pressure gets eased, sometimes, then maybe he won't blow. Maybe if he can play out his sick little fantasy with one of us from time to time, with someone who can handle it, you know, then he won't walk down Beacon Street one night and follow some innocent woman home. Maybe he won't hurt her." She looked around her at the flashing lights, marshalling her thoughts, and then turned back to me. "You see, Jen, I'm in control, even if he doesn't think I am. I have power over him. I can always call Peach. She's the only service he uses, I don't know why, but if she cuts him off he's got nothing, and he knows it. And I think that in his heart of hearts he knows how much he needs it."

"So by playing into his shit you're keeping women from being molested?" I was still working that one out.

"Sure, why not?" Margot shrugged. "Besides, Jen, look at it this way. I don't have a lot of competition for him as a client. So you can either call it altruism or you can call it enlightened self-interest. Either way works."

But I liked Margot's theory. I thought about it a lot. Everything that I'd been reading about prostitution and the sex trade was talking about how it contributed to the oppression of women, how it perpetuated men's fantasies of control and power. And here was this woman, gorgeous, smart, calmly sipping her Manhattan and telling me that in the midst of this profession she was considering the needs of other women.

I liked the thought. I liked the thought of that anonymous woman walking down Beacon Street at night, the streetlamps misting and her footsteps echoing on the pavement. I liked thinking that she was safe because, somewhere four stories up, Margot was there, sleeping with the enemy.

Chapter Four

After the Back Bay call, I definitely needed my fitness club. I went and worked out, sweating and pushing myself past my usual limit, then stood under the shower and scrubbed my body nearly raw. And then I sat for nearly an hour in the whirlpool, getting up every ten minutes to reset the timer. If they hadn't had a closing time, I would have stayed in there all night.

The fact that this was what I had anticipated before I started working, that I had actually imagined feeling soiled and used and unclean, didn't help much. The fact was that I had gotten spoiled. "It's a crap shoot," Peach once said.

Yeah. And sometimes, it seemed, you didn't exactly roll a winner.

But the feeling passed. There were enough neutral or good experiences to balance out my time with Barry; there was no obligation for me to ever see him again. And eventually, as one does, I pushed him into the back recesses of my consciousness and concentrated on what was essential. The money.

The money was essential because by that time – by the time I'd been working for Peach for merely a few weeks – I was beginning to see my way out of my financial problems. Oh, I wasn't there, not yet, not by a long shot; but I could see that it was going to happen.

I was able to pay my rent on time, for one thing. No small accomplishment. I almost wanted to e-mail the rat bastard in California to tell him how well I was surviving.

Well, on second thought, perhaps not.

On the Sunday night after my first week of working for Peach, I sat in my apartment with Scuzzy contentedly purring nearby, and I wrote checks to help pay off debts that had been hanging over my head seemingly forever. I'd already spent some of my money on what I was already thinking of as professional expenses, smart little suits at Next and the Express, lingerie from Cacique. Even with those extravagances, I made bill payments. I was going to be able to start answering the telephone again, instead of ignoring it so I could avoid potential creditors. I was going to stop feeling that tight fist of panic in my stomach when I opened my mailbox, wondering who was threatening to shut me off today.

To say that I was feeling good would have been the understatement of the century.

It showed, too. There was a new confidence about me. It may have been due to my new employment; or it may have just been the fact that I finally wasn't slinking around avoiding bill collectors anymore. Whatever was happening, people were noticing.

The head of the sociology department, for whom I was teaching *On Death and Dying*, was the first to comment. "So – new boyfriend?"

I nearly spilled my coffee. "No, Hannah, why?"

She looked amused. "You're looking so good these days. You

look happy. I heard you humming in the ladies' room, to tell you the truth. I thought that there might be somebody."

No, Hannah, there are a whole lot of somebodies. There is a different somebody every night, if you really want to know. I repressed the thought and replaced the impish grin it engendered with a proper professorial attitude. "I've been working out more; maybe that's it."

The other sociology elective that I was teaching that semester was *Life in the Asylum*, a course that examined the shifting ways in which the well-intentioned but fundamentally cruel institutions of medicine and psychiatry dealt, historically and currently, with the mentally ill. I spent some time focusing on the so-called "paupers' palaces," the immense, grandiose state mental hospitals built in the nineteenth century to try and do the right thing – whatever that was perceived to be at the time.

The day after my shopping and mini-spa, I went into the "asylum" class (as its own inmates liked to call it) with a mixture of feelings that I was hard-pressed to sort out. We were in the middle of what I always found to be a difficult couple of weeks in the subject area: society's use of mental hospitals as dumping-grounds for unwanted women.

I could never treat these classes with any kind of proper academic distance or dispassion, because they never failed to anger me. The superfluous spinster, the outspoken wife, the aging mother, all could be incarcerated if the man who wished to be rid of them found a doctor willing to sign a form attesting to her insanity. Once committed in such a manner, the victim could be released, not by the signature of the committing physician (or by any evidence of mental health), but only by permission of the male relative who had instigated the process.

I found it outrageous. Every time that I think or talk about it, I can feel my blood pressure rising.

The students had that week been reading Geller and Harris' *Women of the Asylum*. They were presumably prepared to comment on the first-hand accounts recorded in the book, the voices of real women who had lived for years and even decades in lunatic asylums, the women who were no more crazy than the men who had sent them there.

Not more crazy, just more powerless.

I had begun to read, in my own newly-acquired independent

study (or independent obsession, take your pick) about how prostitution was sometimes used as proof of insanity, and was feeling rather more passionate anger than usual. Perhaps not a strictly academic point of view.

Some of the women in the class were feeling even more vehement about what they had read than I was. That was usually the case, I have found, which is one of the highs, the joys, of teaching: give people information that they did not have before, and their passions come alive. Tell the truth, and watch it change lives.

Maybe even some day it might change the world.

There was a somewhat heated discussion involving most of the class – well, I'd anticipated that. It is, after all, really difficult to read words that express so much pain in such an eloquent way without having *some* emotional response to it. I let them go at it, walking around the classroom, making a comment here, asking a question there. Inevitably, we were drawn away from the topic, and I let that happen, too, to see where it might go, before reeling them back in again.

"Well, it doesn't really matter, does it, it's just history, that kind of thing doesn't happen anymore."

"Are you kidding? It looks different now. Maybe it's less blatant, but nothing has really changed."

"What exactly hasn't changed?" That was me, the question asked quietly, innocently.

"What hasn't changed? What *has* changed, that's the real question! People still think that there's something unnatural, something abnormal, about women who choose not to do exactly what they're supposed to do."

"That's bullshit! Women are presidents of companies, now!"

"What is it that women are 'supposed' to do?" I asked.

The response was vehement. "Everything! They're supposed to do everything, be everything, and still be nurturing and non-threatening to everybody around them! They have to be sexy. They have to be a fantasy woman and at the same time be as good a cook as their husband's mother! They're supposed to want to have children, and if they don't want children, if they want a career instead, they're seen as selfish, self-centered, and not normal. I'd probably be put in an asylum if I lived a century ago!"

Another female voice chimed in. "And it's sexual, too. Men used to be imprisoned for *doing* something wrong, women were incarcerated for being too sexual. If you wear skirts that are too short, or blouses that are too low-cut, or too much make-up or jewelry, you're not fitting the expectations, so you get punished, you get called names."

I looked at her. "What kinds of names?"

A shrug. "You know. Whore. Slut. Bitch. Either you fit into their image of you, or you're insulted for it."

"But you can't win, because men want that, too! They want you to be a bitch at the same time that they call you names for being one!"

Another student said, "That's the real difference. *We* only get *insulted* for being different. Back then, they got incarcerated for it."

The voices continued as I looked off into the distance. I knew the truth of what they were saying, but I was hearing it as though for the first time. The first time that it applied to me, anyway. To call someone a prostitute, even now, was an insult. Even my students said it, so it must be true.

I gave them a writing assignment, told them to capture their thoughts and anger and passion on paper, because I knew that I would get primal, angry, real words from the women and primal, defensive, real words from the men. I sat down behind the desk and frowned down at the blotter. I was still dressed in my teaching clothes – skirt, knit silk shirt, jacket, flat shoes. I didn't plan to change anything but the underwear before signing on tonight. So I was safe from society; if I didn't *look* like a hooker, then maybe at some level I was still a nice girl.

Later, when I got to know some of the other women who worked for Peach, I would be surprised that no one would ever look at them and guess that they worked for an escort service. They didn't look the part.

What was "looking the part?" I wasn't even sure, myself, anymore.

* * * * * *

Peach called me at seven-thirty. "How late are you going to be around tonight?"

47

I hadn't thought a great deal about that. "I don't know, why?" It wasn't like I had a lot of other things to do. My evenings, since the departure of the rat bastard, were fairly predictable.

"I may have someone for you to see. You'll like him, but he doesn't want to see you until ten, is that okay with you?"

"Sure." I certainly could stay occupied until then; I was going to spend some time on the Internet. Because of the turn the afternoon's discussion had taken, I needed to look into a few things that hadn't originally been on the syllabus.

Those were still early days, when I thought that I could get up from correcting exams and leave on a call. I didn't understand, yet, that there needed to be a little transition time between the two.

"Great. You don't have to call him." I raised my eyebrows. *That* was a pleasant surprise. No sales job required. "He's at Bella Donna on Hanover Street, in the North End."

"Peach," I said slowly, "that's a restaurant."

"Oh, I know. He's the owner. Just go to the bar and say you're there to see Stefano. Be there at ten, and give me a call after you get there."

"Okay." I had actually eaten there before, with the boyfriend who had preceded Peter the Rat Bastard. The restaurant was hard to forget. Northern Italian cooking, sauces that made you swear off Ragu forever. The chef could do things with mushrooms that would make God himself jealous; he had a five-mushroom soup that I would be willing to live on for the rest of my life. This was going to be interesting.

The challenge, as I saw it, was parking. I could take the T, of course, but it would take over an hour to get there from Allston. On the other hand, the North End is notorious for having no parking spaces available, anytime, anywhere. So I went early and cruised around halfheartedly before settling for an exorbitantly expensive parking lot and walking up the hill to Hanover Street.

Part of Bella Donna was a small bar, a place frequented mostly by locals, men of a certain age, the pals and cronies of the owner. I went in and hesitated, a nice girl a little out of her league, until the bartender approached me with a wide smile. "I'm here to see Stefano," I told him, cursing myself for not having gotten the man's last name from Peach. It would have sounded a little less awkward, I thought.

If I wanted to be discreet, however, Stefano obviously didn't particularly care. As soon as I asked for him, there was a ripple of winks, nudges, and nods all around the bar. They all knew what I was there for.

The client himself, emerging from a back room, was not unattractive. He was dark-haired with the beginnings of a belly overlapping his belt, white teeth, and very hairy fingers. Well, you can't have everything.

He kissed my hand, which was really nice of him under the circumstances, and offered me a cocktail. We sipped wine and made polite conversation about the weather, the cronies hanging on every word as though waiting for the punch line from a joke. I said that I had once visited Italy. He said something in Italian that had the cronies gasping for breath through their laughter.

We sipped some more, and then Stefano said something long and graceful to the men sitting around the bar, and slid me off my stool. He led me downstairs, where, next to the wine cellar, it turned out that he had a room that was – how can I best say this? – outfitted for his needs.

He explained the situation to me: no embarrassment there. Sometimes these needs involved women; sometimes they involved a special card game or two. People stayed there from time to time. The room also served as his own home away from home on the occasions his wife Giannetta got fed up with him and kicked him out of the house, occasions that appeared to occur with some frequency.

In any case, it held a table and chairs, a sofa and two or three armchairs, and a small single bed in a corner.

He locked the door carefully behind us, and we sat on the narrow bed and made out for a few minutes. It was fun. The stale air and his eager hands reminded me of summer camps in years gone by. I had a vague memory of a boat house filled with old detritus from beach days, half-inflated swimming tubes, abandoned badminton racquets, and two passionate teenagers finding temporary refuge there in the stillness of a hot summer evening. His lips were rough, and I was again an adolescent kissing a teen-aged boy, a boy unsure of his own needs, unsure of his own power, unsure of what was expected of him.

Stefano pulled away at length, and gestured for me to stand up. "Take off your clothes," he urged. As I started, slipping my jacket off my shoulders, taking off the silk shirt, he unbuckled his belt, unzipped his fly, and pulled out his cock.

By the time I got through the layers to the new camisole, he was already – so to speak – there. Orgasm attained. Tissues employed.

Later, I learned that this was in fact the sum of Stefano's sexuality, though at the time I was a little disconcerted. This was supposed to be *work*, after all, wasn't it? I hadn't really done a whole lot. I wasn't even naked.

I saw Stefano quite a lot after that, and the scenario never changed. It was always a toss-up as to which of us would finish first, whether I would get my clothes off or whether Stefano would have an orgasm. We never made it as far as actual physical contact. It was not expected.

He did, however, have a reputation to maintain, and his friends in the bar knew that he was downstairs with a lady. So I got dressed while he washed up at the small sink in the opposite corner of the room, and then, magically exactly on time, there was a discreet tap on the door and one of the dishwashers (never a waiter) from the restaurant arrived with a tray of food and wine.

We sat at the table and drank Chianti or chilled Valpolicello and ate veal scaloppini. Or some sort of marvelous seafood stew. Or (after I requested it) that incredible five-mushroom soup. We spoke, sometimes; often we did not.

After the requisite time had passed – it wasn't the full hour – he stood up, kissed one of my hands as he slipped the money into the other, and back upstairs we went.

Waiting for me at the bar was a shopping bag filled with take-out cartons of delicacies. He gave me this gift with a flourish, the bar broke into applause, and that was that.

I heard, later, that if the girl seeing Stefano had a driver, he'd find out where the unfortunate person was waiting and either invite him or her in for a dinner on the house, or send still more of his incredible take-out to the car. He was generous, and open, and kind.

That night, after seeing Stefano, I called Peach once I got home. "Does he ever actually have sex with anybody?"

"Don't think he can," she said, cheerfully. "What did you have for dinner?"

I giggled in spite of myself. "Veal. It was incredible."

"Thought you'd like him. Do you want anything else tonight?"

It was eleven-thirty, and I had *On Death and Dying* at eleven in the morning. "I don't think so, Peach, but I'll work tomorrow night."

"Okay, you got it, honey. Sleep tight."

I did. I had enough dinners to last me for the next two nights, a sixty-dollar tip, and I hadn't even taken off all my clothes. This, I thought as I slipped between my sheets with Scuzzy kneading the pillow beside me, is easy. Nothing to it. Amazing that more women don't do it. I'm carrying it off without a problem.

Well, anybody can be wrong.

Chapter Five

In the end, I took a few nights off after that. Stefano had been fun, most of my calls had been okay, but the experience with the guy in Back Bay had shaken me up more than I liked to admit.

So instead of working I sat in my apartment, sipped red wine, and wondered if I hadn't made a mistake, after all. Maybe the world of prostitution was, in fact, as terrible as it had been portrayed in movies, in books. Maybe it *would* end up making me feel bad about myself. Maybe I needed to decide if the Stefanos made up for the Barrys.

What I really needed, I decided, was to get away from it, to get some perspective. I needed a dose of "real life" – whatever that is – to feel like I was really myself again.

So I spent a lot of time working on enhancing my classes. I arranged a field trip to a funeral home, and I followed up some leads I had heard concerning possible full-time faculty openings.

I also spent some time tracking down people I'd promised to get together with socially, but had neglected. I thought that I didn't need a social life. I was wrong.

Friends had fallen out of touch, and I had done nothing about it. That happens a lot when a relationship ends: people who knew you as a couple feel awkward around you once you're single, and I hadn't exactly been active in pursuing anybody. So I tried to make up for it.

I had lunch with my friend Irene, who had been my carrel-partner at school. We ate at Jae's on Tremont Street and talked over pad thai and sushi about our inability to secure tenure-track positions, and we both admitted that we had nothing even approaching a love life. We promised that we'd try to see each other more often.

I went to the Silhouette Lounge in Allston with my gay friend Roger, who certainly, according to his conversation, made up for Irene's and my lack of a love life with his busy nocturnal agenda. We drank blue drinks and he provided a running commentary on every man who entered the room. We promised on parting that we'd try to see each other more often.

I even invited my next-door neighbor over for Indian food (delivered) and a rerun of *Rear Window* on AMC, which was fun; but we didn't promise to see each other more often. She got up early most mornings to take the T to the financial district, where she did something with stocks; my invitation appeared to be an opportunity for her to mention (which she did, several times) that sometimes she could hear my music playing after ten.

Peach obviously felt the lull and wanted to make things up to me. "I've got something special for you," she said brightly on the following Wednesday.

"What is it?" Okay, so I was ready for a break from trying to convince myself that I really did have a social life.

"Not what, honey: who."

Who was a client called Jerry Fulcher, and he wanted to go gamble at Foxwoods. He wanted me to go with him. Three days, two nights, an Earth, Wind and Fire show, and a massage and spa treatment if I wanted them. Just be my date, he said.

Peach had already negotiated a flat fee – you really can't charge by the hour for a whole weekend – and it was looking good to go. Three days away from the city at the world's largest resort casino and a thousand-dollar paycheck. I didn't think it over for too long. I could use a vacation.

So, that weekend, off we went to Foxwoods.

We drove down together, Jerry's plan, which I accepted without thinking much about it. Another mistake; but who knew? This was uncharted territory for me.

To get to Foxwoods, you drive on uninspired highways and then on back roads that look like you're going nowhere in particular, and then suddenly there it is. Parking lot after parking lot ringing it like a concrete moat, and shuttle buses in pastel colors bustling in and out of them. And there, on top of the hill, is The Place itself.

It looks, and not unintentionally I suspect, very much like Sleeping Beauty's Castle, the Disney version – only on steroids. The place just doesn't know when to stop: towers and balconies and turrets and acres of glass reflecting back the green of the surrounding trees (we're still working the Sleeping Beauty analogy here, in case you weren't paying attention). Everything is clean and everyone is happy. The staff is all so perky, they have to be rejects from the Mouse Machine itself.

But hell, I was here for work, too. Perky, sexy, whatever it takes.

There were fresh flowers waiting in our room with a card that said "Tia," which I have to admit was a classy touch. Jerry unfortunately also thought it was a classy touch, and said so, over and over. Nothing like a man who needs to keep telling you how subtle he is.

I was up for a shower and a walk to stretch my legs after the drive, but first we had to try out the bed, and that took longer than expected. Jerry was distracted, and distracted doesn't really work well in this line of work. After a lengthy session involving a fair workout on my part, he finally came. He immediately sat up and explained his distraction. "I've been thinking. I don't think they gave me all the credits I'm supposed to have on my Wampum card," he said briskly, as he hustled us both into our clothes and out the door. "Gotta get this straightened out."

I stood next to him as he spent ten minutes arguing with one of the Mouseketeers (who, to her credit, remained perky the whole time) over what turned out to be a difference of twenty dollars, and about which he was ultimately wrong, but which they gave to him anyway to make him go away. I was, even with only Mouseketeers and a couple of middle-aged gamblers for an audience, slightly embarrassed.

As it turned out, I had only just begun to be embarrassed.

After that weekend, I understood the girls whose policy was to only see clients in private venues. No restaurants, no concerts, no trips. They had a point. A lot of these guys need additional training in social skills before they can be taken out in public.

We had dinner at the Cedars Steak House, in a section of the casino styled to look like Bedford Falls or someplace equally perfect and equally fictional. "You can order anything on the menu," Jerry told me expansively. "Even the most expensive stuff. That's the lobster, I think. So, yeah, go ahead, order the lobster! It's free, I have a Wampum card."

I ordered the lobster. I didn't get into a debate over whether the possession of a Wampum card, earned through hours of losing at the gaming tables, truly constituted a free meal. I had a far more immediate problem.

I was seriously overdressed.

All right, so laugh at my naïveté. Or use another word. Innocent. Gullible. Romantic. They all apply.

The truth is that I'd never been to a casino in my life. What I *had* done, however, was see a lot of sixties spy movies and adventure series episodes. James Bond. Steve McQueen in "The Thomas Crown Affair." Dean Martin as Matt Helm and Frank Sinatra as Tony Rome. All from before my time, but recaptured thanks to modern technology on my VCR. I watched them because I loved them. I loved the smoking jackets and the dinner jackets and the martinis and Manhattans and the slinky women with false eyelashes and real breasts. Those were the days.

Those were also my only exposure to casino gambling.

Now, Jerry had made his needs clear: he wanted to look good. He wanted me standing next to him while he played blackjack. He wanted me to massage his shoulders at tense moments. He wanted me to order drinks for him, and then kiss him as I passed them over.

So this combination added up to one single assumption in my mind: go for glamour. I will be the slinky woman leaning over the hero in the tuxedo, while his steely gaze holds that of his adversary in the final moment before turning over the winning card. Yeah, well, like I said, I'm a romantic.

The only problem was that everybody here had signed on for a different movie. I was in *Casablanca* and they were in *The Cable Guy*.

Jerry was wearing maroon sweatpants and a t-shirt that read, "I Heart N.Y." Nearly everybody around us seemed to have gotten the same memo that he had. I saw polyester. I saw – I actually saw, no lie – t-shirts on a middle-aged couple that read, respectively, "Old Fart" and "Old Fart's Wife." The snazzier dressers were into jeans.

And I, on the other hand, was wearing a little black-nothing dress from Lord and Taylor along with seamed stockings and high-heeled black fuck-me shoes.

Oops.

The food arrived, and was what you'd expect in a steak house in a casino. I was glad I that had followed Jerry's suggestion – it's really hard to fuck up lobster. We ordered a bottle of domestic white Zinfandel and Jerry made a joke when the waitress opened it, something about the ones at home all having screw tops. I tried to pretend that I was somewhere else.

He also watched her walk away with eyes that missed nothing.

"She's got a great ass."

I dutifully agreed, but my heart wasn't in it. I was still worried about my dress.

Jerry pursed his lips. "Bet she digs chicks. I can always tell. She was checking out your tits."

Small wonder, as mine are the only ones showing within, oh, a ten-mile radius. She was probably wondering how much my dress cost. I said half-heartedly, "Do you think so?"

He nodded vigorously. "Hey, I wonder. Maybe she'd like to join us later, when she gets off work. I'll bet she'd get off on me watching her tongue you."

Okay. We need to interrupt this broadcast. I'm going to say something that may burst a few bubbles, but what the hell. You know how there are all these urban myths out there, like the alligators living in the sewers and the kids who put the cat in the microwave and it exploded? Well, there are specialized urban legends. There's a Catholic urban legend that says Mary Magdalene was a prostitute (I looked into this one; thought I could use a patron saint). News flash: she wasn't, but we like believing it so much that we ignore little things like facts, evidence, that sort of thing.

Well, anyway, there are sexual urban legends, too. Different ones for men and for women, of course. And, guys, I'm here to tell you: We don't get off on you watching two of us having sex together. In the privacy of our own intimate moments, we generally do not strap on oversized dildos and encourage our partners to engage in a plastic blowjob. I know that's what you like to see. I know that's what you want to believe. But if you are ever sitting and watching two women doing that, you need to know that they're doing it solely for you and you'd better ask yourself why. You'll pay for the show, one way or another.

At least when callgirls do it, the payment is unambiguous.

So I looked at Jerry and said, doubtfully, "Uh-huh."

"Yeah," he said, addressing his steak. "We'll have to check her out." Please God, I thought silently, please God, don't let him make me ask her.

As it turned out, once dinner was over, Jerry had other things on his mind. Maybe there is a God, after all. "Time to win some serious cash," he informed me, and we proceeded into the casino proper.

I thanked Mary Magdalene for my reprieve, just in case.

* * * * * *

I know a little less about blackjack than does your average five-year-old. It's cards, okay? It's one of the games that the steely-eyed men in dinner jackets used to play on my VCR.

It became obvious very quickly that my understanding the game was fortunately not necessary. I was there in a strictly ornamental capacity. And if I had misjudged how others were going to be dressed, at least I wasn't far off in their responses to my choice of clothes. Of those people who were not intently absorbed in the play of cards on the tables in front of them, it became immediately clear that the men all wanted me and the women all hated me.

Par for the course.

So I watched Jerry settle at a blackjack table and nod to the dealer; the cards were dealt and I tried to look slinky rather than bored. I have to say that Jerry seemed to do rather well, so well in fact that he turned to me soon and gave me a hundred-dollar chip. "Here," he said, loud enough for the table to hear, "Go have a little fun for yourself."

I took the chip – I'm no fool – but hesitated. He looked up impatiently. "Go play roulette," he urged. "You'll have fun. Come back when you're finished."

"If you're sure, baby," I said automatically, but I was starting to walk away even as I said the words. Three hours with him and I was already needing space.

I didn't play roulette. I cashed in the chip and put the money in my bag (small and sexy and expensive, another *faux pas*, since most of the women I saw were carrying large vinyl bags into which they could pour their winnings from the slot machines) and wandered around to satisfy my genuine curiosity about the casino.

My friend Irene had had a lot to say about Foxwoods when I told her I was going ("just with a friend, nothing special"). "Oh, my God, Jen, do you *know* about that place?"

I think I've made it fairly obvious that I did not. "No," I said.

"It's supposed to belong to this Indian tribe, they got all this land and these loans because of some sort of payback for white people having taken everything from them."

That much I knew. "So? That seems fair."

"Maybe," Irene continued, excited now. "Except that it turns out that the guy who started the whole thing was a dirtbag. There aren't any Pequots, they died out years ago, and this guy – Skip something – got his family declared a tribe without having to prove it, the way all the other tribes had to." Irene shrugged. "I actually think the idea is good, too," she said. "I think that there should be some accounting. It's just that the right people should benefit, not some scumbag out to make an easy buck."

I was thinking about that as I walked around. I saw a lot of pseudo-Indians, that was for sure: all the cocktail waitresses were dressed in colorful fringed suede dresses and had headbands with single feathers stuck in the back of them. I'm not sure about the authenticity of the feather, but I am pretty sure that no Native Americans would have recognized the length of those dresses (as in barely covering the ass), nor certainly the fishnet tights and high heels that went with them.

Hiawatha meets Moulin Rouge.

I wandered in and out of several rooms filled with people intently staring at cards or dice, and eventually I got back to Jerry, only losing my way once, which was a pleasant surprise. He hadn't moved, although I saw that several faces around the semi-circle of gamblers had changed.

He noticed me peripherally. "There you are. Get me a drink, will you, hon?" he asked. Then, as an afterthought, "How'd you do?"

I looked contrite. "I lost it, baby. I bet on my birthday and lost." Or I would have, if I had been foolish enough to play.

"That's okay." He squeezed my waist and looked around the

table to see if anyone was watching. "I just want you to have fun, that's all. Get me a drink, will ya?"

I signaled to one of the pseudo-Indians. She hadn't been to the same Mouseketeer training as the front-desk people. Or maybe she just hated me on principle because I was better dressed than she was. "Yes, what is it?"

"A Chivas on the rocks, please." Jerry had already given me a lengthy list of his preferences – sexual and otherwise – during our drive down from Boston. "And I'll have a gin and tonic." Might as well enjoy myself, I thought. Experience has taught me that being slightly buzzed can often be a good thing in an uncomfortable situation.

Jerry was getting twitchy. I waited until the drinks came and took a couple of chips from the pile he had left for me to use. He had told me about that, too, on the ride down: "Those chicks, they work their asses off and deserve something. I always tip them." Like that was an extraordinary act of selflessness. Well, maybe for Jerry it was.

I tipped the waitress, which mollified her not one bit. Okay, I thought, fine, I tried, fuck you too. I put his drink discreetly beside him on the wooden rail provided for that purpose, sipped my gin and tonic, and tried to pay attention to the table.

Jerry, it transpired, was getting twitchy because Jerry was losing.

Even without knowing about blackjack, I could tell Jerry was losing. He didn't have nearly the number of chips in front of him that he had had before. Worse still, it seemed that everybody else at the table had more chips than he did.

Now, what I *do* understand about blackjack is that you're not playing against the other people. They're just there. You're playing against the dealer. You play, then the dealer moves to somebody else and plays against them, and so on around the table, all these separate little dramas acting themselves out in near silence, everybody just waiting for the moment when it's their turn with the dealer. So it doesn't matter in the least how the other people at the table are doing.

But of course it really does. Jerry kept looking at their chips, and with every hand he lost, he got a little more twitchy.

He finished the Chivas and looked around impatiently for more. He got irritable with me when I couldn't get the Pocahontaswannabe over fast enough. He started sighing, loudly, when other people were playing their hands. He was, in short, being a poor loser. And annoying the hell out of everyone.

"I'd be doing better if the *other* people here knew how to play," he said to me, his voice loud enough to carry nicely to everyone at the table. I caressed his back and neck and murmured comforting things like, Baby, it's okay, I'm impressed with you, the next hand will be the best; but he shook me off him and said, "What the fuck do you know about it? Some fucking bitch's trying to teach me to play!"

I froze. Everyone at the table froze, except for the dealer, who must have been used to that kind of thing. What I was thinking was that I had never heard James Bond say anything like that to any of *his* slinky women.

Jerry glared at the other players. "It'd help if there were some fucking *Americans* here," he snarled as an afterthought.

Long pause. I looked at the other players. Three were clearly of Asian nationality or descent. This wasn't going to be pretty.

And I was quite certain that I was the only one to find irony in his reference to "Americans" in the context of a casino that had been thrown to the Native Americans much as one might throw a bone to a dog by way of reparations. And, having done so, had missed.

It was time, in any case, to take matters into my own hands. "Come on, baby," I urged Jerry, again putting the seductive tone in my voice and the promising touch in my fingertips. "Let's take a break. I miss you. Come on, just a few minutes . . ."

Man, I don't care if Mary Magdalene wasn't really a prostitute, I'm lighting a candle to her anyway: he actually left the table with me.

We found a dark bar (there seemed to be any number of them around) and I played with his dick under the table and talked as soothingly as I could while he downed two more Chivases, which didn't seem like a good sign. He was convinced that others' poor playing meant that the cards were lined up against him. Of course, "what can you expect from a bunch of goddamned Chinks? The whole place is full of them."

Yeah, well, there's just so much of this that I could listen to, even for a thousand dollars. I moved closer to him and slid my tongue slowly down his neck, my fingers still lightly fondling his dick that I could feel getting hard through the sweatpants. It's not so much the having sex in exchange for money: it's not being able to tell racist, sexist, self-absorbed assholes like this what you really think of them.

"It's time for me, now," I murmured against his neck. "Baby, I need you . . . please . . ."

He fell for it. Thank God I still had my touch. He grumbled about us always doing what I wanted, about how I really was a nympho and couldn't get enough of him, I was lucky he was a real stud and not like some of those other losers I see, and I agreed with it all and pulled him into the elevator after me. Whatever it takes.

And that was just the first night.

By the time we were packing to go, I could barely speak civilly to him. He had embarrassed me in front of bartenders, waitstaff, card dealers, pit bosses, maids, and polyester-clad patrons. He had made loud boorish comments in the high stakes rooms and had felt up one of the Pocanatas cocktail waitresses. He had sent food back to the kitchen three times. He asked the African-American couple sharing our table at the Earth, Wind, and Fire concert to stop dancing around so much, and muttered something rather loudly about how "those people" had to behave like monkeys.

Fortunately, you don't have to speak to your partner in order to have sex with him. Or at least you don't need to have a conversation. Because I might have said any number of things that might have been regrettable.

I paid for the time I spent away from him at the promised spa session by playing prolonged games in bed. "Tell me I've got the biggest cock you've ever seen. Come on, bitch, say it again. Say it *loud*!"

He had me bring him to the brink of orgasm and then stop, over and over again, until I was dizzy with the effort and he lay back and said, "What's the matter? Come on, kiss me here, I want some tongue this time."

"I need to rest a moment," I protested.

He grabbed my hair and pulled my head to his crotch with such force that it brought tears to my eyes. "You're not here to rest, bitch, you're here to do what I want, so suck me!"

We ended up having long sessions of increasingly violent sex, silent uneasy meals together, and lengthy hours gambling in the casino during which I cringed at his behavior.

Saturday night I fled for a half-hour, pleading the classic headache, and found myself in one of the dark little bars, the only person there. "What'll it be?" The bartender, at least, was not dressed like a Hollywood Indian.

"Grand Marnier," I said, thinking of the comfort of ten minutes of elegance, a balloon glass and a warmed liqueur, something to remind me that there was Life After Foxwoods.

"Sure thing," he said, and a moment later handed me the drink. It was Grand Marnier – served in a plastic cup. I gaped at it, and at him.

"What's the matter? Did you want ice in that?" he asked.

* * * * * *

By Sunday afternoon Jerry was desperate. He had had a short winning streak on Saturday, but had been losing steadily ever since then. Lots of credits on the Wampum card.

We had planned to leave at three, and it was now past four. Our bags were packed. Jerry was still hunched over his cards. "All right, Tia, all right," he said crossly to me. "Just one more hand."

I dropped my voice. "Jerry, it's four-fifteen, we're supposed to have left already." I knew that he was an important client for Peach, or I'd have left on Saturday. She didn't want to lose him; I didn't want to lose her. But what a temptation.

"Jesus Christ!" His roar interrupted my thought and startled people at the tables next to us, and a pit boss looked interested and began drifting in our direction. Jerry saw everybody looking at him, and in a tone that implied they would all agree with him, he said, "What do you want? I pay her more than she's worth, and now she's nickel and diming me about the time!"

I walked out. I waited for him in the front hall. There was a statue there, with a periodic sound-and-light show about the Native American heritage of the Pequots. I thought about Irene's words and looked at the feather headdress on the statue that was more a tribute to John Wayne than to John Smith, and waited for Jerry.

I wondered what the gorgeous women in the slinky black dresses in the casinos frequented by James Bond et al. would have

61

done in my place. I thought about what they would have done for a good ten minutes.

And then I did it. I got in the car and headed home alone.

Chapter Six

And so spring drifted imperceptibly into summer. It was another of those springs that we get so frequently in New England, where if you're not paying attention for a week, you've missed it altogether. One day it's damp and chilly and you're wearing a wool jacket, and then within a week you're waking up sweating with your bedsheets twisted all around you, the sun is blindingly bright, and the temperature is hitting ninety degrees with some regularity.

I had turned in my last grades at the end of May, and in June I started summer school.

Three classes, I thought with relief. It didn't mean that I could do without Peach, but it meant – hopefully – that I could keep my focus where it belonged, in the classroom rather than in the bedroom.

Summers are important – not to mention fun – for not-yet-established professors, because the curriculum everywhere tends to get a little lighter. Students don't want to take calculus over the summer; they want to take their electives then, learn something interesting and a little offbeat. And so in the summer months, most colleges are more open to suggestions for subjects that aren't necessarily part of the general semester's curriculum.

I was teaching the same classes I had in the spring, *Life in the Asylum* and *On Death and Dying*. I was also teaching a Thursday evening class at the Boston Center for Adult Education, giving women tips and destination suggestions for world travel alone. When I was doing my undergraduate work, a friend and I – both of us travel-mad – had written a book on women traveling alone, and while I had traveled mostly on a shoestring since then, I knew that I could be helpful. And, besides, teaching the class was *fun*.

Peach, unfortunately, was less than pleased about my class on world travel. "What if I need you?" she asked. "Thursdays can be busy."

I shrugged. "It's just one night a week, Peach. I never work every night, anyway."

She wasn't deterred. "If one of your regulars calls," she warned darkly, "I'll have to send him to someone else."

I had my own regulars by then. And I am here to tell you that regulars are a very good thing. The thought of losing one was enough to give me pause . . . Well, actually, it *would* have given me pause, were it not for the fact that regulars can also be fickle. A sure thing isn't a sure thing until the money is in your pocket and you're on your way out the door. If the rest of life hadn't already taught me that, working for Peach certainly did.

It wasn't even particularly that I adored my regulars, even, or certainly not all of them. But they have the advantage of being a known factor in a swirling sea of unknowns.

One of the – oh, what is the word that I want? troubling? disconcerting? – things about being an escort is that you often feel like you're going on a series of blind dates. You never know who or what exactly is waiting on the other side of that door when it opens. That uncertainty can get a little wearing.

All right: it can get very wearing.

Besides that, you have to be "on" all the time. Taking an acting course or two might be, in retrospect, the best way to prepare for this job, because the moment the door opens you're committed to getting out of there with two hundred dollars in your pocket and, hopefully, a client who will request you again and again. And you need to work for that. Whatever it takes. Selling yourself all over again. Being exactly who he wants you to be. Chameleons, that's us.

Regulars are a relief from that uncertainty, that edge that is something like fear but not quite fear, that sense of always being onstage, always selling something, always trying to convince, to please . . . and, at the same time, trying to stay tuned to your inner voice for safety's sake. Regulars mean that you can relax a little. You know what to expect with them, what they like and don't like, how the visit is likely to go.

That which is known is comfortable.

So in essence, you could say that we have a goal every time we walk into a new situation, see a new client. The goal is always to make the guy a regular. Unless he's horrible, of course; and you can pretty much figure that one out in the first five minutes. The rest of them are fair game.

Some of these regulars, for me, evolved into something akin to an ongoing relationship, one that differed from other relationships only in that it ended with a financial transaction at the end of the evening. Not all of them I met through Peach – she tended to collect men who didn't want the same girl every week, because she didn't make as much money off that kind of regulars. I met some on my own, was introduced to others. And I loved them. I even developed a friendship of sorts with them, a real affection. Within the parameters of our defined roles, these were, in fact, real relationships.

There was Phil, who liked to show me off to his friends. We sipped cocktails together in trendy restaurants on Columbus Avenue, chatting with all the people he knew who "accidentally" happened by that night, before going back to his place for sex.

Robert took me to wine-tasting parties at Cornucopia-on-the-Wharf, whole dinners constructed around sampling wines from a given country or area. We'd sit at big circular tables and listen to the distributors discuss the wines while we ate and sipped, and Robert watched the other men watching my breasts. He always liked it when I wore low-cut dresses and flashy necklaces. It was a minor indulgence that I usually granted.

For Raoul – far and away my favorite client ever – I dressed in little black nothing cocktail dresses and went to the symphony and Handel and Hayden Society concerts and even the occasional opera. We ate dinner first, wonderful dinners near Symphony Hall, at Tables of Content or Tiger Lily. My time with Raoul felt oddly like an ongoing friendship: the sex always seemed to be a bit of an after-thought, fifteen minutes tacked on at the end of the evening because we both felt it to be our duty. More frequently than not he would ask, apologetically, if I'd mind terribly if we skipped that final portion of the evening; he was in his sixties, and quite naturally got tired. I always managed to express regret.

But even Peach's regulars – clients who would prefer to see me, but would see anybody else if I wasn't around – were important to my mental health. And her threat to send someone else to one of my regulars was real. But in the end a scheduled absence wasn't really all that different from what happened any other night I didn't work for her. Peach tried to be fair, but business was business, and she'd send another callgirl to anybody's regular in a heartbeat.

So, despite her reservations, I taught my evening class.

I liked the two day classes, don't get me wrong. But that night class was – well, honestly, it was sheer fun. Opinionated. Lively. It was exclusively female, all of the students being women with something of an adventurous mind and spirit, wanting to go to Thailand or Argentina or the Ukraine by themselves. Hikers, photographers, writers, adventurers. There was always lots of laughter, lots of wisecracks; it seemed that we had formed some kind of immediate solidarity around the shared facts of our being single, female, and wanting to see the world.

We talked about Muslim countries, and we talked about compromises. One of the younger women in the class who had sat stolidly in the front row until I could convince her that I really did want the chairs arranged in a circle, had assigned herself the role of Angry Young Woman. She wore t-shirts with messages like "A Woman Without A Man is Like a Fish Without a Bicycle," and Doc Martens, had her hair in a buzz cut, and she seemed ready to take on the world as though it had somehow personally affronted her. As, perhaps, it had.

"It's wrong," she said, her voice rising. "They can't make women cover themselves up, like it's somehow our fault that they can't keep their hands off us! What kind of patriarchal bullshit is that, anyway?"

I said, mildly, "It's their country."

She was almost out of her seat at that. "Oh, so if you travel somewhere they execute people without a fair trial, you'd just shrug and say they have the right to do it, it's their country?"

Someone from the other side of the room said, *sotto voce*, "Yeah, some country like Texas, for example."

The first student was undeterred. "Well? Where do you draw the line? Huh?"

I said, again as calmly as possible, "You can choose not to travel to places where you find the customs offensive or degrading. I have always felt that by choosing to visit a country, you have also chosen to accept their customs, or at least to acknowledge them and abide by them. You don't have to like them. And you don't have to go there."

I flashed back for a moment, then, remembering my junior year abroad in France, remembering wincing when American tourists with their inevitable loud voices and broad vowels came into the café I frequented, demanding hamburgers. With ketchup. I remember wondering why they bothered, even, leaving Cincinnati or Denver or wherever it was that they lived.

I cleared my throat. "I lived in Tunisia for two years," I said to the class. "I covered my head when I went out in public, and I wore a wedding band on my left ring finger, and I traveled all over the country, and I never had a single problem, a single unpleasant incident." I held up a hand to silence the Doc Martens woman, already seething, ready to launch a retort. "And no, I don't think that it's comfortable being in a country where you have to pretend that you belong to a man in order to be safe. That's why I don't live there. But if I went there with my set of ideas and my way of life, then I would not have enjoyed my stay as I did. And if you travel expecting people to second-guess your beliefs and your needs and your comfort level, then frankly, there's no point in traveling at all." I glanced at the girl in the Doc Martens. "Otherwise, you might as well stay in Cambridge, where you can dress however you like and take men to court for sexual harassment."

All right, so it was a little cold. But if we're all so evolved that we'll explore and respect and adopt foreign concepts like Feng Shui, and eat sushi and hummus, and dress in ethnic clothing, then we're really being hypocrites if we draw the line at belief systems. It's exactly like the middle-aged American tourists and their hamburgers. What's the point?

And I need to remember the same thing. I realized that the next night as I stood in a hotel corridor, waiting for the gentleman behind door number 148 to open it and invite me in. I'd like all of our clients to conform to my idea of how a man should behave; but that is, after all, only my own needs and values and preconceptions at work. I'm a traveler here, visiting your world for an hour. What are your customs? What are your taboos? How can I learn about you and have you feel good about my visit?

The night after that I decided not to work. I had *On Death and Dying* the following day and was giving back papers – the first one I had assigned to the class, breaking the ice around the difficult subject of children and death. The class had been asked to write a short story in which the writer attempts to explain death to a child. It was, as always, an assignment that left me a little teary. I'd spent the day reading and evaluating the papers, and was emotionally exhausted. Time for pajamas and television, time to order Indian food from the take-away down the street and invest in a little Quality Cat Time with Scuzzy.

Needless to say, Peach interrupted this program with one of her own.

She was brisk. "Jen, there's practically no one on tonight. I'll throw you a little extra. I don't want this guy calling another service."

I sighed. "How much extra?" I was at that point almost – almost – caught up with bills, but money was still tight and Peach knew it.

Lightning calculations on the other end of the phone, and then she sighed. "All right, an extra fifty." That meant, of course, that she was going to ask him to spring for the extra. I never, then or at any time that I worked for her, saw Peach reduce her own fee for any reason at all. She really didn't need to sigh as though I was robbing her.

In any case, the extra fifty had me hooked. I reached for pen and scrap paper. "Okay, Peach, I'll do it. What's his name?"

"Dave Harcourt. He's a regular. He lives in Needham. You'll need lingerie; do you have anything?"

"Sure." But it put an end to my hopes for a casual call, jeans and simple accessories.

"Great. He'll tell you what he wants. Call me back."

Dave surprised me: he was the only client I ever called who didn't immediately want to know what I looked like. He was more interested in my clothes closet. Or, more specifically, in my underwear drawer. "What will you be bringing?"

The word *bringing* seemed odd, but I was used to clients being nervous. "What do you like?" I asked. "I have –"

He interrupted. "Black stockings and a garter belt," he said. "And a couple of different bras. And a teddy. Oh, and what size shoes do you wear?"

"Nine," I said lamely. It sounded like he wanted a fashion show, not an escort. I winced. It sounded like it was going to be a busy hour.

"That'll do. Bring a couple of pairs, high heels, black."

"That sounds wonderful," I said. "I have a cocktail dress that –"

My efforts were unnecessary. "I don't really care what you wear," Dave said. "How long before you get here?"

Peach confirmed what I was thinking. "Put the stuff in a bag," she advised. "He doesn't want you to wear it, he wants to wear it himself. And be discreet, he lives in a residential area."

He had fairly mediocre taste in wine, even less taste in furnishings, and incredible eagerness to see what I'd brought with me. The problem, it transpired, was that we were not even close to the same size.

A fair amount of struggling, breathlessness, and epithets ensued. He gave up altogether on the teddy, but just managed to strap the bra on across his flabby chest. I stood behind him, trying to make the garter belt stretch far enough to hook together in the back, feeling oddly like a Victorian matron attempting to impose an hourglass figure on a debutante who had consumed one snack too many.

My debutante and I finally made it, and soon he had also struggled into the stockings and shoes and was striking poses in front of the floor-to-ceiling mirror that unfortunately constituted one of the living-room walls. He was visibly getting more and more excited by the view, and the only contribution that he needed from me was apparently to sip my wine and tell him how exceptionally beautiful he looked. We did finally have sex in the end, which I found slightly disconcerting, as he was still wearing my underwear, but it was successful from his point of view and he finally, reluctantly, got into his own clothes and gave mine back to me.

I never wore them again. It wasn't the association that bothered me; it was the fact that they were stretched beyond the point of no return.

Just as well, really, since after that Dave started asking for me. I even eventually bought a little Dave-kit, with plus size undergarments, and it worked out well for a year or so.

I kept thinking about the image of the traveler as a conceptual frame for prostitution, and was more and more intrigued by it. It worked both ways: the client gets a taste of exotica, of something out of the ordinary, expensive and beautiful and not at all what the guy who sits in the next cubicle is doing that night. Like Anne Tyler's Armchair Traveler, he visits a new country every time a new girl comes to his door. And the girl travels, too, but she's doing it on a shoestring, she doesn't know what to expect and has to be prepared for anything. It was a neat bit of categorization, I thought.

That weekend, and the following weekend, when I had free time, I went back to the books I had been reading before I started working for Peach, the mass of literature that exists out there about prostitution, madams, brothels. This time I went with the more academic texts, books with titles like *The Response to Prostitution in the Progressive Era,* and *Hell's Half-Acre: The Life and Legend of a Red-Light District.*

What was occurring to me was that there was too wide a gulf between my two jobs, to the point where I was feeling that I was living two lives. I found myself thinking about the one while performing the other, and while it gave me a secret smile, a moment of inner amusement, it did feel jarring. Running out to the post office on a Saturday morning, my hair uncombed, no makeup or jewelry, my sweatpants stained and tattered, I had the impulse to say to the man standing in front of me in line, "Do you know that tonight I'll earn two hundred dollars, that somebody will be glad to pay that for an hour of my company?" It really was a laugh: I looked like no one's idea of a callgirl.

Or on a call, with my head tipped back and my eyes closed while a client pawed at my bra, I'd think about what assignment I'd give to my *Asylum* class the following day. Might as well use your time, I told myself. Certainly it was less tedious if one could simply pretend to not be there.

And eventually I came to two decisions, ways that I could bring the two sides to my life somewhat closer together.

The first thing that I did was begin a proposal for the next summer's curriculum, for a class on the history and sociology of prostitution. I'd get the minimum enrollment, I figured, just out of prurient interest. And it would be a way of integrating what I was doing with who I really was. Okay, so it's justification, I'll admit it. But we all do it . . .

The other thing that I did was decide to tell a friend.

Chapter Seven

I decided that I had to talk to somebody about what I was doing.

I understand, now, why murderers feel driven to confess their crimes – at some level, every human action needs a witness. We don't exist in a void, and we don't think of ourselves outside of a context.

I was leading a completely dual life, teaching by day and being an escort by night, and never the twain shall meet.

It would help, I thought, if I could have just one person who knew both sides of me. Who respected my academic career while knowing about my being a callgirl.

I thought about Seth right away. Seth and I had been on-again, off-again friends for probably the longest of anyone I'd known. We met online before it was fashionable to meet online, had counseled each other via e-mails and the occasional visit through marriages and love affairs and degrees and disasters; and Seth, I knew, wouldn't judge me. Seth *cared*.

So one night between calls I dialed his number long-distance from the cell phone in my car. Seth lived in Manhattan. What the hell: I could afford it, now.

"It's just for a while, you know, until I can pay off the student loans."

His voice was concerned. "Yeah, but listen, are you safe?"

I giggled. "Safer than I've ever been, sweetie. I make sure it's on, believe me. You can count on that."

"I didn't mean that. You know what I mean."

"Yeah . . . I know what you mean, and I really think it's all right, Seth. Peach screens the clients pretty well, and so far the only ones I'm seeing are regulars, guys that she knows, guys who use her agency all the time. I insisted on that. I told her that I couldn't afford to get arrested. It's okay, really it is."

"I just worry about you, that's all."

"I know." A wave of affection washed over me. He was so sweet. "And I'm glad you do. Besides, in a weird way it's been really good for me."

"How so?"

"Well, just imagine. After the Peter Rat Bastard fiasco, with him trying to convince me that I wasn't worth anything – and think of all the other assholes I've dated and believed when they tried to unload their inadequacies on me. Well, news flash: there are a lot of men in this city willing to pay two hundred dollars just to be with me for an hour. They think I'm worth that kind of money. And I'm starting to believe that I *am* worth it. That's a pretty big ego lift, I've got to tell you."

"Yeah, but look at who they are."

I pulled over into a loading zone as my temper flared. Can't drive and tell someone off at the same time. "Yeah, Seth, you want to talk about who they are? Let's see. Last night it was one of the string section of the Boston Symphony Orchestra. And after him, a guy in a townhouse on Beacon Hill; there was a Renoir on the wall. And I'm on my way over to MIT right now. Real losers, Seth. You're right. I should have stayed with Peter the drug dealer. Now that was a class act. I'd much rather have *his* penis inside me." I drew in a shaky breath.

"All right, all right, calm down, honey. That wasn't what I meant."

He wasn't getting off the hook that easily. "The hell it wasn't."

Silence. Then: "Okay, so it was. So maybe I'm wrong about the kind of guy who sees a hooker."

I could feel my blood pressure rising again. "Hooker? You haven't been hearing anything, have you? What do you think, I'm cruising Kneeland Street in shorts and boots, walking up to cars and offering a good time in the back seat? Christ, Seth, I thought you were listening to me! I thought you'd understand!"

"Honey, all right, what you're doing is cool, I don't object, it's just that I don't want to see you hurt." Yeah, the patronizing thing always works with me. I considered hanging up, and very nearly did, but Seth and I had been friends for a long time . . .

"I thought you'd be the only man who wasn't" – I floundered for the right words, I'm not as articulate when I'm angry – "*stereotypical* in his thinking. I thought you'd see that there's class in doing this because I have class, and I wouldn't do it unless I could respect myself. We've had that conversation so many times, Seth, especially after Peter. Remember? I swore that after him I'd make sure that I was always able to sleep at night, I'd never feel that way about myself again?"

"Okay, okay. You're right. I was totally out of line there." Impossible to tell why he was backing down, but I wasn't going to look a gift horse in the mouth. "You're right, hon, okay? It's the stereotype that comes to mind, not the reality. I'm a product of the culture that produces the stereotypes. So educate me, but don't kill me. I was just reacting like a guy, like any guy would. You're like a sister to me, you know that."

"I'm not a hooker." Even to my own ears, it sounded sullen, like I was pouting. Good thing he was long-distance, I could blame it on distortion in the ether, or whatever it was that was carrying our voices.

"Of course you're not. You use the term callgirl? Okay, I will too, it sounds better. Listen, Jen, I didn't mean anything bad . . ." I let him grovel for a little while longer, but I needed to check in with Peach, see what the prospects were for the MIT guy. So I let Seth off the hook, he had squirmed long enough. Maybe he even understood as much as he was saying that he did.

But the conversation replayed itself later that evening as I stretched over the professor's desk and watched the fish swim around in his aquarium while he took me from behind. (Actually, that was one fantasy I thought was pretty cool, a boring meeting with a student the next day and the secret thought that he had been having sex on that very desk the night before, I could get into that one. As I was to find out, several of my clients thought along the same lines, fucking me in places that would later bring a secret sexual *frisson* – the table in the boardroom, the desk in the front of the lecture-hall, the examining-table in the doctor's office, that sort of thing. I wondered if they could still hear my screams echoing off the walls the next day.)

Seth's words intruded into my feeling good about the professor's pleasure. I have to say that some people are so delighted with you and what you do for them, it's hard not to get caught up in their happiness. This guy was like a kid at Christmas, exclaiming happily over my breasts, transported by joy when I touched him, chuckling wickedly as he cleared space on his desk. His orgasms were the closest thing to complete delight I think I've ever observed. Does it matter that it was a callgirl who got him there? Hell, no: joy is rare enough in our world, you've got to grab it and feel it and love it whenever you can. A woman had done that for him. It didn't matter who she was, only that he felt it.

But tonight I had Seth on my mind. The problem was that I had never thought of him in sexual terms, and here he had reacted, as he said, "like a guy." Well, he had the right, didn't he? He *was* a guy, after all . . . Except that for me he had never really been either male or female – he was just Seth. Sex didn't enter into it. When I was going through my I-think-I'm-a-lesbian phase we checked out the same women, but that was just a game. I didn't want him to be like everybody else. I wanted him to stay just Seth – safe, different. I didn't want to fight the same fights with him that I had to fight out there, every day, with everybody else.

So after that first night when I told him what I was doing, we went on with the e-mails and the occasional calls, and every time he asked me if I was still working, and when I said yes, he just said, "Be careful, honey. Just be careful."

And I liked that. Liked that he knew, and accepted, and cared.

Just after Christmas he sent me an e-mail: "Company's sending me to Boston! Woo hoo! What do you say to drinks at the Ritz and dinner at Morton's, their treat?"

I wrote back: "What do you think I say? I can't wait to see you! They're getting stingy, though, last year when you came, didn't they book you at the Four Seasons? Which is fancier?"

My inbox beeped a few minutes later. "Who cares? So long as there's room service, that's all I care about. The *Globe* and eggs and bacon delivered in the morning. My needs are simple. Besides, I got a suite this time. Meet me there next Thursday, seven o'clock, I'll have them chill some champagne for you."

I couldn't resist: "Which one?"

The e-mails were flying today. Beep. "You tell me, I'll order it. When did I ever settle for second best?"

I typed a quick response. "Well, there was your ex-wife . . . ."

Beep. "You *would* have to remind me. See you next Thursday. Be careful."

The week passed, and I took the Thursday night off. I tried to work on a new syllabus until about three and gave up and went down to the river for a brisk walk, ending up at the new Galleria Mall afterward. God, it was cold. I sincerely hoped that Seth would spring for a taxi to take us from the hotel to the restaurant. Five years now he'd been coming up to Boston, five years I'd been meeting him for drinks in whatever hotel he was staying at, followed by the inevitable dinner at Morton's. "There *are* one or two other restaurants in Boston, you know."

"Not in my opinion."

One last faint protest. "What if I become vegetarian?" At Morton's, they bring the cuts of meat to your table and you choose off the cart instead of the menu. The meat, needless to say, is at that stage uncooked. Vegan hell.

Seth was heartless. "Then you can watch me eat."

Thursday night I put on my universally acceptable little black cocktail dress and the pearls that were the only thing I'd salvaged

73

from my disastrous relationship with the rat bastard. I did the usual quick makeup job that had become second nature to me since starting to work for Peach, then put on my absolutely warmest winter coat and drove to the Ritz-Carlton. The company must be doing well, I thought. Rooms at the Ritz are around three hundred ninety-five dollars a night.

I parked in the underground lot beneath the Common, because I didn't want Seth having any awkwardness about a woman visitor charging her parking to his room. I collected the book I'd bought him that week as a present at the Avenue Victor Hugo – a first edition Swinbourne, no less – and headed up to his suite.

He was on the phone, and waved me in. "Okay, Dean, we'll have to get into it in the morning. Yeah. Yeah, okay. No, I'm on my way out for dinner now. Yeah, I've got that covered. Yeah, I'll talk to you then. Bye."

I raised my eyebrows. "The scintillating conversation of the movers and shakers never ceases to amaze me. I hear that Bill Gates can even construct full sentences when he tries."

"Doubtful," he said. "Nobody who's *anybody* majored in English, honey; you're a dying breed." Seth hugged me, then pulled back to inspect me. "How the hell are you? You look great."

"I'm freezing," I said. "And I didn't major in English, I just happen to be one of the few people who uses it correctly. It's a dismal day when one has to major in English in order to speak it." I cleared my throat dramatically. "And it looks like I've got to be the one to tell you, that tie has to go. Who picked it out, anyway?"

He made a face. "Catherine." Catherine was the new girlfriend, a semi-serious contender for the newly-available (since the past spring) position of Wife Number Three.

"I see." I raised my hands in mock defeat. "Far be it from me to second-guess Catherine." I took off my coat and sat down. I felt good, relaxed, so totally at home with him, despite the time and distance since we'd last been in the same room together. "However, it has to be said, her talents aren't exactly sartorial."

"Well," he said, sitting on the sofa across from me, "she may be the first woman I've dated who would actually know what that means, so I must be making some progress, right?"

I laughed. "God, Seth, it's good to see you."

"You, too, Tia Maria." The old nickname slipped out, and it jolted me out of my relaxation. "What's the matter?"

I picked at a nonexistent fiber on the cushion next to me. "Nothing, really. It's just that nobody calls me that anymore." Not since my college drinking days, when I preferred getting sick on Tia Maria to getting sick on any other alcohol. In those days, Seth sent me witty e-mails making fun of my inability to drink, and used the nickname on occasions where he wanted to either taunt or comfort me. It was with that thought in mind that I'd chosen Tia as my working name, when Peach asked me for one. "And, so, anyway, when I was thinking about a name to use for the business, I wanted something that was – oh, you know, connected to me in some way. So I use Tia. That's why it just seems weird hearing it here, out of that context." I felt like I was babbling. I didn't need to explain myself so much, right? Not to Seth.

He had gotten up and opened the champagne the right way, absorbing the pressure of the cork into his hand. Those among my clients who serve champagne seem to enjoy a thunderous popping sound followed by the cork ricocheting around the room. It's pretty adolescent. Yeah, I know, so my point is . . .? And, besides that, we mostly cater to the *nouveau riche*, and Seth was anything but. His name, still inexplicably retained by Wives Number One and Two, is Seth Niven Bradford III. "Champagne for my lady?"

I took the flute he offered. Chilled slightly, correctly. I shivered. "Thank you."

He poured his own and sat down again. It would have been gauche to offer a toast, and he didn't. "Speaking of that, are you doing all right? I worry about you. Sometimes there's stuff I read in the papers . . ."

I sipped the champagne and smiled at him. "That's your hometown, Seth. You've got a lot more crazies in New York, and a lot more tabloids. I told you, it's okay. And let's not talk about work, okay?"

He dropped it. That was the other thing I was loving about Seth: even the most disinterested man became absolutely and idiotically fascinated when the subject came up, and Seth could just stop talking about it.

It's an interesting phenomenon. Try it. I'm serious. The next time you're out for beers with some of your guy buddies, just mention to them that you know an escort. Or a madam. They'll drool all over you, guaranteed.

Of course, you also won't be able to move off the subject. But it's still an interesting experiment, if you have an evening to kill.

At a stifling faculty wine and cheese party I once said casually (and recklessly, but what the hell, it was Harvard, I was a mere teaching assistant, they weren't going to offer me tenure anyway, and I was bored and already had three glasses of really bad port under my belt) that I had an acquaintance who was a madam. I was immediately besieged.

I found myself strenuously wishing that they could be as fascinated with my dissertation research. Obvious prurient interest was couched in suitably detached and almost academic questions.

I didn't look (well, after all, I *did* still want the occasional course they threw my way), but if I had, I'd bet anything on them all having hard-ons at the mere *mention* of prostitution. There's something about the subject that men find absolutely riveting. "But isn't it true that most of the women involved in the industry are in fact nymphomaniacs fulfilling their own sexual needs?" A goatee wobbling over a glass of stale sherry.

In your fantasies, jerk-off.

And it's equal-opportunity fascination, equally enthralling to the liberals who want to legalize prostitution as the fundamentalists who want to preach against it.

But it didn't matter. I had a safe haven, an island in the sea of predictable and offensive male interest. The goatees could drool to their hearts' content: I had Seth.

Seth didn't want to know who, or where, or how many. He didn't want to ask about orgasms or prices or whether the girls doing doubles really were lesbians ("Isn't it true that . . .?"). He just wanted to be sure that I was safe.

I loved Seth.

We drank wonderful champagne and didn't talk about my work – well, after all, it was a fairly dismal subject, since it looked like another fall of sporadic community college courses. We didn't talk about his work, either. Seth was very high up in a company that plans to take over the world once Microsoft, as all empires must, eventually falls. Most of what he did was classified as "I could tell you, but then I'd have to kill you."

We just talked. About a mutual friend who was billed third in a current major motion picture (and am I the only person in this country waiting for the announcement, "Soon to be a minor motion picture?" I'd actually go see that one), and who we both snidely and jealously dismissed as a mere Flavor of the Month. "No staying power," Seth said, and I nodded wisely, being by then on my second glass of champagne.

We talked about Catherine's work on her doctorate, at which point I darkly and bleakly pointed out that she'd do better getting some sort of technical certification: look at all the good my degree did me. A little cynicism here and there never hurts, and I could feel safely superior since she was still working toward the Holy Grail, whereas I had already attained it. We talked about Catherine asking Seth to open up more to her, to trust her, and his knee-jerk response to her questions. "So what am I supposed to say? She asks me what I'm thinking, right now, and I'm sitting there wondering what time the game starts." We talked – briefly – about my current lack of a love interest. "It's hard with working for Peach, Seth. I mean, I'm not available a whole lot of evenings, and where would I tell him I was?"

"You could tell him the truth."

"Oh, right. You're so tolerant and liberal, how would you feel if Catherine went out two nights a week and had sex with somebody else?"

He looked at me over the rim of his glass. "We have an open relationship. Catherine's free to have sex with whomever she chooses."

"Uh-huh." I nodded. "But say you're watching her get ready – after all, it's not anything personal, it's just work – and you watch her put on all this fancy underwear. Fancy underwear that she's usually too tired to put on for you . . ."

My voice trailed off. I had been a graduate student, myself: I knew how Catherine must feel most of the time. Exhausted beyond exhaustion. Open relationship? I'd bet she barely had energy to fuck Seth once a week, much less anybody else. Getting laid can be high maintenance, and she was preparing for her comps, probably studying for ten hours a day along with working on and attending any classes for which she was a teaching assistant. Sex becomes pretty irrelevant at that point.

I took a breath and continued. "So imagine that, and imagine that sometimes she comes home and tells you about her calls . . . you know, she talks about work, we all do it, just to unwind. And she says this guy tonight was into degrading her, calling her a slut, a whore . . . And then she asks you if you want to go to bed, she touches you, and all you can think of is this other guy playing those games with her, touching the same breast you're touching . . . You might get turned on, and you might get disgusted, but you'll sure as hell have a reaction."

Seth was getting red. "All right, maybe. But that's me and Catherine. All right, it would be tough. But it doesn't mean that the right person couldn't know."

"The only people I know of who would tolerate that in a supposed loved one are pimps and addicts." I know I sounded harsh, but it was the truth.

And I never could figure that one out. In all my time in the business, I never saw a "normal" healthy relationship work in which the woman was actively working as a callgirl and the man was aware of what she did. On the other hand, lots of drug addicts functioned that way. Lots of abusive relationships, also.

It was really odd, too, because if you think about it, it could work. It *should* work. I mean, in the abstract. I absolutely compartmentalized what I did for Peach as "work." It wasn't sex. It may have been sex for my clients — well, I should hope that it *was* sex for my clients! — but it wasn't sex for me. I acted my way through a sexual situation for an hour and then it was over and I went out for a coffee and got back to my own life.

One of Peach's girls said to me once that she had mentioned it to her boyfriend, just as a theoretical concept, and he thought it would constitute cheating. That really cracked us both up, because nothing could be further from the truth. Like kissing your child, then kissing your mother-in-law, then kissing your lover. Same physical action. Totally different events.

But then again, we have to remember that the industry exists precisely because men take sex so seriously.

And of course the problems all come when it stops being

abstract. I teach; I'm actually very, very good at teaching. I teach adults who do not look at me as a role model, but as a source of information. Or grades. Whatever. What I do in my own time, or what I do as a part-time job, does not change my teaching, my ability to inspire, to challenge, to excite students' minds.

Yet if anyone knew that I also worked as a callgirl, my career would be over. Not even the community colleges would hire me. No one would be able to define why the two are incompatible, but everyone would be sure that they are. "I may not be able to define pornography, but I know it when I see it." Yeah, right.

Or, just for the sake of argument, bring it even closer. One of the escorts working for Peach, Beth, taught middle school – seventh and eighth grade. Now, we all know that she is precisely the same teacher now that she was before you knew she was working weekends for Peach. Right? And nobody really seriously suspects that she is encouraging sexuality or promoting pornography among her students (as if seventh and eighth graders needed any encouragement in that direction). I mean, aside from the ethical questions involved (and my experience is that Peach's girls fret far more about ethics than any other group of people I've ever encountered), what would be the point? Middle school students can't afford Peach's rates . . . So there should be no reason for Beth not to be able to do both. Theoretically.

Theory has amazingly little to do with reality.

So let's go a step further, let's bring it closer still. You're liberal, I hear you shrugging this off: Sure, it's fine for Beth to teach during the week and work for Peach on the weekends. Capitalism at its best, right? So answer this one: would you want your eleven-year old daughter to be taught English by a woman who is, in addition to a teacher, a prostitute?

Tell the truth.

Gotcha. I rest my case.

Callgirls talk more with each other about morality than does any other professional group I can think of. More than priests and ministers and rabbis, even, because those people are talking about religion, which always puts a different spin on morality. I can think of so many conversations . . . sitting in my car, waiting for a client, having a drink at Jillian's or coffee at the Triton Bookstore . . . and wrestling with issues. Being worried about the wife, what this might be doing to her. Talking about how Peach thought that somebody owed her one hundred and twenty dollars, when the girl knew that she was actually holding one hundred eighty for Peach. Talking about how much it hurts, in one's soul, to lie to one's boyfriend. Talking about going to confession on Saturdays and wondering if one ought to be mentioning one's profession. Talking about the questionable ethics of learning a man's areas of vulnerability in order to use them for one's own purposes. We talked about ethics more than about any other single issue – including money – and I'm not sure that any of us resolved any of the struggles that we discussed. But they were real for us, pressing, urgent, important. And that's one of the reasons I still see red when I hear someone making fun of a prostitute for having no standards. If anything, we set the bar a trifle higher than most of you do.

Maybe we did because we didn't get to disguise our issues the way that most people do. Affairs and marital infidelities can be rationalized away. Corporate cheating can be explained and justified. For us, it cuts a little closer to the bone. Try sitting in a guy's living room, making out with him, while a picture of his supposedly happy family smiles at you from the end table. It never kept me from doing my job. But it always left me with a lot of disturbing questions. And no amount of rationalization or justification – or martinis – was going to just magically make them go away. I had to face them. We all did. Perhaps that's another reason why alcohol and cocaine played such a large role in our lives.

Sometimes you just need a little numbing from all the meanness that you see.

But back to Seth. We'd gone through a good two-thirds of the champagne when he consulted his Rolex. "Well, this is great, but we need to get started."

There's going to be competition for our reservation at Morton's at eight-thirty on a Thursday night? Boston isn't that cosmopolitan, and I was feeling relaxed and comfortable. "Come on, Seth, let's finish the champagne first."

He got up and reached into his back pocket and took out his wallet. He took out a few bills – I couldn't see what denomination they were – and came over to where I was sitting, putting them on the table next to my champagne flute. He was tugging a little distractedly at the unfortunate tie. "No, I just want to make sure that we have time before we leave for dinner."

Did the champagne temporarily remove every one of my brain cells, or am I just incredibly naïve? I looked up at him. I must have looked stupid. I know I sounded stupid. "Time for what?"

And I *still* didn't know where this was going. You, gentle reader, will have caught on by now; but for somebody who can be so cynical about world politics, astute about historical interpretation, enlightened in her participation in the sex industry, I am still and will always be the most trusting and gullible woman on earth. My husband once asked me, "Hey, did you know that the word gullible isn't in the New Oxford Dictionary?" and, indignant and astonished, I was halfway to the bookcase before I caught the amused glint in his eye.

They ought to lock me up for my own good.

Seth stopped next to my chair, put his champagne glass on the occasional table next to the hundred-dollar bills he had just set down there, and without further ado unbuckled his belt. "I want to be sure we have time for you to suck me off," he said.

You know how, when you're in a car accident, the final seconds before you hit the other car suddenly move in slow motion? Your situation is instantly absolutely crystal-clear, and nothing exists beyond you and the vortex that is drawing you inevitably closer to disaster, and you feel almost disinterested, as though it had nothing to do with you, as though it were just a movie. And this happens even though just seconds before it you were saying, "Oh, shit. Oh, God, no. Oh, fuck." Then at the same time another part of your brain is arguing with your senses, doing the full-blown denial thing, saying that it isn't really happening. Now *that*'s real chicken soup for the soul, fuck those stupid books, give me a good hearty slice of denial any day.

Of course, that part of the brain usually shuts up on impact. Even at its most persuasive, denial can't do much of anything creative with twisted metal, with the slow finality of impact, with the color and taste of blood.

They say that when those things happen your life passes in front of you, but I don't think so. I think time just slows down enough for you to fully understand how little control over your life you really have.

I'll bet it's especially slow for people who spend all their time trying to control things.

Anyway, that's what happened that Thursday night at the Ritz-

Carlton. Part of my brain was talking calmly and rationally, telling me that this wasn't really happening, this wasn't real. I was misunderstanding what was happening. No. No. If I could just sit still and not breathe, I'd find out it wasn't real.

At the same time another part of me knew with dreadful certainty what was ending and how terrible was my loss. I was watching everything spin out of control – Seth, our years of friendship, the warmth I had been feeling, my history of leaning on him emotionally, my perception of who he was, to hell with that, my perception of who *I* was . . . and it wasn't the past spinning around there with me, it was the future. I was Alice Through the Looking-Glass, bewildered at the sudden perception that nothing made sense anymore, that nothing that I had always accepted as real was, in fact, reality. If this could happen, anything could happen. I could be the White Rabbit. He could be the Jabberwocky. Our shared past meant nothing. Our future was nonexistent. And I had never imagined a future that didn't have Seth in it.

I finally managed to pull myself together – there hadn't been any impact of metal on metal, after all, but I had to deal with the reality of the disaster anyway. The reality was that the belt was unbuckled and the zipper was going down, and if I didn't do something right away I was going to see Seth's penis, and I couldn't bear that.

Something inside me would break if I did.

My mouth was dry. I looked at him and all the words inside me couldn't get out. All I said was, "Why?"

He paused with his hand still on the zipper. His tone was mildly curious. "Well, you're a hooker now, aren't you?"

* * * * * *

I don't know what the worst part of that story is. That Seth could make that kind of assumption about me, based on my employment? That he had retained, despite my attempts to explain my life, all of his prejudices about prostitution? That he had been everything to me, and I was nothing to him?

Or was it simply that I had lost a friend?

A Barbra Streisand character once said something about, "I may be a prostitute, but that doesn't mean I'm easy." Just as callgirls see sex within a structured work setting and sex with a chosen partner as completely different things, so too is our morality unaffected by our work. I may exchange a sexual encounter for money, but that will never mean that I treat sex lightly, or give it away casually. I'm not easy.

If anything, it's the other way around. I was actually far more promiscuous in the years and months before I started working for Peach. I remember – and can I tell you how ashamed I am at this memory? – having sex once with a guy *just because* it was easier to go ahead and have sex with him than it would have been to argue with him about leaving my apartment. Just because I was tired and it was the quickest way out of a tedious situation.

That's what is humiliating, you see. It's humiliating to hurt myself like that, to treat my mind and my body and my soul like shit, fucking someone whose name I couldn't even remember even as he was entering me, giving in to his obnoxious, degrading words and behavior, simply because I didn't have the energy to do what I wanted to do. That's a horrible realization: that I was willing to hurt myself, to hurt my soul, just because I was *tired*.

I wasn't acting within any particular moral framework back then, needless to say. But nobody then assumed that they could simply thrust their penis in my face and expect me to respond. I was still a nice girl, then.

I took it more seriously, once I started working for Peach. I didn't fuck strangers anymore simply because it would have been easier than standing up to them. I started thinking more of myself. I came to an understanding, a policy, if you will, that I would exchange sex for two things, and two things only: for love, or for money. It sure as hell helped me to sleep better at night.

Being a callgirl is being a professional. I interacted with my clients the same way that any service professional interacts with their clients. Some I liked, some I didn't. I treated them all the same; I treated them all fairly. I charged a fair price for my services and didn't cheat or cut corners. Some of Peach's girls would try to get the guy to come as soon as possible, and then would leave afterward. I always stayed the full hour, if the client wanted me to. Always. If I left with my dignity intact, it was important to me that the client had his dignity intact, too.

So where did this crazy idea come from that just because I do it professionally, I'm available twenty-four hours a day – for free, mind you – to anyone with the requisite equipment and needs? Just because I do it professionally, I love to do it and want it all the time? Do you really believe that we're all nymphomaniacs who can't get enough? You've been watching too many skin flicks, my friend.

Let's rephrase: do you see a whole lot of psychologists begging to analyze people on their time off? Or chemistry teachers who just can't stop trying to cram the Periodic Table of Elements down people's throats at dinner parties? Or a Web designer who goes around offering to put together killer Internet sites on Saturday afternoons for free, just because they like coding?

Oh, please Get a clue.

It's a job. *It's a job.* Most if us can't wait until it's over, and don't think about the next time until we absolutely have to.

It's a job. We know you wish we'd play the fantasy for you all the time, and we'll do it well, but please just accept and be grateful for our willingness to do it as a profession. We'll whisper in your ear, even as we probe it with our tongue, that we'll fantasize about you tomorrow. We'll scream in the throes of apparent orgasm and we'll gasp to you that all we want to do is please you and we'll swear that this is the best, the best it's ever been . . . and all that that means is that we're good at our jobs.

I worked at one time for a software company. The engineers there had me absolutely convinced that all that they cared about in life was the database application they were designing. They came in early, they worked late. They sat in the cafeteria and talked about system architecture. They made jokes about life in cubicle-land.

But do you know what? All that meant was that they were good at their jobs. Because in the grand scheme of things, they knew that it was just a database, a database that stored and kept track of insurance policies. And when they went home they thought about their families, their goals, their pleasures, the book that they were reading, the movie they wanted to see. They didn't think about coding, or databases, or configuration specs. They didn't confuse their jobs with their lives.

So give me a little credit; look at me as you might have looked at one of those software prima donnas. Like them, I may have liked what I did, but I never mistook it for reality.

Never.

Chapter Eight

I had thought that the class on prostitution would work as a summer elective, but as soon as I'd turned it in to the Curriculum Committee, they raced around like crazy to get it into an addendum to the fall catalogue. I'm still not sure why. Maybe someone thought that there weren't enough feminist-oriented classes in the fall lineup; maybe they just needed something a little different to spice up the hour between *World History 101* and *Elements of Logic*. Or maybe they were financially astute, watching the bottom line, knowing that a possibly-prurient class would attract students, donors, and attention. Whatever the reason, it was going to appear, and I was going to have to be prepared to teach it.

So I suddenly found myself immersed in prostitution. One could say that my research was both academic and practical in nature. Theory and reality. By day, I sat in the stacks at the library at Boston University reading, taking notes, waiting for the magical moment that inevitably happens when all the information suddenly takes on a form in my mind, and I see clearly how to present it, like a sparkling path opening up before me. By night, it would be off to the races. I usually arrived at the library already dressed for work; it was easier to leave directly from Commonwealth Avenue than to go all the way back to Allston to change.

One evening I headed over to the BU student commons to get something to eat, having come to the realization that I was tired and hungry and was not assimilating any of what I had been reading for the past half-hour. When I had been a student here, this area had been just a cafeteria. Now it seemed to have become the equivalent of a mall Food Court – perhaps so that when the mall rats arrived at college they would feel right at home, wouldn't have too much nostalgia for their lost teenaged years. God forbid that we should ask anything too difficult of them.

I picked up a sandwich and a soda from a refrigerated display case that appeared to specialize in very small, expensive, exotic juices, and headed over to a table.

It was a while before I noticed the guy at the next table looking at me. I had that part of my brain turned off, or at least turned very low – the part of the brain that notices men and flirts with them and so on. When I finally did realize what was happening, to be honest, I was shocked.

I may well have been accustomed to dealing with undergraduates in my classes; I may well have been accustomed to having men be attracted to me; what I was not accustomed to was having the two come together. But unless I was mistaken, an undergraduate was about to come on to me.

And, in fact, he did. Asked about what I was reading. Indicated that he had noticed that my coffee cup was empty. Offered to refill it for me.

Our little tête-à-tête was interrupted before it really had gotten going by the ringing of my cell phone. It was Peach. "Work," she said economically. "Guy up in Chestnut Hill."

I took the notes as discreetly as I could and disconnected. "I have to go," I told the undergraduate. He had a ponytail. I really like ponytails.

"How about that coffee, later?" he suggested. "I was enjoying the conversation."

"Sorry." And I really was: it was a nice change to be neither callgirl nor professor. I smoothed my skirt and stood up. "It has been nice."

And it was. Real life intruding, with a lingering promise that maybe it isn't so bad out there, after all. That when this is all over there may be a place for me somewhere. That young men find me interesting and attractive without having been informed of my measurements – or of my ability to grant them a grade.

So I was feeling some sort of tender warmth, a longing, a lingering thought that maybe if, just maybe . . . It was bittersweet. I actually used that word, in my mind: bittersweet. I had never really understood the expression before, something I almost wanted, but knew that I couldn't have.

I knew the truth, of course: if I had gone for it, I would have found that it wasn't what I wanted, after all. Maybe I liked the feeling of wanting. Maybe I liked the feeling of knowing that there were options out there, that the world was still turning, that it would still be there when I was ready for it again.

I was smiling when I got in my car. "I could have had a date tonight," I informed my reflection in the rearview mirror. "I could have had a *real* date tonight." I said it with triumph.

You wouldn't have believed that a two-hundred-dollar an hour callgirl could be that insecure, would you? Surprise, surprise, surprise.

It didn't last, of course. And in fact maybe it was a gift that had been given to me, a moment of expectation and happiness and innocence.

Because that very night was to be a lesson in the sadness of the profession.

Nothing happened there that I could use in my notes for the new class. What I learned that night could go nowhere but in my heart; but it took up residence there, and the innocence was gone, and all that it left in its wake was a feeling of irreparable and eternal sadness.

The client Peach sent me to lived alone in a gorgeous apartment in Chestnut Hill. There are Chestnut Hills in various cities all over the United States, I have learned, and they all have one thing in common: money. This apartment was filled with appropriately lit fine objets d'art, furniture that clearly had been constructed several centuries ago, and paintings whose provenance I recognized. Minor works, perhaps, but by far-from-minor artists.

The client was a slender man whose skin was so pale that it was nearly translucent in places. He had a gentle, sad smile and didn't talk a lot. Dvořák was playing in the background, the New World Symphony. He served me sherry and we went to the bedroom.

Once there, he asked me to strip to my underwear, which on that night as on many others was a gauzy camisole over my bra and panties. "Do you have your makeup bag with you?" he asked, still with that sweet melancholic look. "All I want to do is watch you put on your makeup."

"Just – put on makeup?" I was a little baffled.

"Yes, and talk to me." Oh, okay, that made sense, I would talk dirty while he watched me do something. That wasn't particularly new. Last Tuesday I had talked dirty to a client while touching myself. Tedious, but he had liked it.

I settled on to the bed and drew out the required instruments – mascara, eyeliner, eyeshadow, blush. "What would you like to talk about?" I asked, as suggestively as I could, while he settled into a Louis Quinze chair at the foot of the bed.

"Tell me that you're getting ready to go out with Daddy," he said, and his voice had taken on an echo, as though it were coming from very far away. "Tell me that the sitter will be here soon, tell me where Daddy's taking you for dinner," he said.

I froze for a moment. I truly, honestly wanted to cry. I did what he wanted me to do, of course; what else was there to do? I chatted on and watched myself in my compact mirror so I wouldn't have to watch him masturbating while I pretended to be his mother. "We'll call when we get there to make sure that everything is okay here. And I'll give you a special kiss before I leave . . ." I held the tears at bay. Barely.

He gave me a lot of money, later – far too much money, a seventy-dollar tip over the usual. Most girls would have loved it, considered it an easy call, laughed about it later. I drove home to Allston, feeling hollow inside and wondering what had happened in his childhood to have so warped his sexuality. And why he had chosen to work through his obvious pain in the context of a callgirl rather than in the office of a therapist . . .

Some calls I made involved harmless role-playing, the kind of stories that they read in the skin magazines, that they see in the porno flicks: "Pretend that I'm a doctor, and you're the nurse who works for me . . ." Or, "Pretend that I'm your teacher, and you want an A in my class . . ."

This was something different altogether. And I felt it in my soul. Not even Barry, on Beacon Street, had touched my soul. This client had. I wonder about him, even now, I wonder if he still has callgirls pouting in mirrors and assuring him that Mommy really loves him. And I say a prayer. It can't hurt.

That night, it was hard to concentrate on writing the bibliography for my new class. I gave up after an hour and two glasses of red Côtes du Rhône and simply surfed the Net, not looking for books, just looking for something to get my mind off the sad little man in Chestnut Hill. I wasn't altogether successful.

Recently, someone was asking me about the time I spent working for Peach. "But they want you to do really weird stuff, don't they?" It's a standard question. When I answer it – if I decide to answer it – I never talk about the man in Chestnut Hill. I never talk about how I still feel when I think of his needs, and his pain.

As for the other clients having weird needs . . . well, that depends, of course, upon one's definition of weird. I happen to think that it's weird to allow people to keep guns in their homes that kill hundreds of children every day. I don't think, by that standard, that a guy wearing a bra is any too strange.

As I said, we all have our own definitions.

The fact remains that in this profession, one encounters a range of sexual tastes and fantasies that one probably wouldn't experience first-hand if one had fewer partners. Partly, I think, it's because when the encounter is professional rather than personal, a client may feel freer to express the fantasies that may not be considered mainstream. Here, it's safe. A callgirl, after all, isn't going to be shocked or disturbed by odd behavior. She isn't going to call you names or reject you or make you feel bad. If anything, she's going to tell you how exciting you are. Cool.

She isn't in a position to use unusual behavior or desires to question the validity of your relationship with her. A new girlfriend, on the other hand, might look askance when first presented with an unusual request. "You want to do – *what?*"

I think that some men call the agency precisely so that they can play out the "forbidden" fantasy, experience the side that is hidden from colleagues, wives, girlfriends, neighbors. They might enjoy vanilla sex with their regular partner and then call us when they want to explore something more risqué, something less acceptable to the mainstream.

That aspect of it reminds me a little of a conversation that takes place in the film *Analyze This*, between Robert de Niro, who is playing a Mafia don with anxiety attacks, and Billy Crystal as his therapist. De Niro has just said that he had experienced a moment of sexual dysfunction with his girlfriend.

"So, you're having marital problems?" questions Crystal.

"Naw, my marriage is fine."

"Then why do you have a girlfriend?"

"I do things with her I can't do with my wife."

Crystal appears genuinely baffled. "What do you do with your girlfriend that you can't do with your wife?" he asks.

The Mafioso seems shocked by the question. "Hey," he says, "those are the lips that kiss my children good-night, all right?"

It seemed that I was sometimes dealing with men thinking along those lines, men who wanted to play something, or try something, that they didn't want to share with their partner – because, in their heart of hearts, they really didn't want to *be* with anyone who did those things. Callgirl as slut. It's just another level of the eternal problem: men want to have sexual experiences, they want to date promiscuous and sexy girls, but when it comes to marriage – whoa. That's different. The mother of my children. No question here: she has to be a Virgin. With a capital V.

Doesn't make sense, but there it is.

All in all, though, most of the fetishes and unusual activities that I encountered were fairly benign, essentially harmless. And beyond the games and the role-playing and the toys – well, a lot of it was fun. Colored and flavored condoms. Purportedly sensual oils and body rubs. Vibrators and dildos and porn films on big-screen televisions.

Fun, mindless, entertaining, and lucrative.

Except for the guy in Chestnut Hill.

That night, for the first time since I had started working for Peach and stopped worrying about money, I took a sleeping pill.

There are some nightmares that it just isn't worth it to invite in.

Chapter Nine

I resolutely put the Chestnut Hill client out of my mind. I had far too many other thoughts, thoughts of a practical nature, with which to deal. For one thing, eighteen people had enrolled in my class *The History and Sociology of Prostitution*, and, ready or not, it was going to happen.

September in Boston is nothing short of glorious. It's usually still too hot, of course, but the leaves know what's happening and are starting their slow demise into a fiery spectacular death. Mornings are chilly and evenings cold. There is at least the promise of something more than heat, heat, and more heat.

It's special here for a lot of other reasons. Boston and Cambridge are educational meccas; they lie low during the summer months, but suddenly come alive with the influx of students in the fall. The sidewalk in front of the Berklee School of Music – known as the Berklee Beach, for obvious reasons – fills with young uncovered bodies. Dreadlocks and tattoos and piercings and cases containing esoteric musical instruments.

The coffeehouses, bars, and Irish pubs are suddenly so full that they have people trickling out the doors. The venerable old trains of the Green Line are inundated with freshmen away from home for the very first time, and making that fact known to the world, sitting on the steps while people try to enter the trains around them, world-weary and arrogant from their extraordinary experiences in high school in Hudson, New Hampshire, or Seekonk, Massachusetts, or Sanborn, Maine.

Even the air feels different.

They say that January first marks the new year, but that isn't true here: for us, it's the third of September, when there is nothing behind to mourn and nothing ahead but promise. U-Haul trucks are everywhere. Hardware stores fill with earnest young customers. Anything can happen. People smile at one another. For a few charmed weeks, it feels as though anyone could make a new beginning, anyone could start a new life, anyone could become what he or she is destined to become.

There's an indefinable air about the whole city, a sense of expectation, of eagerness. Yes: the real new year is in September, when notebooks are still pure and white, when textbooks and course syllabi look exciting, and when foreign films suddenly start making sense for the first time.

That September, however, was hotter than any one I could remember. It was also, fatefully, the month that my car had to be inspected.

Please understand this: I loved my Civic. This isn't a commercial, or anything, but honestly, I had 140,000 miles on it – and I ride the clutch, mind you – and I hadn't had to replace anything major, ever. It started up every morning, no matter how cold it was.

I can't really blame the car for not passing inspection; I never paid much attention to it between inspections. If I had been a better owner, this wouldn't have happened.

The guy in the shop said he could have it ready by Monday noontime.

The problem was, of course, that in the escort business, Saturday and Sunday nights aren't good nights not to work. Friday was the best night to take off; most of the girls did their personal dating on Fridays. It was a bad night for work, because guys had just gotten paid and thought they could go down to the bar and flash the cash around and get laid for nothing. They didn't admit defeat and call the service until after midnight, by which time I personally was way too tired to go out on a call.

Saturdays were good for regulars and for guys who planned their weekend around the agency. A lot of them wanted to see an escort and then afterward go out to the clubs, or on a real date, or meet their wives somewhere for dinner. So there were always a lot of early calls, the ones I liked the best. I loved calls that had me home and curled up with Scuzzy by ten-thirty.

Sundays were always good for business: it was the last hurrah of the weekend, when Monday started staring people in the face and they didn't like how it looked.

So I called Peach that Friday around four and told her that I was without wheels for the duration. She wasn't happy. That was under-standable. I'm reasonably sure that at least some of my regulars stayed faithful to me because I had my own transportation. It's a lot less ostentatious than pulling up to a suburban house in a brightly-lit taxi – or having one beep the horn outside when the hour is up. It's also a lot cheaper for the client, because he gets charged extra to help cover paying the driver. The cost of transportation to and from the client's place was generally shared by the callgirl and the client, with Peach negotiating as much as she could from the client. None of it ever came out of her fee. Nothing ever did.

So, for the first time, I was without my own car. Peach, however, was nothing if not positive. "Not a problem," she assured me. "I'll get you a driver."

Probably at least half to three-quarters of the girls who work for the service used a driver. A lot of them were college students living in dorm rooms; and the first advice that any school in Boston gives to prospective students is: Get rid of your car. The T – the public transportation system – is efficient and inexpensive; Boston traffic sucks; and the city employs (or so I am convinced) ex-Gestapo guards as meter police. I once met a woman whose son, who hap-pened to be a police officer, ticketed her car in front of the house that they shared. True story. And it's a fact that I have personally paid enough parking tickets to deserve having a small building – at the very least – named after me.

So the girls used drivers. I had already met one of them, Luis, who worked part-time for Peach while he went to business school. During my first week, back before she trusted me to hold cash for her, I'd meet him in Kenmore Square to give him Peach's take from the money I'd received from the client. I'd seen him once or twice after that at social gatherings – Peach had singled me out from among the women who worked for her as being worthy of her friendship, and occasionally invited me over to her house for late-night soirées. Luis had been there, seemed to always be there. He and I looked at each other in a way that said we were both interested, but not yet.

I don't know where Peach got her drivers. She was usually having some sort of trouble with one or another of them at any given time, but I had never asked her about any of it.

That Saturday I showered and put on a clean pair of shorts and t-shirt (no sense in getting dressed yet when you don't know who you're going to be seeing, and what they're going to want you to wear) and flipped on the television. Nothing. So I put a tape of old *Frasier* episodes in the VCR and was just settling in nicely, with Scuzzy purring next to me, to watch Niles have a telephonic tiff with Maris. And then my own telephone rang.

It's funny, you *want* the phone to ring because you want to make money, and at the same time you are disappointed when it does because you know how annoying the next couple of hours could potentially be.

"Jen? Got work for you."

I pulled a pad of paper across the coffee table and flipped the lid off the felt-tipped pen. "Go ahead."

"It's a regular." She always told me that when it was somebody I didn't know. Trying to reassure me, I expect. "Jake. Number is 508-555-5467. You'll have to get directions from him, it's in Marblehead."

"Okay. What did you tell him about me?" This was the most crucial information, from my point of view: it determined my persona for the evening.

"You're twenty-eight, 36-25-35, new to the business. You can be in graduate school or something. I told him you're getting a friend to drive you up there. I said your car is in the shop."

So that meant she was charging him extra without telling him where it was going. That wasn't unusual: some clients didn't like the feel of a "professional" driver; it took away from the fantasy that the girl really wanted to be there. If this guy was in Marblehead – way up on the North Shore – it was really going to cost him.

None of my business: that was how Peach earned her fee. All I had to say was that my car was in the shop. Stick to the truth whenever possible: the liar's greatest secret. "Okay."

"Call John on his cell phone. It's 555-3948. He's been there already. He'll cost you sixty dollars round trip. You'll be getting three-twenty from the client. Give John directions to your place and an ETA, and talk to the client, and call me back."

"Okay."

I put down the phone, feeling both satisfied that I had a call and was going to make some money, and at the same time wishing that I could just stay home and hang out with Scuzzy and Frasier at the Café Nervosa. A double mocha latte here, please.

Scuzzy was glaring at me. He always knew when I was about to leave, presumably deliberately ruining his evening. I sighed and picked up the phone again. "Hello, may I please speak with Jake?"

"Yeah." Scintillating conversationalist, I could tell right off the bat. I'm perceptive that way.

"Oh, hi, Jake. This is Tia, I'm a friend of Peach's. She asked me to call you."

"Uh-huh." He wasn't going to make this easy.

I took a breath. Why the hell do you think I'm calling, asshole? "Peach thought you might like me to spend some time with you this evening. Would you like me to come over?"

"Well, that depends. Tell me a little about yourself."

I was getting good at this. When a potential client asks this question, take it from me, he isn't interested in learning about my favorite author or my thoughts on the political situation in Yemen. "Well, I'm twenty-eight years old. I'm five feet seven, I weigh 126 pounds, I measure 36-25-35 and wear a C-cup bra. I have medium-length wavy brown hair and green eyes." Slight hesitation, slightly more breathless voice. " I'm very pretty. You won't be disappointed." On the television screen, Niles was jumping up and down. Hard to tell if it was frustration or glee. I wished I could turn the sound back on.

"Uh-huh." There was a pause. Great: this was apparently one of the ones who wanted to get off on the phone – on my time. A control freak, usually. Or maybe it was just his version of foreplay. "Gee, Tia, I don't know. What are you wearing?"

Oh, for heaven's sake. You're going to say you want me, you already told Peach that you did, based on the identical information you just asked me to run through. This is a really stupid game. "Right now I just got out of the shower, so I'm just wearing a towel. How would you like me to dress?"

"Hmm." Jake had all the time in the world, apparently. Well, he could: it wasn't his dime. "How do you like to dress?"

In baggy sweats and woolen socks and my old Rykas, if you want the truth. "I always feel best in black lingerie," I said into the phone, as sweetly as I could manage. Remember, Jen: the car payment is due next Friday. This asshole is your car payment. "A lacy bra and panties, and of course a garter belt and stockings." I giggled, a little breathlessly. "With seams up the back. I don't understand why women don't wear stockings anymore. They're so . . . feminine . . . .." I let my voice drift off just enough so his imagination could take hold. Either I had him now or he was gay.

"Umm, yeah, that sounds great." Ten to one he has his dick in his hand. "Um . . . okay, uh-huh. Uh . . . That's okay. When can you be here?"

Finally. Once we got down to specifics, I could relax. Thank God.

I took another breath. "My car isn't working, so I'm getting my friend to drive me. I need to call him, and I need to get directions from you. I'll be there as soon as I can." To soften the blow, I added, "I can't wait. I like your voice. It's so warm and . . . and intimate. I wish that I could be with you . . . now."

"You like how I sound?" Later, he'll tell people that I was crazy about him from the beginning. If I give him any compliments at all, he'll say that *he* should have charged *me* for sex. "She was so hot for me, I'm telling you, she was getting off on my voice on the telephone . . ."

Can you spell projection?

I rolled my eyes for Scuzzy's benefit (I wanted, after all, to retain at least *his* respect) and did the husky sex voice thing again. "Yes. You sound . . . nice. Warm. Sensuous." Again the sexy *sous-entendre*. No subtleties here. "So, Jake . . . where do you live?"

Long set of directions. I repeated them back, then gave him an hour and a half estimated time of arrival, to be on the safe side. He grumbled, but he had already known it would take that long; he knew that I was coming from the city. He just wanted some leverage, something he could use to make me feel bad. It was amazing, the number of clients who liked that kind of control, who liked to put you at a disadvantage, make you feel from the onset that you needed to work even harder to please them, to make up to them for something. I was already tired of him by the time I hung up the phone. It had taken me ten minutes just to confirm the call. He was a pro at this.

John answered his cell phone on the second ring. British accent. "John here!"

"Jen here," I answered, bemused. "Peach says you can take me to Marblehead."

"Right you are. Where do you live?"

"Allston, just off Brighton Ave. I need a few minutes to get dressed."

"Be there in twenty minutes, then."

Final call to Peach. "It's all set."

"Of course it is," she said calmly. Peach always expects the world to conform to her plans. "Call me when you get there, and tell John to give me a call, too. I want him to pick up some cigarettes for me while you're seeing the client."

I turned my attention to my closet. Great. One of the hottest nights of the year, and I've just committed myself to Full Hooker Jacket. Such is life.

I made it in the twenty minutes, putting a reasonable slightly short but not too cheap print dress on over the much-discussed lingerie, brushing out my hair and putting on makeup, earrings, bracelets, and perfume while trying to watch the end of *Frasier*. Honestly, that Maris. What a bitch.

I hovered uncertainly in front of the entrance to my building until a Corolla pulled up and the driver leaned across to open the passenger door. "Jen, right?"

"Right." I slid into the seat and shut the door, thanking all the gods within hearing that the man had air conditioning. My brief wait outside had been enough for sweat to start clinging to my neck and trickle down my upper thighs. The stockings weren't helping.

I pulled out my set of directions. "Not him," John protested as soon as I started reading them. I glanced up sharply. "What? Why? What's the matter?"

"Gives different directions every time. The girl's always late and he always uses it against her, and when she says it was his directions, he says she's stupid and is the one who got it wrong."

Wasn't that special? And I was going to have to have some form of sex with this idiot in the near future. That's why they pay me the big bucks. "Don't tell me this," I protested.

John was cheerful. "Don't you worry," he said, taking the entrance ramp to the Pike inbound. "Been there enough, haven't I? I'll get you there in no time, surprise the hell out of him."

I smiled. "You're my hero," I said. Obviously still in flattery mode.

"No problem," he said. "Just remember when it's time for my tip."

Sixty dollars, and I was supposed to tip him on top of that? I managed to keep my surprise silent, but just barely. Thank God, I thought, for my Civic. I was loving every rust spot and frayed bumper sticker on it. This Driving Miss Daisy stuff was way too expensive.

He didn't ask about my musical tastes, just flipped on WFNX, and so we listened to alternative rock all the way to the North Shore. It was an educational experience. I am here to tell you, yes, there *is* a band called the Butthole Surfers. Frightening. I spent quite a few miles wondering how I could reference the group in one of my classes, give the students the impression that I was cool. Not a chance. So after that I just relaxed and listened.

After that, I figured, *he* could tip *me*.

We made it to the oddly pillared colonial (who said that rich people have taste?) nestled above the harbor behind a mile of grass, trees, and driveway, in thirty-five minutes flat.

"The poor fellow will be disappointed," commented John.

"I'll help him work through his pain," I said flippantly. "Don't forget to call Peach. I'll see you in an hour."

He waited, his headlights on the door, until Jake answered the doorbell and I walked in. Gallant. Or maybe just practical. If there were a problem, he didn't want to have to turn around and come right back for me.

If I didn't get paid, he didn't get paid.

I went through the motions with Jake. For all his posturing, for all his selectiveness on the telephone, he himself was five foot three, had to weigh two hundred and fifty pounds, and was one of the most unattractive men I've ever seen in my entire life. Thus was justified what I liked to think of as my Second Law of Prostitution: *The least attractive are always the most demanding.*

And even as I played the slut for Jake, I wondered what it must be like for someone like John to drop a woman off at a house, knowing that he's leaving her off in order to have sex. Possibly unpleasant sex. What does he think about while he's waiting? Does he imagine what we might be doing? When he picks the girl up, later, does he smell the sex on her? Does he think about it? Does he see her as more desirable, or less desirable, because of what she's been doing?

All in all, an odd occupation, it seemed to me.

He was right on time to pick me up, which was a relief, since Jake and I had run out of things to say to each other within the first five minutes. "Everything all right?" John asked. "Yes, thanks," I said, a little surprised. It was nice of him to ask, almost a comfort. Like someone knew that it *was* an act, a game, an occupation. After an hour with Jake, I needed that. Clever man, John.

"God, you try finding a place to buy cigs in Marblehead at night," he said. "Place closes up tighter than –" He thought better of continuing that thought. "Anyway, Peach says I'm to take you home; she'll call you if anything else comes up."

"Fine." I recognized the code. That was Peach-talk for this is probably it for the night.

That was perfectly all right with me, to tell the truth. Jake had not had air-conditioning, and sea breezes had been notably absent during our brief bout of gymnastics on his bed. "Wife's at her mother's house," he smirked, making a production of dramatically turning her picture facedown on the dresser. "Can't have her watching us, can we, now?" A little late to show feelings for her, asshole.

"I'll call her when I get home," I said noncommittally to John. I had been running numbers in my head, not as easy as it sounds, arithmetic never having been my strong point. The call was three hundred twenty: sixty for Peach, sixty for John; that left a total of two hundred for me. That probably meant that Jake hadn't been able to find any other service willing to send someone all the way to Marblehead for him, and that Peach had had no problem asking (and getting) whatever she wanted.

I thought about him turning over his wife's picture with such drama, and wondered briefly why he hated her so much, to intentionally and deliberately make her so much the center of what we did there. And then I dismissed the thought. If I started thinking about the wives, I wouldn't be able to work again.

The money was okay and John had been nice. I slipped him an extra twenty, wondering if I was being a total idiot in doing so.

There were no more calls that night. I pulled off the dress, stockings, garter belt and fuck-me shoes, and slipped gratefully into a pair of ripped shorts and an AIDS Ride sweatshirt, and tied my hair back with an elastic band. I spent the rest of the evening happily reunited with *Frasier* and a bowl of Haagen Daz frozen yogurt, signed off at midnight, and went to bed.

The next night I found out why John was worth the extra twenty I'd decided to give him.

Peach called around seven. "Work," she said, briefly, all business.

I'd divided my day between sleeping in, working out at the gym, and thinking about my first lecture for the new class. Well, my second lecture. The first lecture was always housekeeping stuff – how you get graded, what I expect, what books you'll have to buy. The second lecture was when the relationship really began.

"Okay, what've you got?"

"Mark in Chelsea." My smile was immediate and spontaneous. Too cool, a regular client, one of *my* regulars in fact. The good thing about a regular is you don't have to play games ... well, that's not quite true. You always play games. With a regular, at least you're familiar with the rules of the games you do have to play. It's the unknown element that's always unnerving.

Mark in Chelsea was pretty straightforward. I could run the program through in my head, even time it to the minute. We would sit and drink a really awful wine (my money was on it coming out of a box) and look at his view of Boston's skyline across the river (admittedly beautiful) for exactly fifteen minutes. While we were doing this, he would complain about his work and how everything and everyone conspired to keep him from the raises and advancement that were rightfully his. The fact that he was a whining weasel who, by his own admission, would sell out his mother if the price were right apparently didn't enter into it. It didn't matter. I would make

dutiful and sympathetic noises at appropriate places in the mono-
logue and think about my grocery list, or whether it was time to
change Scuzzy's litter.

He would then kiss me, passionately and a little clumsily, and
we would pretend that we suddenly couldn't bear to wait another
moment, and mutually undress each other quickly in the darkened
living room. We would have sex on the carpet, the only dialogue
here being his grunt, "You got it?" as I handed over the condom. He
would last as long as he could, he'd come, roll off me, and head off
to take a shower. Premature ejaculation may be distressing in a husband or boyfriend; but, believe me, callgirls love it.

The other extreme – and we see a lot of that – is tedious beyond
belief.

I would dress and be back on the balcony with the rest of my
glass of wine by the time he reappeared. "Great view, huh?" he'd
ask. "The whole evening was lovely," I'd assure him. He'd say,
"Whenever you're finished . . ." and I'd say, "Oh, I really shouldn't
have any more . . ." and he'd pay me and I'd leave. Thirty-five minutes, start to finish. Consistently. Yes: Mark was one of the good
ones.

"You know I need a driver?" I asked Peach that Sunday.

"Oh, sure, no problem. I've got Ben coming by. Tell me your
address, again."

I gave it to her, and she said, "Okay, I'll have him call you when
he's downstairs."

"Okay, and Peach, remember: Mark doesn't go the full hour."

"Yeah, no problem. Just tell Ben when to come back. He's
thirty-five dollars."

Rapid calculations. Mark paid one hundred eighty. "Peach, that
leaves me making eighty-five for the call."

"Oh." I could hear her running the figures. "Okay, why don't
you call Mark and tell him you have to get a driver, so it'll be an
extra twenty-five."

No, Peach. That's why you get sixty dollars a call, no matter
what I make: so I don't have to say things like that to a client.

Many – if not most – of the services in Boston charge by
the event, so to speak. Say it's sixty dollars for the girl to walk in.
Then you and she negotiate the rest of the evening, a little like an à
la carte menu. A blowjob adds fifty to the base price. Fucking adds a

hundred to the base. And so on through the more exotic options, with prices that are set both by the agency (general guidelines) and by the callgirl (specific to the situation). It is assumed that the client will have one orgasm. If he wants a second one, it gets negotiated. Nothing is left to chance, and nothing is given away.

If I had worked for one of those services, I'd have starved within the first week. There's something really Rabelaisian to me about arguing prices with a guy in an obviously stressful and adversarial way, and then opening your legs for him two minutes later.

One of the things I liked about Peach is that she took care of all that. If the client complained, I could purr, "Oh, baby, you know that if it were me setting your rates I'd help you out, but I can't help it, you have to talk to Peach." So at least there's a pretense that he and I have a little respect for each other, that we're in this together. It helps the fantasy.

Well, it does for me, anyway. Maybe it's just my issue. It's been my experience that men have never had problems fucking women they hate or with whom they're angry. Sometimes they even prefer it that way. Another difference between the genders that I will never understand.

Besides, I liked Peach's premise. The client isn't paying for sex, for specific acts or games or behaviors. He is paying for an hour of the callgirl's time. He can come as many times as he is able or wishes. He can talk, or request a fantasy, or fuck. He can play games, he can maintain at some level the illusion that the girl is there because she likes him. It's a valuable commodity. Clients went to those other services – clients were consistent only in their fickleness when it came to escort agencies – and most of them returned to Peach in the end. She gave them what the others couldn't. Validation. Dreams. Fantasies. Illusions.

In any case, I wasn't about to forego this benefit of working for Peach. I cleared my throat. "No, Peach, I can't call him, I have to get dressed."

A loud sigh. I was supposed to feel sorry for putting her out. "All right, Jen, I'll take care of it, just be ready for Ben, okay?"

"You've got it, Peach."

The other great thing about Mark in Chelsea was that he didn't care what you wore, as long as he could take it off in a hurry when it came time to tussle on the living-room carpet. Lots of buttons were out. Comfort, happily, was in. I put on a pair of sandals and a light summer dress with a zipper down the front for easy access. It was, in addition, the coolest thing I owned. Mascara. A hint of perfume. Here endeth the preparations.

Ben called about a half an hour later. "I'm downstairs."

"Be right there."

I grabbed my keys and the purse I used for work – no money, no ID, just lipstick and mascara, a couple of tissues, and three or four condoms. Just in case.

Ben was in a large old American car of some sort. The first thing I noticed was that all the windows were rolled down. The second thing I noticed was that there were already three women in the car. Neither of these observations was exactly rocking my world.

"Get in, get in." A bit on the impatient side, our Ben. Not sure exactly where he meant, I opened the back door and joined the girls already sitting there. "All right." He had a list in his hand. "Tracy first. Brookline, right?"

The red-haired woman sitting next to the far window in the backseat drawled, "Yes. Coolidge Corner."

Ben pulled aggressively away from the curb, swerved to barely avoid an ancient couple attempting (the nerve of them!) to cross on the crosswalk, and hit the radio. Rap. Loud, pulsing rap.

Curiously enough, there was a time when I liked listening to this. The anthropologist in me, no doubt. The message, then, seemed more sincere, more raw and more real. That was before it started talking about getting bitches pregnant and blowing people away, back in the days when it was a snapshot, a message, a story of lives conceived and endured in poverty and hopelessness. When it reflected a lived experience, rather than a celebration of the worst consequences of the life it had previously witnessed. I even remembered, unexpectedly, some of the words that had been an influence in my life and thought. "Rats in the front room, roaches in the back, I can't take the smell, I can't take the noise . . ." Who was it? An odd name . . . right: Grandmaster Flash and the Furious Five. Back in the eighties, back when it was communication rather than posturing, before the gangsta rap, the denigration of women, the celebration of testosterone. I must be getting old, I thought – I was about to say: back when the world was innocent.

My grandmother always said that the world lost its innocence with World War One. She hadn't seen nothing yet.

Back to the present, which was difficult to ignore. Just breathing was a bit of a challenge, even with all the windows down. Shalimar and Obsession were battling for precedence in the back seat. They didn't blend well, and I began thinking fond thoughts of John and his air-conditioning and his alternative rock.

By the time we made it to my stop ("Yo, Tia, Chelsea, right?") we had gone from Brookline to Newbury Street with a brief detour to allow the blonde in the front seat to alight in front of a wrought-iron gate on Beacon Hill. Ben kept bending over something next to him in the front and I had a sneaking suspicion that all his subsequent sniffling wasn't the harbinger of a bad cold. I paused as I got out and leaned in through the open front window. "I'll be ready in thirty-five minutes."

"No can do, babe." I could see him better now, and unless I was paranoid *and* delusional, he was snorting coke out of an issue of *People* magazine that was on the seat next to him. The requisite credit card and rolled-up bill were in plain view. I was taken aback for a moment with the enormity of what I had just seen.

Heaven help us if we were pulled over. Heaven help *me* if we were pulled over. Good-bye, job. Good-bye, future. I was seriously pissed off.

I jerked my attention back to what he had just said. "What do you mean, you can't do it?" My voice was sharp.

He sniffed. "Got a schedule to keep. Tracey's two hours over in Brookline, but Tiffany's hour's almost up and then Lisa's time's gonna be coming up. Be back in an hour." He gunned the engine to impress me with the importance of his schedule.

I held on to the door. "The client doesn't want me to stay an hour," I said. "He's a regular, and I'd like to keep him happy."

"Hell, just give him another blowjob, that's what'll keep him happy."

Had he been standing in front of me, my response would have been immediate, physical, and temporarily disabling. As it was, there was only one obvious course of action. "Oh, okay, you're right," I said brightly. "Oh, wow, you've got *People*? That's cool, it'll give me something to read while I'm waiting for you to come pick me up." Before he could react, I grabbed the magazine and stepped back from the open window, fanning myself with it as I did so, opening all the pages, practically in his face. Who knows how much coke fell out of its pages into the car, onto the street? I didn't care. There are people who think that men don't say things like that anymore. I know better – most women know better – but here at least I didn't have to just take it.

I paid the price, needless to say. Ben never returned. Try finding a taxi in Chelsea on a hot summer night. Now try being an attractive woman finding a taxi in Chelsea on a hot summer night. You get my drift.

Peach was furious. "Ben's pissed at me now. What happened? You think drivers grow on trees?"

"No, apparently you get them out of cesspools!" I was just as mad. It was one in the morning, my easy call had turned into the Trek Home From Hell, there was obviously no chance of a second call, and now *she* wanted to yell at *me*?

"He told you to get an extra blowjob. So the man's a pig. You've got to be able to take a little misogyny," said Peach. "You get it from clients all the time."

"Yeah, and that's why I don't need it from somebody who's supposedly working for me. I get *paid* to take it from them, Peach. But let's not even go there, because that's not all. You know he had coke out in plain sight on the front seat?"

Silence. She hadn't known.

I pressed my advantage: "That's why he's pissed, Peach, I accidentally messed up his stash." Well, maybe not so accidentally. But she didn't need to know that. And he hadn't worked it into his tight little schedule to score some more. "You know what would happen to us if he got pulled over? With us in the car?"

What I really wanted to rant on about was the assembly-line approach to escort transportation, but I knew that this would get her where she lived. Peach prided herself on her record. Since she had been in business, none of her girls had gotten badly hurt, and no one had been arrested. This was risking the second alternative, big time. I pressed my advantage still more. "You've got a fucking time bomb there, Peach. He's not just using, he's using in public. He's using while he's driving your girls. He's a fucking disaster waiting to happen."

She believed me. That was one of the good things about Peach: once she had decided to trust you, she really trusted you. Peach knew me better after a few weeks than people who had been in my life for years knew me . . .

She knew I wouldn't lie about something like this. "I'll get back to you," said Peach, using her distant voice, the voice she used when her brain was in high gear.

"Just don't do it tonight," I snapped. "I'm signing off. I'm taking a long bubble bath and drinking a gallon of water. News flash, Peach: there aren't any taxis in Chelsea. And the bus is on hourly rotation. It was an education, truly. Good-night."

"Wait –" But I'd already hung up on her. I liked that. It wasn't often that you got to hang up on Peach: she usually did the hanging up.

I got my Civic back the next day and did everything but kiss its new tires. Since then, I learned that Ben was, comparatively speaking, mild.

Some of the other services *require* callgirls to use their drivers. They require it as a means of control, and they overwork the girls at the beginning, saying that there is a five call minimum per night, and then when the girl is falling asleep on her feet the driver offers her a line or two of coke. Just a little pick-me-up, on the house, just because he thinks she's nice and wants to help her out.

But the next time it's not on the house, and the girl is up to a six-call minimum, and the driver always has something on him. (Peach tries to get women drivers when she can, but with those other services, it's always a him.) Before long the girls can't function without doing lines first, and their money is all going into the driver's pocket.

So Ben wasn't too bad, I guess, when you consider the alternatives.

Cocaine was what everybody was doing then. Ecstasy hadn't yet made its comeback in the clubs, heroin had lost its chic, and, thanks to a significant South American population in the Boston area with ties back home, cocaine was the drug *du jour*.

It was impossible to avoid if you spent any amount of time out at night. Cab drivers made suggestive remarks concerning procurement. There were lines in the ladies' rooms in all of the clubs, girls waiting not for the toilets but for the counter space.

Most of our clients got high. I did it, too, but for an entirely different set of reasons. I did it because No-Doz and espresso coffee just weren't cutting it with me anymore.

What I hadn't considered in my brilliant Master Plan, you see, was exactly how much I'd be burning the candle at both ends.

On Death and Dying was conveniently scheduled in the late afternoon. Most of the nurses taking it got off shift at 3:30, so the class started at four. Not so *Life in the Asylum*, however. As a very junior faculty member, I was given the dreaded eight o'clock slot on Mondays, Wednesdays, and Fridays. I am convinced that a.m. stands for "(I) am miserable." I had never been one for early mornings to begin with; and my current moonlighting made the aversion even more pronounced.

Try getting home at two in the morning, still in work mode: nobody comes home from work and goes straight to bed, right? You have to unwind first, to decompress. So you have some wine or some herbal tea, maybe take a bath, maybe read a little or watch TV. I mostly read: late nights were the best time for the mystery authors I love, Michael Connelly and Kathy Reichs and Tony Hillerman. Eventually you fall asleep, and just as you're coming to the really good part in your dream, the alarm goes off. It's six-thirty in the morning, and in another hour and a half you will need to be bright, entertaining, and – most of all – awake. And you hit the snooze button one too many times to have the leisure to wrestle with the espresso maker in the kitchen.

It's bad on the other end, too. You decide that tonight you'll only do one call, an early one, and then get to bed because you only got four hours' sleep the night before. So you go on a call at eight o'clock, a perfectly reasonable time, but the client likes you and decides to extend . . . and extend . . . and extend. By eleven you've run out of witty and/or sexy things to say, you've run out of little games and trade secrets, you've run out of – well, energy. But you want him to call again, you want him to ask for you, so you need to recapture that *joie de vivre* that picked up and left about an hour ago.

The short-term solution for both, of course, was simple. A line of coke in the morning ("breakfast of champions," as one of Peach's other girls liked to call it) that at least clears away the cobwebs and gets you functional. Then, at night, you make a brief trip into the client's bathroom for a pee and another line, and suddenly you do get that second wind after all, and you leave with a great deal of money and the knowledge that he will indeed ask for you again.

Logical. Simple.

Not particularly healthy.

Even without unscrupulous drivers forcing drugs on the girls, it's easy to see why so many of them end up with problems. There's a lot of alcohol involved in this line of work, a lot of drugs. If one is at all susceptible, one is inviting the Bogie Man to come right on in and take up residence.

It wasn't just us, either. It seemed for a few years there that everybody in town was doing coke. That was in the days before so many of the cokeheads committed suburbicide – got married and had kids and bought SUVs and spent all their money on soccer camps and a new deck in the back of the house, and couldn't buy cocaine anymore. It seemed too bad: they were the ones who ended up looking so tired all the time. They probably could really have used it.

I was lucky. That's all; it's not through some special skill or attitude that I survived my years working for an escort agency without developing serious problems with drugs or alcohol. There is, apparently, nothing addictive in my personality. I did way too much cocaine and drank way too much alcohol and didn't get caught in the Bogie Man's lair. Pure dumb luck.

Otherwise, if I had had the requisite addictive personality, if I had come to need the substances . . . well, if I were one of the fortunate ones, I'd be writing these lines from rehab. If I wasn't one of the fortunate ones, I would have given up teaching, given up my life, I'd be living in a crack house and exchanging blowjobs for rocks. I've seen it happen.

I got out. Not everybody did.

Chapter Ten

I met so many addicts when I was working as a callgirl.

You meet a lot of people, of course: all sorts of people. You do that in any profession; but prostitution seems to attract the extremes.

I first met Sophie when I went on a call for Peach. Sophie, who worked independently then, was already with the client when I arrived. He had contacted her directly, then called the agency to turn it into a double.

It turned into one of the best calls of my career. Sophie and I were immediately in synch with each other. She was gorgeous, Chinese, with perfect glossy black hair and a body to die for. We amazed the client, had great fun together, laughed and played and finally found ourselves at eleven o'clock in a hotel corridor with a lot of cash in our hands.

"Come back to my house for a drink," she suggested. "Let's take the rest of the night off."

It sounded like a good plan. We had gone through three bottles of Mouton-Cadet with the client, and aside from everything else, I wasn't too enthusiastic about driving further than I had to. We were in Framingham; she lived in Natick, the next town over.

Besides, I really liked this woman. She had quoted Pascal while we were in bed working together. She spoke English, Mandarin, Cantonese, French, some Vietnamese. Most of her sentences, unaffected and spontaneous, sounded more like a poem, or a song, than like a real conversation.

I called Peach and signed off, and went home with Sophie.

Her apartment was quirky, filled with large papier-mâché animals. A giraffe towered over the chair where I sat down; a tiger prowled in front of the big bow window. Wildly colored birds hung overhead. A zebra guarded the entrance to the kitchen; some unidentifiable marsupial perched in the bathroom. They were everywhere, their bright colors contrasting with the heavy cherry furniture that took up the rest of the space.

Sophie handed me a bottle of Sam Adams and got on the phone. Within twenty minutes we had visitors, three very young men, all of them very attractive, friends of hers. None of them Asian, but I didn't make anything of that. Not then.

They brought with them what seemed that night to be an infinite supply of cocaine.

So we sat and drank and talked and passed round the CD jewel box to do lines. Sophie kept disappearing, and when I went to find the bathroom I took a wrong turn and found her in the kitchen, cooking the coke, making it into freebase to smoke. "You don't mind, do you?" she asked. I shrugged. It was her house, I was buzzed and extremely attracted to one of her guests. She could have been shooting it into a vein, for all I cared.

But I did care, in the end. Sophie and I became friends. And through our friendship I learned, the hard way, what everyone who knows an addict learns eventually. Sophie's only, real, primary, exclusive relationship was with the drug, no matter how hard she tried to convince one otherwise. It would always be with the drug. People were ancillary, secondary. She could like people, she could love people, but she did not need them in the same way that she needed coke. She would have betrayed anyone, or done anything, for cocaine. In the end, that was all she wanted, needed, or cared about.

Of course, I knew nothing of all that at the beginning. I could handle doing drugs and still have a life; naïvely, I thought that she could too. I thought that most people could; and, besides, she didn't fit the profile of an addict. She was strong, bright, intellectual, caring.

It took me a long time to learn that the one had nothing to do with the other. To learn that the Bogie Man doesn't discriminate; and why should he settle only for the poor, the uneducated, the desperate? Why not take someone vital and brilliant and filled with potential instead?

I tried very hard to save her, and got extremely hurt in the process. I lost a great deal of who I was, of what I had, to my belief that I could save her.

I remember hearing someone talking about heroin, once, I think on a PBS documentary. "You know what?" he said. "The first time you shoot up, you might as well just go right out then and there and rent yourself a U-Haul. Bring it to your place, load up your stuff, your house, your girlfriend, your friends, everything. Might as well lose all that stuff upfront. Get it over with. 'Cause, guaranteed, you will, eventually. You think you won't. But no one gets out. It's just a matter of time."

I didn't understand those words when I heard them, but it didn't take me long, once I was in the business, to catch up. And it didn't just have to be about heroin. Crack was just as damning.

That's all very well in theory, of course. But if you want to rip your soul apart and ensure a minimum number of nightmares per month for the rest of your life, then care about an addict. You'll never be the same again, I promise you that.

I'm not sure how to articulate this, to explain my fascination with Sophie. I loved our conversations, her insights, her sudden high giggle. I loved the way that she talked, her words reflecting her native language's ability to communicate through allegory and symbolism, a way of arranging thoughts that translates poorly into western prose. When she wrote, it was like reading haiku. When she talked, it was like listening to a poet, the words creating bright images of things one had never imagined.

As I said, we worked together, whenever we could. But we spent other time together too, scheduling around my classes and her part-time day job where she sat in a stuffy fifth-floor office in Chinatown and translated economic reports for a nonprofit international think tank.

Well, that was what she was doing when I met her, anyway.

We drove out to Walden Pond in Concord one day, following the trail that leads around the lake. It was late fall, and the leaves were turning, falling; they crunched beneath our feet. There was a hawk, I remember, circling over the lake, opening its wings, riding some unseen current, silent and magnificent.

To be honest, I hadn't seen it. My eyes had been down, on the path, and I didn't know that anything was happening until Sophie grabbed my arm. "Look!" she breathed, her eyes following the figure dipping in graceful circles above us. I followed her pointing finger with my gaze, then turned and watched her instead, watched Sophie's amazement, her absorption, her obvious overwhelming awe in the presence of the beauty of the hawk, the day, the lake.

I remember thinking that I wished I could feel with that kind of intensity.

Sophie had been sexually abused when she was a child. Her enemy was her own blood: her father, adoring her until she reached puberty and then brutally rejecting her once she started looking like a female. She had no siblings – her parents were faithful adherents to China's one-child policy. There were no brothers, no sisters to witness and contradict her increasingly warped perceptions of love and family and truth.

Her mother should have, of course. But her mother was the child of a traditional household and did not have the inner resources that it would have taken to reject its dogmas. She did not question her husband because she could not question her husband. So she tiptoed down the corridor, shutting her bedroom door behind her, and she sat in her marriage bed waiting for – what? Expiation? Forgiveness? Redemption? I imagine her there, staring straight ahead, deliberately blind, deaf, and ignorant, not knowing because it would have killed her to know. I imagine her quilted robe, her expressionless face. I cannot forgive her. I can accept that I will never understand the pressures and constraints that she was dealing with; but she also had this child, flesh of her flesh, blood of her blood. I wonder if she cried out in pain as that child was violated.

I imagine the father, too, but I cannot think of him rationally. There is too much anger coloring those thoughts.

It's odd: on the admittedly dubious strength of my undergraduate work in psychology, I had assumed that a lot of the women in the business would have been abuse or incest survivors. I saw them with the older clients, wretchedly trying to create a love and acceptance they had never known in their families of origin. Or I imagined them using their positions for vengeance, to punish men – men as a generic, as a species – for what had been done to them.

It turned out that I was wrong. Either I was way off-base in my assumptions, or else Peach did a really good job of identifying issues, of making sure that the damaged did not get more damaged through working for her. I tend to think that the latter is true; Peach had her own collection of ghosts, some of which were inexpressibly toxic. She wasn't going to contribute to anybody else's.

The French have a saying: they talk about "travelers of the interior," those who find the richest and most satisfying explorations to be those that take place within their own souls. Sophie made that expression come alive for me; she epitomized it. She was forever pushing her own limits, trying to ascertain what and where they were.

I don't know what she was reading in her native Chinese; but I saw the English-language books to which she gave her hours, her energy, her intensity. Unlikely combinations, but making their own kind of sense if you thought about them long enough: Jung and Anne Rice, Sartre and Mary Shelley, Françoise Sagan and Dostoevsky, Calvino and Hemingway.

She talked about them, too, but not the way that the rest of us talk about books. We see fiction in terms of story lines, characterizations, action, dialogue. Sophie didn't care about any of that. She followed more esoteric pathways, looking for truths hinted at, for answers half-revealed. She lived inside the words, tracing the geography of the souls' progress, unerringly identifying the precise moment when the author had been unable to take the one additional step that would have turned their work into something bigger, more significant, more genuine. Sophie talked about that a lot, obsessed about it perhaps: that everyone is willing to settle, to accept the ordinary, because we're unwilling to put our beliefs, selves, and souls on the line, to challenge ourselves to go further.

She gave me a ceramic jar once, a simple cylinder covered with Chinese characters. "It is a poem, a very beautiful poem," she said. "Written by a man who had been very great, successful in politics and in literature, but who fell out of favor and was imprisoned. He wrote this poem in prison. It is filled with visions, with thoughts that he never would have had before." And I was reminded of some of my own readings, back when I was in parochial school and looking among the great minds of the Church for answers to my restless questions. I had found none – had nearly given up, in fact – until I got, curiously enough, to Thomas Aquinas, that most rational and intellectual of theologians. "I have seen things," he wrote in a letter to one of his students, "that make all my writings seem as straw."

I think that Sophie had caught a glimpse of some of those things. Or, if she hadn't, she at least knew that they existed somewhere, which is more than most of us go through our lives knowing.

I still have the jar she gave me. It sits now on my desk, filled with an odd eclectic assortment of pens and pencils and old faded ribbons, and sometimes I look at the calligraphic characters and wonder what words they enable to take flight, what dreams they might unlock, what magic they once whispered to Sophie.

There was so little in her apartment that told you she was Chinese. There was a rice-paper lamp over her bed, with delicate characters brushed on it. There were chopsticks in her kitchen drawers, a rice-cooker, generic bits of life that could have belonged anywhere. There was a Chinese stuffed lion, that she kept in a closet; it had been a gift from an old lover, brought from a province famous for making lions just like this one. She never talked about the lover. After she told me about her abused childhood, she never talked about her family. Only once, in a dreamy, unguarded moment, she said that she missed the rice-porridge that had been her childhood breakfast, the smell of it, watching her mother stir it, her features set and determined.

It was deliberate, I think: in turning her back on her tortured childhood, Sophie had also turned her back on her country, and she had come to a place where she could no longer separate the two. She spoke of China only when I asked her about it, responding to specific questions with precise, unrevealing answers.

After a while I stopped asking.

We worked together when we could. Sophie had private clients, and she often could persuade them to include me in the call when she went to see them. I never told Peach; they weren't Peach's clients, it had nothing to do with her. Those were good times, lots of laughter and champagne, Sophie's giggle spontaneous and happy – I could have sworn that she sounded happy. Maybe, in those moments when she played a role, slipped into a persona, maybe then she really *was* happy. I don't know.

I do know that as soon as we got back to her apartment after a call, she couldn't wait to start smoking. Often she already had the cocaine; sometimes if we had been doing lines with a client she would ask him for a gift bag to take home with her; the rest of the time she called for a delivery. Just like Dining In, I thought irreverently, only these guys never closed. When business is good twenty-four hours a day, there's no reason to keep banker's hours.

I'd take whatever I was drinking, wine or beer or a cocktail, and would stay with her in the kitchen while she prepared the coke. I was usually a little high, a little buzzed from whatever we had done with the client; the last thing that you want at a time like that is to be sitting alone in a room with a giraffe staring you down. You want to talk, and so I did, babbling on as though what she was doing was perfectly normal.

She would light several cigarettes to burn down while she was cooking – crack pipes need ash in order to draw. She'd mix the coke and the baking soda in a test tube, add water, and swirl the mixture as she held it over the flame of her gas cooker.

And after that we'd sit and listen to music and talk and talk, and I'd do the lines that she'd left out for me, and she would take carefully-spaced hits off the pipe. She would close her eyes and lean back, an expression of sheer physical orgasmic pleasure enveloping her face. That made me curious: I liked the effect of cocaine, but nothing in my experience with it had ever affected me like that.

Eventually, of course, she started passing the pipe over to me, and that was when I began to understand what the guy in the PBS documentary had been talking about. It was sudden, immediate, pulsating pleasure, completely unlike anything else I had ever experienced. A slight ringing in the ears, and then a rush of – well, ecstasy may be a little too strong a word, but the feeling was very close to that. It was better than any sex I had ever experienced. It was better than anything I had ever experienced.

I wanted to both keep doing it and to go back to never having done it.

Perhaps it was a good thing that we fell somewhat out of touch for a while after that night. Well, a good thing for me, anyway. I liked the feeling I got from freebasing. I liked it, I thought, a little too much.

I didn't see Sophie, in point of fact, for nearly two months, though we spoke several times on the telephone. And then one evening she called, her voice casual; she had rented *Fargo*; did I want to come over and watch it with her?

My name had been on the waiting list for that movie for nearly two weeks. And, besides, I missed Sophie. I gave Scuzzy some of his special expensive treats to keep him company and headed out to Natick.

And walked straight into one of Dante's circles of Hell.

If I had not known it was Sophie, I would not have recognized the woman who opened the door. She had cut off most of the long glossy black hair; it was short and untidy, and she was wearing clothes that had surely been slept in. More than once.

I sat down in the living room and watched her move about nervously. She had cued up the video and turned it on almost at once, then went to the kitchen for bottles of Sam Adams and the plastic water bottle she had converted into a pipe. I took a hit when she offered it to me, and the immediate sharp sensation was as good as I had remembered.

Halfway through the opening credits, Sophie pressed the pause button on the VCR. "Do you have a camcorder?" she asked.

"No," I replied, mystified. "How come? What do you need taped?"

"Nothing." She flicked her lighter and inhaled off the pipe, savoring the hit, then inhaling the smoke that had remained in the bottle. She put another rock on the filter, lit it again, one hit following the other, before eventually passing the makeshift pipe back to me. I realized that she had upped the ante since the last time that I had been there: she was doing about four or five hits for every one of mine. From my own perspective, that was fine. I had ambivalent feelings (to put it mildly) about freebasing anyway, and each time I did a hit I told myself that I wouldn't do another. Well, maybe just one more. So having someone else control my intake was not a bad thing.

The fact that she was smoking practically nonstop, on the other hand, was a very bad thing indeed.

"It's just," Sophie said at last, not looking at me, talking as if what she was saying had no meaning, no importance, "It's just that there's this guy, he said he'd pay me for movies. You know, skin flicks. Me and guys, me and girls, if you had a camcorder you could do some of them with me, I'd cut you in with this guy. He said he'd pay for anything . . . It's like a job, you know. Not just one time, but over and over again, as many movies as I want to make." She shrugged. "Never mind, Jen. It doesn't matter."

I didn't know what to say to that. Vinnie, a client I saw regularly at the Chisholm Motel, had wanted to film me, too. "I'll never show it to anybody," he had said, straight-faced. He even offered me more money so he could film us together, film me going down on him, film me fucking him. And maybe from his point of view it made sense, it might have given him something to watch in between visits to the Chisholm.

In fact, to show just how trustworthy he was, he offered to put on a video then and there that he had made with one of Peach's other girls. "She loved being filmed," he assured me. "She loved taking it up the ass in front of a camera." I didn't to ask him if he had told her, also, that he wouldn't show the video to anyone else.

There was, in any case, no amount of money in the *world* that was going to induce me to leave behind a permanent and accessible record of what I was doing.

I looked at Sophie pityingly. I wouldn't have done it for her, either, but in that moment I wished I had the camera. I wished I had the answers, anything to take away the pain in her face, in her voice.

She would have done well, too. A lot of amazingly racist good ol' boys like the idea of women of color . . . in bed.

We watched the movie in silence for some time, and then Sophie said something about Frances McDormand's accent, which she was having a hard time understanding, and I talked about the Scandinavian settlements in Minnesota and North and South Dakota, and after that, finally, wonderfully, we were talking again. The snow and the accents and even the fairly grisly murders that were happening on-screen in front of us were meaningless. We sat there, oblivious, the words pouring out, talking like we used to. Sort of. Close enough, as the rat bastard used to like to say, for government work.

It wasn't until I was leaving that I noticed the missing furniture. I guess that when I had come in I was too busy noticing Sophie.

She immediately shrugged it off. "I had kind of a yard sale," she said. "I didn't need it all."

I looked at the denuded living room and foyer and couldn't think of an appropriate response. Or any response at all, to tell the truth. The cherry armoire in the corner . . . the heavy sideboard, with all its intricate carvings . . . "What about your desk?" I asked at last. "Don't you need it for when you do work from home?"

And then she told me what had happened.

* * * * * *

The next day, having struggled with the issue over a restless night of blurred dreams and tense wakefulness, I invited one of my colleagues from the state college to lunch. "I'll be honest with you," I said on the phone. "This may sound racist, but I want to talk to you because you're Chinese, because I need help with something and you're the only Chinese person I know."

Henry wasn't offended. He was kind, and extremely clear.

"First of all, in a situation such as the one you have described, the girl would never make progress. If she had stayed in China, she would never have a responsible position, she would never have respect. And she would not expect it. She would be held back by her guilt, and by having brought shame to her family."

I stared at him. "*She* brought shame to the family? Henry, her father was abusing her. Surely the shame belongs to him." But of course in the real world it didn't; even in our supposedly liberal and gender-equal country, in cases of rape, domestic abuse, and even sometimes incest, more often than not the victim is still blamed. Why should China be different?

Henry pursed his lips, thinking about it. "Perhaps that would be so, if behavior was how we measured worth. But there are other things, more important things. She told people – not specifics, you say, but enough to cast a shadow on the family name. She did not take the place at Beijing University that was being held for her – Beijing University, it is very prestigious, it is our Harvard. It is an insult to her family, to the important people, Party officials perhaps, who had sponsored her for the position. There must have been many talks, many exchanges, for someone such as her to be offered a place there. She had to have been an excellent student. Every student in China works hard, but only a very few go to Beijing University. It says that she was the best of the best, and it also says that she had some sponsors, somebody willing to – how do you say this? – put themselves on the line for her. Somebody did this, and then she said no. To say no is very bad, Jen. It is an insult to the school. And, of course, to the People's Republic."

I struggled to find something to say. I was stuck with the image of Sophie, emerging from the hell that was her childhood, and even despite all that, becoming one of "the best of the best." I was right about her brilliance. "Kids in the States do it all the time," I said. "I guess that education isn't taken as seriously here as it is in China."

He looked at me pityingly. Every developed country in the world is eons in front of the American educational system. He pursued his own thoughts. "It is not just the issue of the university. For us, family is the most important thing. Family loyalty is a great virtue. Taking care of your parents as they once cared for you is expected. And I would suggest to you that even though this friend of yours is far away from China, no matter how successful she is here in America, the guilt and shame of what she has done is pressing down on her. She is expected to be there, now, with her parents, caring for them in their middle and old age. It is an honor, for us, to care for those who have cared for us, who have so much wisdom and experience. It is what she has been taught, it is what she believes in her inner person, even though her mind may think that it believes something else."

I pushed my sandwich away. I had lost my appetite, and decided that it probably wasn't appropriate to sit there nervously shredding the bread between my fingers. "She doesn't seem to feel that – well, she never talked about it," I said. "I guess I don't know what she's feeling."

"Yet you were concerned enough to wish to talk to me." His eyes were gentle, almost mournful. "I cannot predict behavior. And your friend is not behaving in a Chinese way, so I cannot see what path she is taking. But – I hesitate to say this –" He looked away, then finally brought his eyes back to my face. "What I am about to say is repudiated by many," he said. "It is not considered modern. And many people are saying that it should not be done. But when a person, and especially a woman, does something – well, let us say *wrong*, then an acceptable way to . . ." He broke off, shaking his head in frustration. "I am a scientist," he said, apologetically, with a wan smile. "I do not have the vocabulary required for this explanation."

I prompted him. "Maybe what you mean is, an acceptable way to be forgiven?"

He frowned; that wasn't quite it. "To erase what was done," he said, finally, still dissatisfied with the words. "To take away the shame, and to clean the soul, then the person is encouraged to take her own life, to commit suicide." He hesitated. "I bring this up because I wonder, if it is so bad that your friend is causing you this concern, perhaps this is a route that she might take." He shrugged, touched his napkin to his lips, and rose. "I must now go for my one o'clock lab," he said, his tone polite and slightly regretful. "I can be available to you again, if you have other questions."

I nodded. "Thanks, Henry. I appreciate your time."

The news was bleak. The early abuse had taught Sophie that she could only be attractive to a man if she was childlike, even frightened, if he imposed the rules and she obeyed them, even at tremendous cost to herself. And then when she did everything right he rejected her anyway, teaching her that love was conditional, inconsistent, unkind, random. Had she run away to the States as an act of assertiveness, of strength, as a way to care for herself as her parents never had? Or was she running from the guilt that Henry believed she was feeling, the guilt of her early years, the guilt of refusing that precious place at the university? Had she felt, here, that she had escaped and could start over, or had she learned that there are some things that you can never escape?

I knew the answer. Sophie had escaped from nothing. She had surrounded herself with fantasy animals and adoring men and books and thoughts, and still she was pursued. I imagined her in Conan Doyle, running down that infinitely long avenue, the hound of the Baskervilles slavering at her heels. It must feel like that, to her. Running, as we all run in the worst of our nightmares, running and running and never getting away.

Small surprise that she had looked for other means of escape.

I sighed and signaled the waiter for the check. I already knew the answers to my questions. And I also knew what she was doing. The crack pipe isn't as efficient as jumping off a building or slashing one's wrists, but in the end it's just as effective. She might not know it herself, but she was finally doing what was expected of her. In the end, she was being the good Chinese daughter.

And then the anger came, seizing me with an intensity that made my hands tremble as I searched in my purse for my wallet, my car keys. Not if I can help it, Sophie, I thought with determination. Not if I can help it, you won't.

I had barely noticed the slip of paper that had just been put in front of me; I was too busy trying to figure out how to save her. Then I found myself staring, somewhat stupidly, at what was in my hands. The bill for the lunch.

And my wallet, which had contained just under two hundred dollars the day before, before I went to watch *Fargo*, was now completely empty.

* * * * * *

I didn't see the point in asking Sophie about the money. I didn't waste time wondering if I had misplaced it: I am very careful with things like money. There was only one place that it could have gone.

She had had plenty of opportunity. I had been drinking beer; I visited the bathroom several times during the evening, peeing under the watchful gaze of whatever marsupial it was she kept there.

I sat in the restaurant, and I felt hurt, and shocked, and then eventually I felt sad. Still, I wasn't going to give up. She wanted to steal from me? Fine. She wasn't going to drive me away that easily.

I was going to make Sophie see that she wanted life.

The first step, I decided, was to show her that I wasn't angry about the money. In fact, what I had to show her was that I could help her. That I cared about her, that I wanted to help her.

Peach would have decked me if she had known, but that night when I went on a call, I put on my most honeyed voice and persuaded the client that he really did want a double, and that I had a friend. "We're hot for each other," I purred; and I just *know* she's going to be hot for you." When he agreed, I called Sophie. It's not that Peach dislikes doubles; she just wants *her* girls to do them. Together.

The telephone in Natick rang eight times while I massaged my client's thigh to keep him interested. I was about to give up when Sophie answered.

I didn't wait for her to say anything. "Isabelle, it's Tia! Listen, I'm over here in Weston with this absolutely fantastic friend of mine, and I told him about you, and so we wondered if you wanted to come over and join us for an hour."

She cleared her throat. "How much?"

I forced cheerfulness into my voice, though her question was not reassuring. "The same as usual, don't worry. Can you come? I'm so anxious to –" I slid into the Sex Voice for Andy's benefit " – *be* with you again." Come on, Sophie, I thought. You can do this.

She came. She came forty-five minutes late, which did not please the client and entailed some creative manipulation of the truth when Peach called; but she came. She had even tried to do it right; she was wearing a gauzy Indian dress that floated around her small frame, lipstick, earrings.

But her face frightened me. Her cheeks seemed somehow to have flattened; there were shadows where they used to be. Her eyes were glassy and staring, a clear indicator that she was pretty railed. And, unless I was mistaken, she was missing a tooth. I didn't even want to think about what that meant. I didn't want to feel the fear clutching at my stomach.

No time for speculation, anyway: we were on the clock.

I tried to get the party going. Sophie was passive, making half-hearted attempts at going down on me, at sucking Andy's cock, at slipping her finger into his ass after he asked her to. I sighed inwardly and got to work, making love simultaneously to both of them, giving him pleasure physically while feeding his fantasy about our lesbian status by trying to rouse Sophie. It was an uphill battle.

Why had I called her? So that the memory of times we'd shared might make her feel better? Or might make me feel better? Who had I done this for, in the end? If things looked the same, maybe I could pretend that they really were the same?

"Isabelle" finally asked to go to the kitchen for a glass of water, and wandered out of the room even as Andy, pumping into my pussy while at the same time getting his ass fucked by my finger, was nearing and then reaching orgasm.

I got her out of there as quickly as I could. She had arrived in a taxi, so we both got into my Honda. "Hey, Sophie, are you all right? I asked. "You didn't seem like yourself in there."

No answer. She was busy counting the bills he had given her.

We got back to Natick and climbed the three flights to her apartment. She seemed more animated now, more energetic, as though she were coming back to life. We got in and she went immediately to the phone in the kitchen and called her dealer. I had known she would, but I was still irritated. I wasn't used to being ignored.

There was no furniture in the living room except for a futon mattress on the floor.

I marched into the kitchen. "You sold all your furniture," I said hotly. "And that's fine, who needs furniture, who needs a TV, but Sophie, what the hell did you do with the animals?"

She was preparing a glass tube in anticipation of the upcoming delivery. She shrugged. "I was tired of them, anyway."

"I know what you're doing," I said, keeping my voice as calm and steady as I could. The state of her apartment had distracted me from my purpose. "You think that you're worthless, you feel guilty because of your father and because of the way they blamed you for what happened, and you feel guilty for leaving them. But you don't need them, you have me, I'm your friend, I want to help you. I know that you're hurting, and that it's not your fault. It's fucking unfair, Sophie, and I *know* that. Don't you see? You're not alone. And I'm the one you should be leaning on, I can help you, really I can!" I took a deep, shuddering breath. "Because the worst part of it is this: I'm here to tell you, Sophie, that there's not enough men or alcohol or cocaine in the world that will keep you numbed from feeling all that."

There was a knock at the door and her eyes slid away toward it. My irritation flared and I turned and left. As I reached the door and jerked it open I heard it, so soft as to barely be audible, Sophie's reply. "Maybe not," she said, in the frightened voice of a very small child, "But at least it does for a while."

The next day, just as I was getting home from *On Death and Dying* (and who says that God doesn't have a macabre sense of humor?), Peach called. "Well, we lost that one," she remarked.

"What's up, Peach? What are you talking about?"

"Andy Miller. Your call last night." I could hear her lighting a cigarette, listened to her inhale. The smoke she was holding in her lungs made her voice tight. "Seems that there was a robbery while you were there." She exhaled, while my stomach clenched in dread. "As soon as you left, he started noticing things missing. His watch, for one thing. It had been by the bed. And then there was some cash he kept in a box somewhere, I don't know, he didn't say. Some decent jewelry that was in his daughter's room." "I'm not saying this for you to feel bad, Jen. You had nothing to do with it. I know there was another girl there, from another service, he told me that. I don't know which agency, he couldn't remember, but anyway he says he's not using us anymore, that the whole experience turned him sour."

I was still assimilating that fact that the client had covered for me, claiming that it was he who had called Sophie, not me. Clients didn't do that sort of thing, as a rule. "Gosh, Peach, I had no idea."

"Well, of course not." She sounded completely unconcerned. "There's a lot of that in this business. Don't worry, Jen. He'll be back. He won't call for a few weeks, and he'll try some other agencies, and then he'll decide that we weren't so bad after all, and he'll call. I've been here before. They always come back."

Her lack of concern wasn't particularly contagious. As soon as I got off the phone, I looked through my purse until I found the scrap of paper where I had scribbled his number the night before, when I called to confirm the visit. "Um – Andy? This is Tia, from last night."

He didn't seem surprised. "Yes, what can I do for you?"

I swallowed. "I just talked to Peach. She said that – that some of your things got stolen. I want to say that I'm really sorry that happened." I hesitated, but there was no response, and so I went on.

"Peach told me that you – that you said – um, you told her that Isabelle was an agency call. I wanted to thank you for doing that. I would have lost my job with her if you had told her the truth."

"Yeah, I figured that it was like that." There was the briefest of pauses. "Listen, Tia, it's none of my business, but I'm going to give you a piece of advice anyway. You'll be all right, I can see that you've got what it takes, but you're close to making a bad mistake. Stay away from that girl. She's drowning and she'll take you down with her."

I said, stupidly, "I don't think –"

He cut me off. "I told you, I've been around. I can see what's going on. And I have a brother doing his fifth stint in rehab, and I know what you're doing. It's called co-dependency. I know because I did it for a while, too. You're trying to help a friend, and that's commendable. But she's not your friend."

I thanked him and hung up the phone. I resented him for saving me, and then for using that leverage to lecture me. I could take care of myself.

But the voice in the back of my head was saying something else altogether. Sophie had nearly lost me my job. Sophie was stealing from me. Sophie was using me. Sophie was encouraging me to use the same substance, to do the same activity, that had so harmed her. Addicts do that, I learned later on. She wanted company in her death march.

Andy was right: she was not my friend.

But I wanted her to be. If I pretended that she was, maybe all the bad things would go away, and she really would be my friend again, like we had been in the beginning.

But I lay in bed and watched the changing patterns of the shadows on my ceiling, and I knew that I wasn't willing to put my flimsy theory to the test. I didn't call Sophie after that, and she didn't call me.

Three weeks later, my *Death and Dying* class was organized around funerals, how different cultures practiced funeral rites, what these rituals provided for those who grieved. And even as I was talking about Buddhism's concept of Bardo, that intermediate step so important to ensure proper reincarnation, assured only if the family of the deceased enacts the rituals properly, I had a sudden vision of

Sophie, trying in my fantasy to do the right thing, going back to China for her father's funeral, and being turned away. I was glad that the class was nearly over. I was finding it hard to breathe.

I didn't even bother going home after that. I drove straight to Natick, pounded on her door until she opened it, carelessly, water bottle-cum-crack pipe in hand. "Hey, Jen, what's up? Do you want a hit?"

You may ask yourself, gentle reader, what I was doing there. What kind of sick rescue fantasy was I feeding? Was I trying to help Sophie, or was I trying to help myself?

I had a simple idea. Sophie had lost her furniture and was slipping into addiction. Maybe, just maybe, if she had furniture again, she'd get better, she'd remember how things used to be. Well, I believed it at the time. Hard to believe that I have a doctorate. Hard to believe that I have a brain.

I propelled her out the door and into my car. She probably resisted, she probably protested; I was impervious. On Route 9, I pulled into the parking lot of the first furniture store I saw. I was obsessed; I was on a mission. I bought her a bed, and a coffee table, and two easy chairs. "You have to live," I hissed at her as I paid with my credit card and arranged for delivery to her apartment. "You'll pay me back, that's your responsibility."

She was amazed. "This is so kind," she said. "You believe in me, Jen! I won't let you down. You know I won't let you down, don't you? I will pay you back, as soon as I am able. The next call I make, I'll give you some money."

"I know," I said, and drove her home, where she cooked some more crack and I – to my shame, can you spell enabler? – joined her on the futon for some hits. When it was finished, she proposed calling her dealer for more, but I had had enough.

I took a very long shower when I got home, washing away the sweet smell of the smoke, letting the hot water massage my metabolism as well as my scalp. Coming down off a cocaine high is extremely uncomfortable. Coming down off a crack high is hell. I didn't want to deal with it, and I didn't want to think about her anymore. I took some sleeping pills, washed them down with a shot of Oban from the bottle that I kept around in case I ever had guests with decent taste in single malts, and went to bed.

Sophie came by a few nights later, bringing with her an envelope to give me, her first payment toward the furniture. I wanted to trust her, but I watched her anyway. Apparently my vigilance leaves something to be desired, however, because after she was gone I realized that my own watch and my diamond stud earrings had gone with her. I opened the envelope; it was filled with sheets of lined paper, torn from a notebook.

I cried and cried and cried.

In the end I finally decided that Andy was right. This wasn't the way that I wanted to live. I didn't want to keep freebasing, which Sophie expected of me and which I was agreeing to a little too quickly. I didn't want to lose my career, my apartment, my cat, my furniture, my life. I didn't want to lose my reputation with Peach. And I sure as hell didn't want to keep getting robbed by a friend.

Of course, it didn't stop just because I wanted it to.

Sophie became more and more needy as time went by. I suspect that, one by one, people were dropping out of her life. She started calling me all the time, at all hours, begging me for money, for a ride somewhere, to do a call with her so she could get some crack. Or she needed me to make a buy for her, she'd pay me back the money, she promised. Come on, Jen, please, just this one time. Please, okay? I'm asking you to do this for me. Please do this for me, Jen . . .

She always had a good story – no, a *brilliant* story. It would just be this one time. She was making plans. She was going to go back to school. She was thinking about going into rehab. But in the meantime, if I was a friend, I'd help when she was hurting. Don't you care that I'm hurting, Jen? Don't you even care about me anymore?

Or she had perfectly plausible reasons for wanting my help. It wasn't about drugs, she hadn't done anything in days, almost a week, wasn't that good? No, it wasn't about drugs, I had been right about that, she just didn't want to be alone tonight. Just for tonight, Jen, please come over, don't let me be alone.

She sounded so very reasonable. That is the addict's gift, the gift of the silver tongue. They are always convincing. They can make you believe anything. I was then, and am, reminded of the Rod Stewart song: *"Even though you lied, straight-faced, while I cried/ Still, I'd look to find a reason to believe."* And, oh my God, did I look to find reasons to believe Sophie. And she knew it.

There were excuses for everything. She didn't have money, she hadn't eaten in three days. So I brought her food, and was treated to a spectacular fiery temper tantrum for my troubles.

The new furniture was there. The mattress on the bed was already pockmarked with burn holes from her cigarettes, from her crack pipes. It was a wonder the whole place hadn't burned down while she was in the kitchen cooking up another rock.

I found a television-cum-VCR on sale in the *Want Advertiser* and bought it for her; I brought it over to Natick with a bag of videos for her to watch and a bag of groceries. Once in a while I gave in to her insistence and drove her somewhere, usually up to Lynn or Revere. She was going further away to buy her coke, now. She had burned all the local dealers; at that point, there probably wasn't a single one to whom she did not owe money. Unlike me, they were used to dealing with addicts; they could say no. It was unfortunate for Sophie that not everybody was willing to take it out in trade.

The reality was that I was watching her dying and she was asking me to help kill her. The night that I finally understood that, I stopped; it was one of the hardest things I ever had to do.

She had badgered and badgered me, calling every three minutes on the phone, just asking for a ride for which she would pay me if I couldn't find it in my heart to do it for her out of friendship. Her words. So I had given in yet again and picked her up out in Natick and we set off for Lynn.

It was hardly the best of times. It was eleven o'clock at night, we were seriously lost, and it turned out that Sophie had no coherent idea of where we were going, just a vague assertion that she would recognize the house when she saw it, because she had been there the night before.

The night before, I had been up until nearly four in the morning with a client, I had had an eight-thirty class that morning, and I was in no mood for this bullshit. I handed Sophie my cell phone. "Call these people, get directions," I said crossly. My patience was nearing the red line.

She looked at me blankly. "I don't know their name. But I'll know the house; let's try some more streets."

I took a steadying breath. As far as I could tell, she could have made a buy at any of the last six corners we had passed, had I agreed to it. To say that we were not in the best part of town would have been a severe exaggeration. "Sophie, you said that this wouldn't take more than half an hour."

"Well, that was what I *thought*," she said, pouting. "Jen, just do it, okay? We're here now."

Not for long, I thought grimly. I gave it another ten minutes, and then bailed. "Sophie, this isn't going to happen. I'm going home."

"How can you do this to me?" It was a wail.

"How could *you* do this to *me*?" I countered. "Sophie, you're using me, and I've had enough. Do you want me to leave you here, or take you home?"

"If we could just go down that street, I think that it is looking familiar . . ."

I whipped the wheel around and achieved a screeching of tires that I have never duplicated since. I took her home. I didn't say a word, not when she was crying, not when she was begging. I waited in stony silence for her to get out of the car. I went home and didn't pick up the telephone that kept ringing all night.

And, damn it, she had managed to clean my wallet out again, too.

I couldn't do it anymore. I couldn't keep loving her and hating her at the same time.

I started saying, "I'm sorry, but I can't talk to you," when she called me. I made the payments on her furniture and was torn between anger at doing it, and intense sorrow that it hadn't helped.

And even then, there was a very small part of me – the Peter Pan part of me that's in all of us, the one that resists growing up and resents responsibility – part of me was jealous of her, closed in her apartment with the shades down, ignoring the real world, sucking that sweet intense oblivion from the crack pipe, and not feeling anything at all.

One of Peach's girls once told me that she had tried coke, and didn't like it. "It numbs you," she said. "In every way. I was surprised how much it works on your heart as well as your brain. It takes away your capacity to feel anything. You just stop caring. You stop feeling. I don't ever want to stop feeling."

Yes; but she was young and healthy, with her whole life stretching out in front of her, full of mystery, excitement, promise, and hope. It's easy, then, to want to feel.

On the other hand, she was right about the cocaine.

I stopped talking to Sophie, and eventually – after a seemingly endless time – she stopped talking to me. The last I heard before I left the business was that she was doing blowjobs in the doorways of apartment buildings down in the Fenway for a rock or two of crack.

I am writing these words years after all of this happened, and there are tears in my eyes as I write. My throat is burning, my stomach is tight: I still feel it. It's as if we were survivors of a shipwreck, Sophie and I, and I tried to keep her afloat, and she sank anyway. I'm left wondering if there wasn't something else I could have done to keep her there with me, on the surface, treading water, hoping to be rescued.

Of course, Andy was right when he said she wasn't going down alone. If she could have, she would have taken me down with her. Not because she hated me, but because she was indifferent to me. I had become for her a means to an end. She had lost the capacity to care. Her only love was the drug.

I have to tell you: I'm not sure that I'm stronger than Sophie was. I'm not better, and I'm not smarter. The only difference between us, maybe, is that I had a lighter load to carry through life. I did not have to carry the memory of a father who tortured, of a mother who turned her back.

Or – I may still be making excuses for her.

I knew another woman who worked for Peach. She had been gang-raped when she was fifteen, survived an illegal abortion and a suicide attempt and three abusive relationships. She was doing drugs, and she got out. So perhaps it's not about the size of the load, but about the size of one's courage.

Or maybe it's just about pure dumb luck.

If so, I was lucky, and Sophie wasn't.

There's hardly a day that goes by, even now, that I do not remember her. I hold many memories of that time in my life; but it is only Sophie who haunts my dreams, making me cry out in the night. My husband has become accustomed to my nightmares. He holds me close, and asks no questions.

A few years ago, I attended a seminar on drug abuse, and I learned precisely what cocaine does to your body. There's a substance in your brain called dopamine, and dopamine is your friend: it's what makes you feel good, happy, even sometimes elated. Your brain pretty much figures out how much of it to keep dropping into your system for you to stay in a good mood.

Cocaine comes in fast and hard and with a lot of intensity. It blocks the dopamine, but your brain doesn't care, because the coke is so much *better* that the usual stuff. Who needs dopamine when they can have elation? But no one can stay high forever, and once you come down, so does your mood.

The catch is that in the meantime the dopamine producers have looked at your cocaine-induced euphoria, and they have decided that you don't need anything else. So the production of dopamine slows and sometimes even stops, leaving you feeling a lot worse than you did before you decided to stick a straw up your nose. Not only has the cocaine high disappeared, you've also lost your normal baseline, your natural happiness.

The saddest reality of all is that you will never, ever, *ever*, feel as high as you did the first time you did the drug. You will keep believing that you can, that if you just have one more line, one more hit, everything will be fine . . . but you're fighting chemistry. You're fighting reality. Addiction is a story that can only have one ending.

Sometimes, the degree to which I flirted with it scares the shit out of me.

* * * * * *

I think of Sophie, and I realize that there would never have been enough of *anything* in the world to heal her. Not enough dopamine, not enough cocaine, not enough alcohol, not enough sex. Not enough friendship. Not even enough love

Chapter Eleven

The one thing in my life that I protected jealously from my difficult relationship with Sophie was my teaching. Even at the beginning, some sixth sense warned me not to let her get involved in that part of myself. I may not have seen her or what was happening to her as clearly as I might have; but at some level I understood that allow-ing her in any way to touch my other world, the academic world, would have been catastrophic. Even when I was spending evenings or afternoons with her, even during my brief flirtation with crack, I made sure that I could continue to teach.

I was lucky in that, too. Maybe that sixth sense was really the voice of Mary Magdalene, my (sort of) patron saint. *I* certainly can't claim credit for it.

I was apparently to be rewarded for my efforts, though, because as it turned out, the class on prostitution was easily the most interesting class I'd ever taught.

I don't say that lightly: I've had some really interesting experiences. I was a teaching assistant for two years at MIT, in the humanities department, and corrected papers written for classes called *Mysticism and Gnosticism in Literature*, and *Evil as a Literary Theme*. The papers had no assigned topics, and the sheer breadth of subject matter selected by the student authors was staggering. It's hard to top those, and I have never since seen anything remotely like them. They stood out, even in that venue, where brilliance in the sciences appears to go hand in hand with a purposeful and studied weirdness.

But this one was shaping up to be even more of a fascinating experience.

Sometimes you see a pattern to enrollment in certain classes. Every time that I taught *On Death and Dying*, for example, I knew that I would have to spend the first few sessions weeding out those who really shouldn't be in the class. People who had just experienced a death and needed therapy rather than academic discussion. People who dressed in black robes with long black fingernails. That sort of thing.

I anticipated that at least two groups of people would enroll in *The History and Sociology of Prostitution*. I anticipated feminists, women on a mission, coming to either denounce the topic as oppression or to argue for its legalization. I anticipated a certain number of students whose primary interest was prurient and who hoped to be able to talk about sex. I anticipated at least one Young Republican, gathering information on the issues that might ignite his or her way to the political arena. And I hoped I'd have a few people with genuine curiosity and open minds.

The opening class was the one that that would set the tone, which I planned to be one of low stress and good communication paired with significant learning. I should say here, right at the beginning, that I don't believe in content-less classes, places where *only* discussion takes place. If that's what you want, look for the nearest Starbucks. There has to be some reason for the hiring of educated and thoughtful people as university professors, and my participation as a resource and mentor is intrinsic to my teaching style.

So we did the usual touchy-feely introductions that actually are quite helpful to me, going around the room, each student saying who they are and why they chose this particular class. Then I said a few words about my own academic background, heard myself saying that I was considering writing a book about prostitution (the idea had just at that moment entered my mind), and added that, as a lecturer, I had no permanent office, that "office hours" are immediately before and after each class.

We went through the class syllabus together. I explained the various papers and projects for which they would be responsible, and pointed out the books that they had to purchase and read.

Then I spoke for a while about what we were going to be focusing on for the next four months. "Talking about sex is no longer the taboo that it used to be. But talking about prostitution, on the other hand, *is* taboo, that is, unless it's in the context of a lewd remark or a dirty joke."

I walked around the room. "What we're going to be doing in class this semester is exploring both the history of prostitution – what forms it has taken over the centuries – and how the mainstream of society has interacted with it. Then we'll look at its meaning in a more anthropological context. We'll visit the ancient civilizations of the Mediterranean; we'll go to China and Korea and South America. We'll see how it flourished in every age throughout world history, and we'll start to ask why. We'll talk about the reasons that prostitution exists, why it is needed, and why it is reviled."

One of the students was snickering quietly. I moved slowly around the room until I was standing directly behind him, then stopped and continued to speak. He quieted down immediately. I knew a thing or two about control. "We're going to look at the place and meaning of prostitution in society, efforts to legalize and regulate it, and the different movements that have tried to get rid of it. We're going to contrast prostitution as a career choice with prostitution as another word for slavery. We're going to ask the questions that are uncomfortable and try to come up with a clear and unprejudiced concept of prostitution. I'd like to end this semester with everyone in this room having a sense of where you stand on the issue, based not on hearsay and your own vivid imaginations" (a ripple of nervous laughter flicked across the room; I had said it with some emphasis and a smile); "but on a dispassionate, academic study of the topic."

I left feeling buoyant. The energy was positive. Several students had stayed after class to ask questions or share comments; it all boded well for the future. They were even already asking the right questions, some of them at least, already showing interest, involvement, and some openness.

That feeling I had, that buoyancy, that sparkle, that high – that's why I teach. Not because I'm passionate about my subject area – after all, as an untenured lecturer at large, I was teaching classes that were fairly tangential to my subject area – but because of that connection that gets made when it all goes well. Because of the interest and energy that lights up students' faces when material is presented to them in a way that gets past their defenses.

There are a lot of people who believe that the subject of one's specialization must be the focus and the *raison d'être* for anyone aspiring to teach, but I firmly believe that if I can understand something, I can teach it – and in fact teach it well. The subject area is of somewhat lesser importance – it is in the act of teaching itself that my passion lies. In a sense, the subject matter is a means to an end.

Which is not to say that there aren't subjects that I *prefer* to teach. I'm not sure that I could generate the same amount of excitement around a software application class as I can around issues that I have spent years studying. But in a real sense, in the real academic world, the significance of those years and that study has been greatly exaggerated.

Let's face it. If you enjoy school at all, then staying for more advanced degrees makes all the sense in the world. In high school, you study what somebody else decides that you should study. College offers more choices, you get to narrow your field of study to a general area that you like – but there are still those pesky required courses that have nothing to do with you and in which you have absolutely no interest. A master's degree allows you to refine your classes still more; in my case, for example, I was able to take nothing but classes relating to anthropology. Yet even within that concentrated field you long for even more specialization. I wanted to study people in the real world, yet my Course of Studies dictated three classes in archaeology. Not as horrible as the torture I endured in my undergraduate math courses, but still not riveting.

It is not until you arrive at the doctoral level that all of your classes become passionately interesting to you, speaking directly to the issues that you care about. Two years of that, then your comprehensive examinations, and finally comes the ultimate specialization; the dissertation.

You must write about something that no one has ever written about before. So you do. It gets you what you need: your degree, and a topic that you can pursue in terms of the journal articles and conference lectures that are *de rigeur* for advancing in your field; but, honestly, it's not going to make a teacher out of you. The topic of my dissertation was *The Role of Immediate Family Members in Rites of Passage*. Not, you will note, a subject that everyone would find fascinating. Not something likely to inspire scintillating cocktail-party conversation. So while you may have become an expert on a small, infintesimally tiny area of your field, you'll never be called upon to teach it. What you will teach are the courses that you took so long ago that they are all but forgotten: *Anthropology 101. Introduction to Anthropology. The Origins of Humanity.*

In case I'm sounding too altruistic, let me add that I also love teaching because of the way it makes me feel. Connecting with a student, changing him or her forever, even in the most infinitesimal of ways, helping him or her find out something important . . . it makes you feel that you can fly. There's no drug that can touch that feeling. Nothing is better.

Not even freebasing. Odd how, after having taken the crack pipe into my hands and into my life, everything got compared to it. But a crack high is tenuous, uncertain, even sometimes frightening. This high was different. This high empowered and enabled. It had as much to do with what I was giving as it had to do with what I was taking.

* * * * * *

I had an appointment with one of Peach's clients at four, so I just had time to go home, shower, and change – he liked jeans, the casual look. He lived south on 128, in Needham, one of Boston's white-bread suburbs that was still trying to convince itself that American flags on the streets and specialty grocery stores will hold outsiders at bay indefinitely. Outsiders are defined, of course, as anybody who is not white, preferably Protestant, and making a minimum of eighty thousand a year.

No one had told them that Norman Rockwell was dated, and may not even have been true to his time anyway.

I hate Needham, but I liked the client well enough. He owned one of the boutiques on Great Plain Avenue, and he closed the shop in late afternoon in order to have a callgirl visit. We did it there, too, in the back room of the shop, on a sofa that was just inside the door.

We get a lot of clients from places like Needham, clients who play the suburban success game, but see the hollowness inside it, and don't know what they can do with that unhappy insight. Being men, they naturally think first of making their escape a sexual one. So they continue to do the Patio Daddy-o routine on the weekend and to work hard during the week to get ahead in their chosen professions. They attend their children's myriad sports competitions and practices, and they allow themselves to be dragged by their wives to PTA meetings, suburban cocktail parties, and church rummage sales. Their tragedy is that they're bright enough to know that something's wrong with this picture, but too fearful to do anything about it.

Except hire a callgirl.

I find it pretty scary that the act of hiring a callgirl (whenever you have an extra two hundred squirreled away where the wife won't see it) is the most daring and meaningful act in your life. But it seemed to satisfy them. Well, that, and the two martinis they drank every night as soon as they got home, the ones that enabled them to face the scripted evening activities that lay ahead, the predetermined life that stretched out in front of them.

Carl fit the profile perfectly. Sometimes I felt sorry for him. Sometimes I thought that he was pathetic. But nothing, not even Carl and his empty life, could have brought me down that day.

I was already bubbling over when I got to the shop and went in, pretending to be a customer. That was the procedure. I fingered expensive pins and horrifying little knick-knacks until Carl figured it was safe to lock up, and as we walked back to the back room, I talked about the class, how well it had gone.

I should mention here that I wouldn't have done that with very many other clients. For one thing, it probably wouldn't have come up. Most clients don't want you to be a person at all. They want an object. A pinup. A cuddly plush toy. A representation.

A few clients – and Carl was one – want details about your real life. My theory is that it gives them a *frisson* of something forbidden, knowing personal details about a callgirl. I usually made those stories up, of course. I didn't want these people knowing about me, prying into my life, pretending that they had the right to be part of it for anything more than the required hour.

But today, with Carl, I couldn't resist. "It's going to be a great class," I babbled happily. "Already they're asking questions, and they're *good* questions, not just excuses for talking about sex."

Carl smoothed a hand over his bald head. "I never needed an excuse for talking about sex," he said, which of course wasn't true. He couldn't talk to his wife about it, or I wouldn't have been there. But I let it go. "I can see one or two students who may present problems, later on," I said. "But overall they seem to be really engaged in it, and that's only after the first class."

The conversational topic was sinking in. "You teach school?" asked Carl, as we reached the back room and he kicked off his shoes and loosened his tie.

"Yes," I answered, caution belatedly coming back to me. "I teach at a couple of different colleges."

His eyes lit up. "Wow, that's sexy. Doesn't that really turn you on, standing there in front of a class and thinking about getting fucked the night before?"

"I never think about my job when I'm in class," I said, primly, although he was hitting dangerously close to home. I did, in fact, entertain similar thoughts with some frequency, although I suspect mine had a different spin on them. I did sometimes flash back on an encounter I'd had the night before, and marveled at the contrast between that memory and what I was doing by day; but those flashes of memory were never sexual in nature. I honestly was never sexually aroused by anything I did through the agency. It was just a job.

Besides, I simply cannot imagine standing in a classroom and getting turned on at all. Maybe some women could do that. To me the concept always seemed to be bordering on the farcical. Woody Allen material, perhaps.

If I thought about it at all, it was with the same delight I had felt in keeping secrets, back when I was a child.

Let's face it: secrets are *fun*. My Other Life kept a steady energizing flow going into my Real Life, precisely because the two were so different, because working for an escort service was so forbidden, so clandestine. So illegal. I was walking a tightrope there and I knew it, and there's nothing like a tightrope for a little adrenaline rush.

Carl had his mind on less lofty subjects. "Think about this tomorrow in class," he urged me, his excitement growing apparent as he removed his underwear and pulled me down on top of him. "Think of me fucking you, think of me deep inside you," he added, matching his actions to his words. "I will, baby, I will," I promised.

He believed me. They always did.

After class the next day, one of the students waited shyly outside the classroom for me to emerge. "Dr. Angell," she said, her voice low and earnest. "My mother doesn't think I should be taking a class on prostitution. What can I tell her?"

"Why does she think it's not good for you?" I asked, surprised.

An uncomfortable shrug. "I don't know. I mean, it's not like it'll make me become one, or anything."

She may have grasped some of it, though. There was the reality of the same bizarre argument put forth by opponents of sex education in schools – that somehow knowing about something will make a person want to do it. Or those who think of gay men as constantly on the lookout for young boys to "convert," as though their life were so incredibly irresistible that others needed to be protected from it.

I took a deep breath. "Your mother doesn't need to worry, and neither do you," I said firmly. "This class is going to be about as sexy as learning trigonometry, or studying wind velocity. We're academics engaged in an academic look at a sociological phenomenon." She still looked uncomfortable, so I went on. "Is she afraid that you might end up disagreeing with her views, once you've been through the class?"

A nod. "I think that's it," she said miserably.

"Is this your first year in college?" I asked, as tactfully as I could. I knew the answer already.

"Yes."

I put a hand under her arm and guided her to a bench. We sat. "This is one of the hardest times in your mother's life," I told her.

"It's not new; in fact, it started when you turned two and discovered that you were a separate person from her. And it continued when you were in high school and stayed out late, when you dated boys she didn't approve of, when you said things to shock or provoke her." I was out on a limb, here, but I was taking a chance that her adolescence wasn't entirely unlike my own.

She seemed to be following me, anyway. "This is sort of like dating someone she doesn't like?"

I shrugged. "In a way. All parents want their children to be independent thinkers. Or at least they say that they do. What most parents don't realize is that in becoming independent thinkers, their children may make choices that are different from the choices that they made. They may make choices with which the parents fundamentally disagree. And no one likes that." I hesitated. "I don't plan to have children, you know, but sometimes I think about it anyway, and you know what my greatest fear is?"

"What?"

"That I'd do my best to raise them with correct values – that is to say, *my* values – and they'd end up becoming Republicans in spite of everything I'd taught them!"

That got a laugh, as it was meant to do, and she nodded. "So it's not about a class on prostitution," she summarized.

"No, I don't think that it is." I stood up. "The best thing that you can do is share your thoughts with her, even if you're not sure what it is that you feel or believe. That way, she gets used to the changes you're going to be going through gradually, and she'll see that it's not the effect of brainwashing that got you there, but careful consideration. She should be proud of you for that."

I watched her walk away, but instead of following, I sat back down on the stone bench. It was really odd, I thought, that this hadn't occurred to me before, in all of the times I'd examined the juxtaposition of my two current occupations, but it sure as hell was occurring to me now.

If this girl's mother was concerned about her taking a university-authorized class on prostitution, how exactly would she feel if she knew that the instructor was, in point of fact, a prostitute?

Theory is fine. Knowledge is good. Understanding is commendable. And as long as we continue to look at the subjects of our study from a distance, as though they belonged to some primitive distant tribe that has nothing in common with us, then we're all safe. Academia can continue to form, judge, pronounce, dictate.

I was beginning to feel a lot of sympathy for the members of that tribe. I knew just how they felt.

Chapter Twelve

I think that somewhere earlier I may have mentioned something positive about the influx of freshmen into the Boston area every fall, how it was somehow energizing, part of the whole new beginnings theme that we celebrate here every autumn.

That may be both the first and the last nice thing that I have to say about them as a group.

I know that sounds awfully curmudgeonly, and I'm not the right age to be able to claim that title; but, honestly, it's the truth. It's not just a matter of being stuck in a stuffy subway compartment sitting in front of pimply adolescents who are absolutely certain that their knowledge, their perceptions, and their reactions are true, right, and real. It's the fact that they feel compelled to carry that attitude with them into class as well that bothers me.

I gave an assignment to the prostitution class. I also defined the format in which it should be delivered, mostly to save myself from the complicated rambling diatribes often produced without such guidelines. The papers duly came in, and two had ignored the format issue altogether. One of the two, in place of the expected annotated academic paper, had produced a one-page poem on the subject. I sighed, not looking forward to the confrontation that was going to have to happen here. If anyone wants my opinion on the dumbing-down of American public schools, I would be more than happy to give it.

I gave the unacceptable papers, uncorrected, back to the students in question – both of them freshmen – and asked that the assignment be rewritten following the format I'd indicated. "I'll even be nice," I said. "I won't penalize you this time, because perhaps you didn't understand the directions. Write it over and I'll grade it as though it came in on time."

Far from being suitably grateful for this extremely generous interpretation of their works' shortcomings, both of them were indignant. Loudly indignant.

"I can't believe that someone this narrow-minded is teaching in a so-called center of learning!" snarled Jesse, wasting no time in going straight for the jugular. He was the poet. Probably practicing for his next foray into angry verse. Unfortunately for him, it had been done before, and by persons with a great deal more talent than he was currently evidencing.

I began, "I'm merely asking you to –"

"So your way is the only way to do it?" countered Bob, managing to interrupt and be boorish at the same time. "Like we don't have brains. Like there's nothing that we have to contribute. The point of being in school isn't to teach us how you want things done."

I reminded myself that killing him would not help my career. "Actually, it is," I said, mildly. "How can you know that you disagree with a way of doing things if you haven't tried that way out?" I hesitated, wondering if I was reasoning with the unreasonable, then hurried on before they could jump in. "Tell you what, I'll give you an extra-credit assignment: examine the format that I want you to use, and take it apart. Intellectually, not while you're mad at me. Tell me what's wrong with it, and why you don't want to use it."

"Oh, yeah, so your answer is to get us to do your work for you?"

Something like this happens every year in the fall. They come in, some of them having been at or near the top of their classes in high school, and they're used to one way of doing things – the way that worked back in Pawtucket or Fort Lauderdale or St. Louis. They're cocky and convinced that they have the right to have an opinion on every subject under the sun.

The problem is, of course, that in order to have an opinion you have to have something to judge it against. You can't pick Freud apart until you've really studied Freud. You can't argue against a concept that you haven't bothered to examine. But no one wants to make the effort of actually studying, and too many public schools are letting students get away with that. So instead of insisting on excellence, we've made opinions – anyone's opinions – count as much as actual knowledge and understanding. And we wonder why we produce some of the most uneducated people on the planet.

What *I* wonder is why we don't seem to care that we do this.

"You can rewrite the papers," I said steadily, "or you'll get a zero on them."

They went for the zeros. They might learn, in time, but not during this round. The next thing you know, they'll be complaining that my grades were adversely affecting their self-esteem.

I was actually starting to see my night job as a pleasant escape.

Peach farmed out the telephone to one of her assistants that weekend, and gave a party at her apartment in Bay Village. I say "party," though the term is employed somewhat loosely; what it really was was Peach's salon. I was tired, but I went; of course I went. I was still fairly new in the business, still enchanted by Peach and her persona and ideas and energy. I was thrilled, to tell you the truth, that Peach seemed to be singling me out for attention.

I loved going to her house. I would have loved it even if I hadn't started my flirtation with Luis there. I loved the fact that everyone was so cool, so sophisticated, and so *smart*. I think that at some level I may have been guilty of stereotyping, too. Maybe it's okay to be chic and intelligent too.

You have to understand that everybody who met Peach absolutely, fanatically adored her. It wasn't just that she was known in certain circles as a madam, although that didn't hurt. It was something inside of her, some bit of vulnerability, something vaguely childlike, that attracted people to her.

She chose carefully those whom she allowed to surround her. I was among the only women who worked for her who were ever invited. These were people who tended to be bright, well-read, able to carry on witty conversations on nearly every topic. I think that's what I'm referring to when I call it a salon – that intellectual ability, those lively conversations, which were often the only things that any of us had in common.

So let's talk about Peach.

What can I say about her? She simultaneously projected caring and vulnerability, so that you both wanted to cry on her shoulder and then take care of her for dealing with the trauma of your tears. You did things for Peach that you wouldn't have ever dreamed of doing for anybody else. It took me a long time to figure out that this wasn't natural, that she had created this persona because it worked. She had decided who she wanted to be, and then she became that person, summoning this new being from deep inside her. She was the madam who ran an illicit and successful sexy business, she could discuss Faulkner, she knew the right people, she was the darling of the club circuit. But I knew – she had allowed me to know – that she was most at ease in her sweatsuit, that she read the *National Inquirer*, that she wrote poetry deep in the night. I didn't tell anybody. I was just as dazzled by the persona as everyone else was, and gratified by my participation in it.

Her callgirls would have done anything for her. She counted on that.

That was essential to her business, and it can only happen with a madam. You have to understand that having a madam and having a pimp are, like callgirls and streetwalkers, two very different things. Peach herself had an undergraduate degree (in Communications, which if you think about it makes perfect sense) from a well-known and respected college. She knew more about the classics of literature than I (and, I'll venture to guess, you) ever will. She read voraciously, novels and nonfiction and philosophy and poetry. She shared her books, which lined the walls of her apartment, with generous and reckless abandon. She was exceptionally beautiful, hair flowing around her face, eyes that seemed to understand everything. She made the best coffee in the world, played killer Scrabble, and was famous for losing things.

She worked out of her apartment, sitting surrounded by books and Diet Coke and cats. She had a phenomenal memory for numbers, and no client of hers ever needed to worry about the embarrassment of having his name and information ever show up in any little black book, for there was none. All the information was in her head. The occasional client – a traveler staying in a hotel, a first-time caller – would have his telephone number scrawled in the margin of whatever she was reading that night. Even now I will sometimes pick up a book that Peach once gave me, and find in its pages cryptic notes and numbers competing with the chapter headings.

Likewise, she stored mental information about who was on, who was off, who might be persuaded to work if a regular called, who needed transportation. She could rattle off measurements, bra sizes, accents, occupations, and preferences without ever missing a beat. It never failed to astonish me. She'd be brilliant in sales.

Come to think of it, she was.

Back when I was working for her, Peach's fee was a flat sixty dollars per hour. She was clear about it: when she quoted a price to a client, she'd always say, "and that includes your tip and your fee." I have no idea if anyone knew what she was talking about; and there were some of us who wished she'd drop the "tip" part of that phrase. "It's not the eighties anymore," Peach would say airily, and rather repetitively. "No one tips these days." And she was right: very few did.

She'd negotiate if necessary to include the cost of a driver, or if the client lived really far away; but her fee was always the same. One hour, sixty dollars. Two hours, one hundred twenty dollars. She never asked for more, even when her end of the deal was labor-intensive. That made up, I suppose, for the times when it would take her two minutes flat to set up a call.

Of course, she was doing much more for that money than just setting up a call. I reminded myself of that fact on the nights when I was out in rain, or sleet, or humidity, and would think of her in her pleasant surroundings reading novels between telephone calls, and resent the comparative ease of her part of the transaction and the difficulties inherent in mine. She did all the screening, which you couldn't pay me enough to do; and she ran the risk up front, having her name and telephone number published in the *Phoenix*.

And she really did take care of her girls. I've seen the most extraordinary things happen. One night I was over at Peach's apartment when a call came in from one of the new girls, an eighteen-year-old college freshman, crying because a client had spoken roughly to her. Peach was furious, and had the client on the line in a matter of seconds. "I don't care," she said. "You had no right to say that. Don't fuck around with me, Cory, she's crying. You're just being a bully, and she was young and scared and you took advantage of her. I'm ashamed to know you!" She hung up on him, and she cut him off for weeks after that.

That was one of Peach's fundamental rules, and one of her secrets of success: mess around with one of her girls, and you won't see another one of them soon.

Of course, I have a feeling that, for a lot of the regulars, that was part of the game, part of the attraction of it all. It was almost a kind of aural S&M, with a fantasy "Mistress Peach" yielding a symbolic whip and telling them that they'd been bad boys.

If you were a client and Peach was mad at you, she'd just hang up when you called, no matter how bad business was. You'd have to work your way back into her good graces. Contrition went a long way: "Please, Peach, it'll never happen again, I was wrong . . ." Presents also helped: Peach always seemed to have almost magical access to free tickets to sold-out concerts, cocktails "on the house" at trendy restaurants and bars, stacks of chips appearing out of nowhere when she went to Atlantic City.

She loved it, of course. Who wouldn't? She loved the glitter and privilege and the limousines. She loved the role-playing and the perks and the attention that it brought her.

True story: it was Thanksgiving, the first Thanksgiving that I was working for her. I didn't have anyplace in particular to go, no one to be with, and she invited me to her apartment in the South End, where a small number of people would be celebrating the holiday together. I was beyond thrilled.

As it happened, I was in Louisiana for the funeral of an elderly aunt at the beginning of Thanksgiving week, and I spoke to Peach on the phone from New Orleans. "Do you need me to bring anything?" I asked, automatically; it's what one does to be polite. "Yes," Peach said, "I need a VCR, mine's broken; can you get one? I'll reimburse you. There's a tape I play every Thanksgiving."

Did it occur to me to say, "I'm coming straight in from the airport, that means I have to get it here, in Louisiana, why don't you ask someone closer"? No, of course not. Peach had asked *me*, had entrusted me with this mission. "Okay, sure," I said.

Try flying coach class with a VCR. I got there too late to check it, and it was too big to go under the seat in front of me or in the overhead compartment. I sat in my place, grimly hanging on to it, and the take-off was delayed while flight attendants conferred as to what to do. Other passengers, all too well aware of what (or, more specifically, who) was causing the delay, glared at me. I can't say that I blamed them; I'd probably have cast the first glare, myself, in their place.

The situation was resolved when an alternate place was secured for the box, and we arrived at Logan not too much later than planned. Snow was swirling and a cutting wind bit into me I staggered to the taxi stand, with my purse, my suitcase, my carry-on briefcase . . . and my VCR. I'd lost a glove, a swatch of hair was in my eyes, my makeup had worn off hours before, and I was anything but grace personified. If at that moment I had told anyone that I was a prostitute, they would have dissolved into hysterical laughter. I looked like a refugee from a particularly competitive electronics sale. And the most amazing thing of all was that I didn't mind. It was for Peach. She made the most demanding and inconvenient requests and favors sound logical and even appropriate. It was one hell of a skill.

Peach always found a way to make things work for her. Even her business – she managed special deals with clients, with employees, even with the newspapers that ran her ads.

She was extremely competent. And what she was doing, at the end of the day, was not exactly rocket science. In terms of numbers, it's not all that expensive – or difficult – to set up an escort service. You need to advertise, of course; but even that needn't be outrageous. Some of the bigger services in town – Blue Moon, Temporarily Yours, Midnight Express – took out half-page ads in the Yellow Pages, which I assume were phenomenally expensive. They could afford to: they had staff, offices even, marketing budgets. They also had the potential for really scary arrest records.

An agency like Peach's flew under the radar: she was one person, maybe twenty girls at any given time. She was simply not worth arresting.

She carried two ads in the *Phoenix,* week in and week out, one advertising the agency, a separate one for employment. Back then, that cost three hundred and forty dollars a week, payable in cash. She never paid in person, of course. I frequently had that job, for which she offered the princely sum of twenty dollars: she'd wait until I'd done enough work to be holding that much money for her (it only amounted to six calls, after all) and would have me go over to their offices and pay for the next week's ads. Sometimes it was me, sometimes Luis, sometimes one of the other callgirls.

I often wondered what the sales people at the *Phoenix* thought of this procession of people paying the charges for an escort service. I can't imagine what they thought on certain of the days that I went there, my hair unstyled, wearing no makeup, sometimes in sweats if I'd been working out.

The second ad she ran was for attracting employees.

I dislike the term recruitment; that gives an impression of shady characters standing around schoolyards or something, or else evokes brightly colored lies about the joys of military service. It's not even like Peach ever actively recruited anyone, at least she never did while I was working. In general, people found her.

Like me. I went looking for her. I at least knew where to find the ads; I'd already seen the relevant section of the *Phoenix*, and I expect that its counterpart exists in most local community and alternative papers. Open any of them and you'll see, usually at the bottom of the ad for the service, some phrase like, "Accepting Applications," or "Discreet Attractive Ladies Wanted."

Don't get too excited about your timing: they're all accepting applications, always, all the time. One of the first questions that even a regular client asks is if there's anyone new. New to the agency, new to the work. No matter how beautiful and sexy and compelling a woman is, they'll still reject her in favor of novelty, of variety. I don't know if it's about wanting to put their penis in as many women as possible, or if it's a forlorn hope that the next girl will be the one, the best lay, the sexiest woman on earth. Whatever the reason, it's one of the things that gets us a little cynical about men. But we're in the business of meeting their needs, not questioning their motivations, so every service wants new faces, fresh bodies, all the time. Employment is almost guaranteed.

The problem with the newspaper ads, from Peach's point of view, is that there's a fair amount of screening that has to take place. Women call her for all sorts of reasons. The curious, those looking for an illicit thrill, those who do not understand the nature of the business ("But I just want to have dinner with him!").

She screened out the too young, the too desperate (they are the ones with the potential to make mistakes, to get hurt), the too dull. Then she shepherded them through their first encounter, after which, if they found that it was *not* for them, she might have to do some crisis counseling.

Of course, she stacked the deck in her favor. She almost always sent new callgirls to Bruce, or to one or two of her tame clients who were like him. Kind. Nice. Reassuring. She tried to make it as good for the girls as possible, and because she did, her girls developed a fierce loyalty to her, a loyalty that survived bad calls and bad times, that made them want to be part of her world, part of her agency, part of who she was.

Peach used her own judgment about trusting new employees – and she wasn't always right, either. I remember one new girl who stole a lot of money from Peach and then took off for parts unknown. Two of her most reliable callgirls, women she considered to be friends – one of them went on calls, the other worked the phones – learned the business from Peach, then left to start their own service, taking a number of clients with them when they went. It happens. It's not exactly a situation one takes into small claims court. But for all the times that Peach was wrong, there had to be a hundred times that she was right. She knew and understood people. And she made you feel that she cared deeply about you. Sometimes she would call, and my voice might be off a little, and the first thing she would say was, "What's wrong?" And you knew, you absolutely *knew*, that Peach would do whatever it took to make things good for you again.

Her secret? Simple, but seemingly impossible in the world of the night. She was sincere. She really, honestly, cared.

And that was why, occasionally, she got taken. But she also got some terrific callgirls, and she had some great clients. In general, life was good.

The best way to avoid getting cheated by your callgirls is through referrals.

A lot of the girls who worked for Peach actually were in college, and most of them had friends. It's not something that they generally advertise about themselves, of course; but one generally knows one's friends well enough to know who might be open to the idea, and who might be repelled by it. A referral means that there's a better chance that the girl knows what she's getting into, that she's already familiar with the pay rates, the expectations, the requirements, the limitations. It makes Peach's life much easier – not to mention safer.

And safe sex, as we all know, is the best sex of all.

* * * * * *

If you look through the advertisements for escort services, either in the yellow pages or the newspapers, you'll occasionally come across some promise of honesty. And I'm here to tell you that that is the biggest lie of all.

I remember one of my early clients, the first week that I was working, was absolute torture on the phone. He kept grilling me and grilling me about the specifics of my appearance. Was I *sure* about my weight, was I telling the truth about my bra size? He kept going back to make sure that my story was consistent with what Peach had already told him: "And what did you say your actual measurements are again?"

As it happened, I was calling him from the parking lot of a shopping mall, where I had just spent an unpleasant hour looking at my reflection in the fitting rooms of Cacique, buying lingerie, so it was a bit of a sore subject, my physical imperfections. He agreed to see me, and I immediately called Peach back to confirm. "Peach, he kept going on and on and on about my looks, what was that about?"

She shrugged it off. "Oh, he had a bad experience with another service; they told him the girl was gorgeous and she was missing teeth or something."

I went to the specified hotel with a sense of dread, because of course (following Peach's instructions) I had lied. In my case it was truly a technicality: I worked out, but the reality is that muscle does weigh more than fat, and I weighed far more than my appearance suggested, so I routinely told people what they wanted to hear. No client, hearing the truth, would have considered seeing me; but once he did see me, he never had any complaints.

In the end, it turned out to be one of my best calls ever. The guy was nice, the telephone attitude had totally disappeared, and we shared a lot of laughter and fun. He eventually became one of my regulars, a huge bonus, as I never had to go through the telephone question-and-answer thing with him after that.

But the issue of lying is a major one in the escort business.

I asked Peach about it, after that first episode. "Why would the service lie about the girl? They'll be proven wrong as soon as he opens his door."

We were sitting at a booth in Legal Seafoods, and she was more interested in the menu than in conversation. "Well, something that blatant, yeah, you don't do that. That's really stupid. No one's going to call back if they think you're trying to screw with them."

I had already decided what to order, the only thing I ever order at Legal's: mussels in fragrant seafood sauce. "So . . . ?"

"Face it, we all lie. You know that the client is going to want to see you once he *sees* you, right? But you also know that if you told him your real weight, or, for that matter, your real age, he wouldn't. So you lie. Doesn't hurt anybody. He gets what he wants, you get what you want." She closed the menu. "Mussels in fragrant seafood sauce," she told the waiter.

"I'll have the same thing, please," I said, and waited for him to leave. "It still doesn't leave us with a great reputation."

Peach frowned at me. She always hated talking about the business. Oddly enough in view of her profession, she would only discuss sex if it was absolutely, positively necessary. "Men are sheep," she said. "They're told what they want by the media, the porn industry, the advertising agencies. They don't really understand what they're looking for. They *think* they want Pamela Sue Anderson. They also *think* they know her measurements and what she weighs, and I guarantee that they're wrong on both counts. Guys don't have a lot of imagination when it comes to what they find sexually attractive: they like what they're told to like, and assume that's the only path to sexual nirvana."

So that was why Peach lied. She told her clients what they wanted to hear. She knew that her girls were good, that whomever saw the client would delight him; but he wouldn't believe that if her description of the girl was too far off the Pamela Anderson model. So she lied, the clients loved the girls she sent, and everybody was happy.

Lenin said somewhere that a lie told often enough becomes truth. We are, all of us, inventing ourselves over and over again, every day.

I was talking about Peach's late-night salons, gatherings at her apartment after she shut the phones off for the night, where a selected group of us would sit, drink, do lines, and discuss everything from politics to architecture. Wittily, of course. Some nights we'd play games, Pictionary and Taboo and Trivial Pursuit and Scrabble. We were as contrived and clever and self-absorbed as any French eighteenth-century salon of would-be literati, the difference being that we knew it, and were not above poking fun at ourselves.

And it was fun – I have to say, it was great fun while it lasted. I'd do one or two calls, then head over to Peach's place around one o'clock in the morning, play and stay until five, go home and sleep. Not every night, of course: I was teaching, I had lectures to prepare and papers to grade. But it happened often enough to give my life a sort of edge, a sense of being someone exciting, of having Another Life. It may all have been a chimera, in the end; but it was still a lot of fun while it lasted.

On this particular night, Scrabble was being played, and wine and lines of coke being distributed. I misplaced my wineglass somewhere, and the man next to me touched my arm and extended his own glass. "Here, have some of mine."

I looked up. It was Luis, who sometimes drove for Peach and went to business school by day. I accepted the glass and he held my eyes as I drank from it, then returned it to him. "Let's play," he said.

We shared that glass of wine, and then another. We played Scrabble and Luis won. Eventually people started trickling out of the apartment, and Peach yawned and went to bed; still Luis and I stayed there, talking to each other as though mesmerized, a large quilt over our shoulders, snuggled together, a perfect fit. We talked about his childhood, and mine; we talked about the ethics of business and the ethics of academia; we talked about . . . oh, I don't even remember, anymore, what we talked about. What I do remember is that we fell in love.

Which presented some interesting and unanticipated moral issues. When love is for sale, how do you give it away?

Chapter Thirteen

And so I got involved with Luis Mendoza.

I didn't notice any deterioration in my teaching, not at first. I'm honestly not sure that anybody else did, either. At first. I was getting less and less sleep at night, and yet was managing to carry it off, mostly because being in front of a class was so incredibly energizing and exciting for me that the adrenaline high saw me through.

But papers were being passed back late because I wasn't getting around to reading and grading them, or because I fell asleep at the table while trying to.

Okay, so I was a little late. I rationalized my concerns away: I knew professors who were extremely late. Hell, my dissertation advisor had *lost* my French language proficiency exam, pretended for six months that he still had it, and passed me purely on the basis of not being able to prove otherwise. So I was in decent company.

I didn't think about it a lot. It would just be for a little while . . . a few late papers . . . a few under-prepared lectures. I could survive it.

In the meantime, Luis was filling a lot more than my thoughts. He was the perfect boyfriend. He sent me flowers. He called me just to hear my voice. He presumed that I had an extraordinarily high level of intelligence, knowledge, and wit; and I found myself stretching to live up to his expectations. Our sex life was sweet, friendly, pleasant. He wrote me a poem. In Spanish.

And, curiously enough, my working for Peach didn't appear to have any impact on the relationship at all.

I've said it before, but it bears reiterating. In all of the time that I worked for the escort service, I never confused what I was doing with anything else. The words might have been the same, the acts and gestures might have been the same, but it was work. There are very few callgirls who are unable to make that differentiation; and those who cannot do not survive.

I think that it's a lot easier for a woman to be clear about sepa-rating out sex for money and sex for love than it is for a man to do so. Mind you, men *think* that they're good at differentiating. The husband caught *in flagrant delicti* will protest, "But, honey, it was just sex! It didn't mean anything!"

Well, okay, maybe it didn't, but that's only because sex doesn't have that much meaning for men, no matter who they're doing it with.

For whatever reason – and the anthropologist in me can think of several excellent ones, though this is not the time or place to lecture on them – women have attached a feeling (love) to a physical activ-ity (sex). Men have more or less bought into this notion, because doing so afforded them the opportunity to keep at least one woman around and available. But the old double standard invariably raises its ugly head, and while men are assumed to feel the need to go out-side of the "love" relationship and have meaningless sex without it affecting the primary relationship, women do not have that option. For her, sex is only supposed to have one meaning: love. If a woman engages in the same meaningless sex that men claim as a birthright, then she's considered a slut. Nice girls don't.

But men aren't that much better off. First of all, they have the whole prostitution thing pretty confused. Because most men have either employed a prostitute or considered employing one, it is already outside of the realm of business for them. Meaningless sex, as they might explain to their wives, but, guys, it didn't just fall from heaven in a Glad Bag. They wanted it and pursued it and enjoyed it. That doesn't sound all that meaningless to me.

So for most men, prostitution isn't a profession, it's part of Real Life. Something that they do. A rite of passage for a high school graduate, a last fling for a soon-to-be-husband, a change of pace from one's usual routine.

And sex with a prostitute is great sex, because you get to pick the menu. She's there exclusively for you, to do exactly what you want her to do. There's no nonsense here about having to wait for her to have an orgasm or needing to engage in tiresome foreplay: she's there, ready to do whatever you want her to. She has no needs, no desires, no demands. This is what sex should be like, damn it!

Prostitution plays right into all these fantasies. The callgirl is there to be seductive, to fulfill his wishes, to give him an hour of what he only imagined could be real: a beautiful woman with nothing but sex on her mind. Better, still: a beautiful woman with nothing but sex on her mind who is totally and completely focused on him. On what he wants. On giving him pleasure. All that matters to her is him, his pleasure, his needs, his desires. See, these girls really do exist! Why haven't any of his dates, girlfriends, wives been like this?

Well . . . the short answer is, because they're not getting paid to take care of him.

When you call a service, you can make requests. When the girl calls you to confirm, you can tell her how to dress, you can tell her how to act, hell – you can tell her that she has to act like Queen Elizabeth if that's what gets you off, and she'll do it. If she's at all good, she'll even convince you that she's as turned on by whatever your thing is as you are. "I never thought that being Queen Elizabeth could be so erotic . . . such a turn-on . . . so sexual!" she'll breathe.

And men are so naïve, so gullible. You do everything that you can to make them feel good, to make them feel princely. "You're the best I've ever had. I never have orgasms with other men, but you made me come. If we had only met under different circumstances . . ." And they believe it. That's the most amazing part. Men who are rapacious in the boardroom, men who could spot a securities fraud a mile away, these are the men who will believe anything that you tell them, as long as it's positive, as long as it's about their sexual performance. Many times – and I mean *many* times – a client has listened to me sing his praises and then comment that I was so hot for him, I probably should have paid him, instead of the other way around. And I would listen and wonder in utter astonishment how an intelligent person could fall for something that blatant.

The media, reflecting popular culture as it does, doesn't help. I watched a television program that was portraying a prostitute as sympathetic, trying to show that she *was* not what she *did* for a living. And they did pretty well with it, too, until some asinine screenwriter had her open her mouth and say, "I work hard for my money! Well – *sort* of hard . . ." Great. Spectacular. It's not really work, because it's also fun.

Acting out those fantasies, fulfilling those desires – from the man's point of view, that's normal. Pleasant. It's what you do. And if I'm having such a good time, she must be too, right? So it's not *really* work for her.

Well, it sure as hell isn't sex.

Most women expect sex to be composed of give and take, a more or less equal exchange in which both partners' desires and needs and requests are met. It's never just about one person. At best, it's sharing; at worst, it's taking turns.

What we do as prostitutes, therefore, does not constitute sex in our minds. The callgirl is catering completely to the client's needs on a very one-way street. She gets about as much excitement out of a call as she does out of going to the supermarket. I often mentally composed to-do lists while moaning in apparent rapture, a little multi-tasking to help the time pass more quickly. I have faked more orgasms than I can count. Sorry, but that simply isn't sex.

It is for him; but while *he*'s having sex, *I*'m at work.

It is highly unlikely that a woman will confuse the two experiences. Men, on the other hand, very well might.

So I continued to work for Peach, doing three or four calls a week; and when I wasn't working for Peach, I was seeing Luis. I kept the two completely separated. When I did it with my clients it was work; when I did it with Luis it was sex. And the only drawback to this new situation was that Luis kept me awake as far into the night as most of my calls did. The fact that Luis and I were playing Scrabble and drinking and doing lines with a sprinkling of sex at the end of the evening, as opposed to my exerting myself for a client, really didn't matter at the end of the day. The clock was the final arbiter.

Which is not good at all for being bright and patient and enlightening at eight o'clock the following morning.

Not that things weren't going well for my long-term day job prospects. The prostitution class was new, it was sexy, it was cutting-edge; and it was inevitable that news of it would leak out. I got a call from somebody in Alberta, for heaven's sake, wanting me to post the class syllabus on the Internet so that his students could follow along with the readings for extra credit. The college where I was currently teaching assured me that I could continue basically unendingly with this particular elective.

The dean himself had even invited me in for tea and a chat. "And you could teach some other classes as well, or maybe two different sections of the prostitution one. We realize that to keep good talent like yourself, we need to offer some incentives. This college likes to think of itself as a caring institution. So we're proposing to raise your base pay rate and make sure you have as many sections as you want to teach."

I sat there and smiled stupidly, wondered where he had been last year, when I couldn't make rent and was living on freeze-dried ramen noodles and ended up becoming a prostitute myself because his benign and caring institution hadn't seen fit to give me more sections to teach.

I received a number of invitations to go to various places and do a single guest-lecture spot on the topic, sometimes to a group of board members or alumni, sometimes to sociology, anthropology, or history classes. I tried to do as many of these as possible: the money was reasonable, but more importantly, it was giving me name recognition. And that's one of the most precious commodities in academia.

All the while, I was feeling absurdly pleased with myself. I was going to make it – no, I *was* making it – and on my own terms, not theirs. I was going to get what I wanted, and I was going to do it without destroying anyone else along the way.

I remember a lecture that I received during my orientation, back when I started my doctoral program. Another dean was speaking then. "What you will have to develop, ladies and gentlemen, and develop quickly, is a pit bull mentality. You cannot afford to help each other out. Look around you. Half of the people in this room will not be here for graduation. If you want to be in the half that stays, then it is up to you to get there. Don't think about who you're stepping on to get there, because you can be sure that they wouldn't think of you if your roles were reversed."

I hated hearing that, and I am absolutely sure that my less-than-meteoric rise in the ranks of academia is entirely due to my refusal to play that game. It was the right decision. I want to be able to sleep at night, and I want to be able to look at myself in the mirror. What they were asking us to do was ethically wrong. Becoming a callgirl, in response, was a far more ethical decision.

But now, as Steve Winwood would say, I was apparently "back in the high life again."

I went up to the North Shore to present a guest lecture at Salem State College, and ended up spending the day, even though it was freezing, walking down along the harbor. Luis had wanted to come along, but had a study group. I was just as happy being alone.

Peach called as I was driving back down Route One from Salem. "Are you anywhere near the Chisolm?" she wanted to know.

"About ten minutes," I answered. Peach thinks in minutes, not miles.

"Great. How do you feel about doing a call with another girl? You'll have to fool around with her some."

"Not a problem." I'd spent most of my undergraduate career vacillating on the topic of whether I was straight or a lesbian. My conclusion had been – and still is, for that matter, if anyone wants to know – that both men and women are in fact bisexual and that limiting yourself to only one half of the population is – well, limiting. Yeah, I could handle a double.

The Chisolm is a motel just north of Boston that advertises whirlpool bathtubs and available X-rated cable. No one glances at you, not even casually. You park outside the room you're going to, and the walls are made of the same faux wood that used to be on the sides of station wagons before everybody decided that they needed four-wheel drive vehicles to negotiate the speed bumps in suburban parking lots.

The client's name was Vinnie. He was an overweight Italian-American with a gold crucifix nestled in his abundant chest hair and few social graces.

My partner – who had driven down from New Hampshire to make this call, according to Peach – was already seated on the room's only double bed, wearing a set of matching flowered bra and panties. Her name *du jour* was Stacy, and as Vinnie didn't seem to be into small talk, I took the initiative and stripped down to my lingerie, slowly, trying to get a feel for the room. Just to get things started, I sat on the bed and caressed Stacy's shoulder, while remarking to Vinnie, "She's beautiful, isn't she?" I had learned long ago – before Peach, even before the rat bastard boyfriend – that guys like it when you seem to be into the other woman. Not a problem.

There was, however, a different problem. As soon as I had touched her, I felt Stacy stiffen and almost imperceptibly pull away from me. Oh, shit.

Too bad Peach hadn't quizzed Stacy on *her* feelings about "fooling around with another girl." Or maybe Stacy defined it differently.

All that I knew for sure was that if she didn't like me touching her shoulder, she sure as hell was going to *hate* where I touched her next.

Her eyes weren't telling me anything; they were fixed on Vinnie, waiting to see what he wanted. She was probably okay on her own, the kind of helpless sweet thing that some of the guys liked – no personality, ready to serve. The opposite of what was needed here. We were in big trouble.

I moistened my lips. "Why don't you join us?" I invited him. Maybe if he wasn't just standing there watching us, she'd relax a little.

Vinnie didn't need a second invitation. He stripped quickly and lay down on the bed, stretching out an arm toward where we were sitting. "Come here," he said.

It wasn't clear who he was addressing, so we both slithered over to where he was lying, one of us on either side. This was better. Stacy started kissing him while I moved my hands down his chest, down lightly over his stomach, then encircled the root of his cock. He was stiffening, getting bigger under my touch, and I encouraged him, my fingers caressing, my hand stroking. He grunted and broke away from Stacy, gesturing toward himself. "Lick me," he instructed. "Both of youse."

Stacey slid down until her head was even with mine. I held his cock while she ran her tongue up its whole length. I licked the other side, and, inevitably, our tongues touched. "Close your eyes and kiss me," I whispered to her, pretending to kiss her cheek and ear as I did. "It'll be okay, it'll get him off faster."

I drew away again to play with the tip of his cock with my tongue, then turned my face toward her again. She seemed resolute, her eyes closed, but as we kissed I could feel her relax slightly. Great. I was doing most of the work here, but at least we'd make it through most of the hour with another satisfied customer.

We ended the embrace and I immediately slid up to kiss Vinnie, my tongue moving inside his mouth. "She's so hot," I whispered to him, then leaned over and caressed the top of her head. Stacey had gotten into the rhythm of a blowjob and seemed oblivious to me at the moment.

We muddled through the hour somehow. That's one of the great things about this job: no matter how awful things get, you can glance at your watch and tell yourself: in thirty minutes this guy is history. In twenty minutes I'll not have to deal with this ever again.

Vinnie wasn't awful, and it was hardly his fault that Peach had sent someone who wasn't comfortable with threesomes. Stacey really needed to work on that, I thought as I slipped my key into the ignition and drove away. We got a lot of calls for them.

It's no secret that a nearly universal fantasy shared by men is to have a sexual encounter with two women at the same time. All you have to do, really, is read the *Letters to Penthouse*, any volume, any story, and you're right in the middle of that particular male sexual fantasy. I used to think that the stories were something of a joke – I read quite a lot of them at one time, because erotica was always a huge turn-on for me; I often used to masturbate while reading porno-graphic stories or descriptions of scenes. I was never able to suspend reality, however, the way that the writers (and presumably readers) of these letters could. "My wife is petite, blonde, sexy and wild. One day I was home with the flu when the TV repairman arrived to fix our cable reception. I got out of bed and peeked through the crack in the door. There he was, this big, hairy-chested stud, ramming his thick cock into my wife's juicy pussy . . ." Yeah, that could happen.

Or your girlfriend's two roommates will start kissing each other in the kitchen while you're visiting, treating you to a view of new and creative ways of using cold fruit and vegetables. Or . . .

Let's say you're a man, a fairly average, ordinary man. There's this part of you that gets off on imagining two perfect, beautiful, desirable women together, turning each other on, really into having sex with each other. But the bigger thrill is that you're in the picture. Ultimately (your fantasy informs you), their sex with each other cannot satisfy them, not fully, not completely. Only you can do that.

The adoration that a callgirl gives you is multiplied when there are two women there. Your fantasy may be that they were lesbians who needed a real man to make them straight; or that you're just too much man for one woman to handle; or that you like a lot of stimulation at the same time. Your fantasy may be that they fight over you, or that they share you; that they love each other, or that you're the one who brings them together. To tell you the truth, whatever is going on in your head and exciting your cock is your own business, and it is the center of attention. There is no competition, no other male body parts in sight, just yours, and these two gorgeous women who are begging to touch, to lick, to suck, to bite, to perform, to fuck, to offer, to give you anything you want: it's all about you. Any insecurities that you had are gone: you're a stud, you've got two chicks. Two tongues on your cock. So many breasts. . . . You don't even know where to begin, you're a kid in a candy shop, mouths and hands and pussies and asses, all there for you.

If you don't believe me . . . well, if you don't believe me, then you're a woman, because every man reading this got a shiver of arousal thinking about that scene, and every man reading this knows exactly what I'm talking about. But, ladies, if you don't believe me, check it out with any heterosexual man you know – your partner, brother, friend, office-buddy. They'll tell you: they're fairly sure that it's a "normal" thing to do, think about threesomes, watch football on TV, part of a man's way of life. When pressed for details (and if you're interested, they'll be more open than you perhaps want them to be), they'll even tell you specifically who they imagine to be with in this threesome. Men don't imagine the shadowy sexy stranger: they think about real women. Women they know. Women they see at the market, the health club, the office.

Some of us find that a little creepy. If you can imagine having sex with me, without my knowledge or participation, that's at the very least invading my privacy. If you can imagine having sex with me, if you can masturbate and bring yourself to orgasm while imagining having sex with me, then can following me, even forcing me to actually have sex with you, be so very far away?

In any case, women in general don't share the threesome fantasy. For one thing, women are pretty much taught that another chick around your man is bad news: she's the competition, the predator, the enemy. So it's hard to really get into an imaginary scene where you're sharing him with another woman. And immediately on the heels of that thought is the inevitable voice of insecurity: what if she's better? What if he likes her more than me? What if he can never go back to straight sex? Does this mean that I can't satisfy him by myself?

The guy is thumping and pumping and thinking about how he can keep from coming too fast, and she's already got the divorce papers made out, her own future as a sexual failure assumed, the weight of rejection and loss already heavy in her gut. Then he looks at her and says, "Come on, lick her pussy, get into it!"

Threesomes that are what you might call amateur, so to speak, that involve people who are already in a relationship of some sort and know each other prior to the sexual encounter, are really difficult to pull off. I've tried, and I'm pretty good at detaching sex and love and possession and fun, and I haven't had a lot of success, so I can't imagine what other people do. Maybe that's why callgirls do so many doubles, because it's so tricky to do a threesome with people that you know.

And it really is tricky. The reality is that almost always somebody ends up getting hurt. Frankly, folks, don't try this at home; the fantasies you have require (even though you may not know it) trained professionals. We just *make* it look easy.

I had a threesome once with the rat bastard boyfriend and a woman who had until then been my best friend. Maybe I had told her too many times that I couldn't leave him 'cause he was too good in bed. Or maybe there was something else happening. . . . It wasn't planned; I tried to stop it when it started, and it was awful. I ended up sitting on her bed with tears running down my face while he fucked her; and when I attempted to go down on him, she pushed me away, saying, "I'll show you what a real woman can do."

Something like that takes a while to get over.

Callgirls do doubles, as a two-girl-one-client situation is called, all the time. After all I just said, you may be surprised to hear that most callgirls really like doubles. Not, however, for the reasons you probably imagine.

First, there's the money. He's paying double – the same rate, once for each of you. So you know right away that he's got money, and that if you play it right, you might be able to get him to extend for a second hour. And that's so much better than leaving and then going on another call. It's not that we mind the sex, or the time: it's running around, convincing someone else on the phone that he really wants you, finding the place, trying to figure out what he wants; all that is difficult, sometimes stressful. Even when you end up liking him, the time you spend setting up the encounter and beginning it was not pleasant. So, if you play it right, you could stay here where you already are, comfortable, in control, for the same amount of money. And it's easier to talk a client into extending the time if there are two of you. You can pout. You can caress. You can compliment, you can feed whatever fantasy or need or desire that he's already revealed to you. And if by some miracle he hasn't come yet, or still wants to come again, you can put that off to a second hour. (Pouty, semi-childish voice: "But we were just getting started! There are *so many more* things I want to do to you . . . you excite me so much . . .")

Unless he was determined not to stay, or had an appointment, or not enough money, I could usually persuade clients to extend when I was doing a double. I had my techniques, my phrases, and my repertoire. And I loved doubles because they gave me a chance to see another girl interact with a client, see what was in her repertoire, maybe pick up a phrase, learn from her, make my own interactions fresh.

Besides all that, doubles are just plain less work. If the client is someone who takes a lot of effort to bring to orgasm, you can take turns. If you've already been on two calls and feel a little sore, she can do most of the fucking. If one of you really doesn't like kissing, and the client wants to, chances are the other can fill in. It's not competition, it's never that: on the contrary, there's a sense of solidarity, of being in this together. Something like the bonding between actors, I think, and the giddy relief afterwards when the show went well. It's a peculiar bonding – there are women that I know solely because I've gone down on a man with them – but it is real.

If the client is difficult, you're not dealing with him alone. You have eye contact with each other, send messages. One woman I worked with was faking an orgasm while the client licked her pussy; meanwhile, I was trying to make her laugh. I had my hand on her breasts, of course, in case he looked up; but we were holding in our giggles. Those are good calls. Sometimes the reality of what you are doing for a living can get oppressive, and laughing at the absurdity of it helps.

One night Peach called me to do a double, and – unbelievably – on the way to the call I started my period. No one wanted to miss the call: not Peach, not the client, not my partner. Had I backed out he may have been patient while Peach located a replacement – or, more likely, he might have cancelled the call. We didn't want to take that chance.

I put my arms around the other woman – whom I had just that moment met – and kissed her cheek, murmuring sexually, licking her jawline so he could see. Then I moved up to her ear. "I just got my period," I whispered. "Can you help me cover?"

She pulled back and gave me a long kiss on the mouth. "She's incredible!" she exclaimed to the client as the kiss ended. "You have such good taste, to find someone so special. I am going to love making love to her." She turned to him and ran a hand up his inner thigh. "And I'm going to love having you watch me eat her pussy."

And it worked. By feigning a spontaneous and powerful attraction to me, she set up a situation where she could essentially control my body. She could pretend to engage in oral sex with me, while entertaining him with her ass, or me with my tits and moaning so that he didn't watch too closely. If he attempted to go down on me or fuck me, she could pout and pretend to be jealous. "No, no, that pussy is for me, isn't that what you wanted?" And then she could segue into an invitation to keep his attention away from me: "Come here, I can't wait another minute, she's gotten me so wet, I want your big cock in my pussy while I suck her tits."

In exchange I filled in with a lot of the activities that took more effort: I concentrated on his cock, so that *he* wouldn't get too jealous; I sang his praises as she was singing mine. He fondled my breasts and pinched my nipples as I licked his balls and ran my tongue all around his cock, teasing him over and over until he groaned and I started in earnest, pumping up and down on his cock with my mouth. He had let go of my tits and was watching me give him head, and all the while my partner was caressing my ass and talking dirty, talking about fucking me, how I liked to take it from a girl, just like she was giving it to me. And I moaned in apparent agreement and excitement.

It was one of the few times I didn't mind that the client didn't want another hour; I was cramping and wanted to be in bed with Scuzzy and a hot water bottle and some idiotic sitcom. We rode down in the elevator in near silence. "Do you need a ride anywhere? I asked tentatively. "No," she said. "I have my car. Are you holding Peach's money, or anything?"

"I can if you want," I said. "I'm seeing her on Tuesday."

She handed over the bills, already separated out from her own, folded into a neat little discreet packet. There hadn't been a tip, but that was all right. It had been a good call. We weren't too tired. The client had a good time. Later he complimented Peach on being the only service in town that had real lesbians who also loved to be fucked. He felt he had gotten his money's worth.

We walked through the lobby in silence. Only one person behind the desk: it was one of the big anonymous hotels at the Winter/Wyman exit in Waltham, hotels that grew up around the technology start-ups and giants and technical wizards of route 128, for geeks flying in from Cupertino and Seattle and Japan. No one was interested in geeks. If it had been a downtown hotel, he would have given us a knowing smile and would have masturbated later, thinking about us.

At the door, I hesitated. "Thank you for being so cool about that," I said. "I didn't know until it happened on the way over."

She shrugged, her eyes and mind already on the remainder of the evening. "No problem," she said. "See you around."

And so the same woman who twenty minutes before had been kissing me deeply and passionately, her tongue skimming around my teeth, the same woman who had been sliding her index finger into my ass and inviting a stranger to watch her do it, the same woman who had been sucking my nipples . . . that woman walked briskly away, her keys already in her hand, clicking off her chirping car alarm, unlocking her car before I could even remember where mine was parked.

This woman had made it work. I had done nothing, really, but follow her lead. She had taken the news and gracefully and professionally made sure that the curtain went up, the actors played their parts, and the audience was happy. I wasn't sure how to thank someone – especially someone I didn't know – for doing something that intimate.

The point was moot: I never had the opportunity. She left it all here, in this lonely parking lot beside a businessman's hotel in Waltham: it was over, there was nothing to express. All that she knew of me was the contours of my body, the feel of my lips, my ability to synchronize with her in a rich intricate sexual dance performed exclusively for one man. She wasn't thinking about the performance she had just given, the show that had just ended. She was already thinking about the next one.

A real professional. You come to appreciate that, in this line of work.

Chapter Fourteen

The semester ended, I handed in my grades, and got paid. The checks went into the bank, some of them actually into a brand-new savings account. I paid cash these days for nearly everything else: it was callgirl currency.

Despite the fact that I was apparently becoming the darling of the lecture circuit, and had four classes guaranteed for the spring semester, I wasn't feeling especially good. Not like I had felt in the fall. Maybe it had to do with things not looking fresh anymore, the snow all brown where the plows had pushed it aside, the dirty slush on the sidewalks, the deep-freeze state that we call winter.

Or maybe it was because I was doing too many drugs.

Luis was not particularly helpful in this regard. He had friends, Colombians, who gave him a special price, so he always had coke on him, and we nearly always did it throughout our evening and night together. It was usually fun, making love and stopping for a swallow of wine, Luis laying out a line of coke on my naked breast to snort, lots of laughter, the feeling that you could go on forever.

But the reality was that I was thirty-five, and I couldn't go on forever. I was doing coke regularly now in the mornings, just a line, but what does that mean, when you have to do a line every morning just to be able to function? "Breakfast of champions," I'd mutter, ritually, as if the phrase I had borrowed from one of Peach's other girls were a talisman, and I'd bend over the scratched CD jewel box and transfer the line of cocaine from there to my nostrils. Then coffee, two or three coffees, and then class. I couldn't imagine not doing it. It was my habit, my routine; it was what I did. It never occurred to me just how sick it was.

Then, at night, I'd have done more lines, either out with Luis, or out on a call, lines that kept me alert, focused, and able to keep going. By the time I got home I was physically exhausted, yet unable to sleep, so I turned to pills.

I was grateful for the winter break between semesters. I didn't have to feel as pressured, as manic about everything that I needed to get done. The break would be good for me, I decided. I would start working out again. I would take long walks. I would get lots and lots of sleep. I'd cut back on the cocaine. These were all necessary changes: four classes were awaiting me at the end of January. When school started up again, I would have to be ready. I would have to be at my best.

I promised myself, also, that I'd do a lot of calls over the break, so that I could do fewer of them once classes started again.

So I told Peach that I could work a little more frequently for a few weeks. She was, predictably, delighted. It was then that I finally got to see Mario.

I had heard about Mario long before I ever met him.

I had done a double with another girl named Lori at the Ritz, sometime back in November. It had been a great call; we snuggled together and petted each other for a while and then she went down on the client while I kissed him. He came fast, which was hardly surprising, as he had been masturbating the whole time he was watching us play together. He didn't appear to mind. He paid Peach's astronomical price (we were getting one-eighty each, above and beyond Peach's fee), and was beaming in sheer delight as we left. He had confided in us that we were the first white women he'd ever had sex with. I wondered how the comparisons were panning out.

"That was a great call," I commented in the elevator. "He was really nice." I meant it, too: you get so you really like people who treat you well. In this business they are sometimes hard to find.

The elevator stopped and we got out and crossed the lobby. The doorman held the outside doors open for us, his face expressionless. I always wondered if they knew. I expect so; I understand that at many hotels the doormen double as procurers. "Totally," Lori sighed when we were out of his hearing. "I'm having the most totally ultra week."

I guessed that was positive. With Lori's version of English it was sometimes hard to tell. "Where you parked, Tia?"

"Under the Common."

"Me, too." We crossed the street and skirted the park itself, an automatic nighttime precaution for women. She sighed. "I, like, saw Mario like twice this week, can you believe it, I'm thinking skanko week, and then I got him and now this dude tonight, it, like, rules, ya know?"

"Who's Mario?" I asked idly, more to be polite than anything else.

She stopped in the middle of the sidewalk. "No way. Tia, no way, you don't, like, know who Mario is? Oh, my *God*. Oh, my *God*, Tia. You haven't seen Mario? Oh, my *God*." Lori made up in vehemence for what she may have lacked in eloquence. She also, to my relief, started walking again. It was way too cold to be hanging about on the sidewalk. I've never been to Chicago, but I'd lay even odds that in the winter, the wind whipping down Boston's boulevards and across the Common puts us right up there in the competition. "Listen, it's like, you've *got* to ask Peach to send you, oh, my God, he's like, the best. Well, like the easiest, you know what I mean?"

I wasn't entirely sure I did, but I nodded encouragingly. "So why are you telling me about him?" We did not, as a rule, want to share our best clients with each other.

Lori didn't even hesitate. "As if it would bother me. As if. Don't even go there, 'kay? That's so lame. This guy has girls in every night, he sometimes has lots of girls, there's enough to go around." She lowered her voice confidentially. "He's, like, somebody in the Mafia, you know, but I don't think he whacks people."

I managed not to smile at her appropriation of Hollywood's version of organized crime-speak, and I said instead, "Well, I'd imagine that not everyone has to actually do that. What does he like to do, besides being in the Mafia?"

I really was asking about sexual preferences – well, that's *our* job, after all – but Lori had other things to say first.

"Well, it's like he owns this really cool store, it totally *rules,* ya know, it's over on Newbury Street, it's all leather stuff, jackets and purses and stuff. I went in once, and he was there, and gave me this huge discount on a skirt, it was too cool, he treated me like I was special, like I was his girlfriend or something. It was like, hello, is anybody home, I wasn't exactly like his *age* or anything, the dude is so old, but everyone in the store was smiling and bein' nice to me anyway. And you should see the skirt, Tia, it rocks! I wore it the next time I went to see him, you know, to thank him."

She went off to find her car and I didn't think of the conversation again until one night in January when Peach was complaining about how slow it was.

Just to have something to say, I asked her, "So, Peach, who's Mario, and how come I don't get to see him?"

Peach sighed. She had to send girls out together to do doubles or share rides, but she didn't have to like the ensuing exchanges of information. Peach was a great one for centralized control. She would have made it big in the Soviet Union; she probably had a Five Year Plan for the agency stashed away somewhere. She told people what she decided they needed to know, and got irritated when they found out other things on their own. "He's a regular," she said. "I've never run you by him because he likes really young girls, the college students, the ones that look seventeen or eighteen." And, presumably, who communicate in mall-speak.

The age issue was a persistent concern, though it rarely became a real issue. By that time I was thirty-five, although thanks to good genes and persistent working out I passed easily for ten years younger. Anything more was pushing it. I usually was billed as mid-twenties, and a graduate student rather than from the other side of the podium.

Peach was apparently pursuing the thought on her own. "You know, Jen, that's actually not such a bad idea," she mused. "I think he'd like you, you know, if he can get past the age thing. I'll think about it. You've got a car, that's a plus, he's way out in Weston somewhere with no T access and it's expensive as hell to take a taxi. I'll see what I can do."

Two weeks later, out of the blue, she called. "Work," she said.

Peach was never one to waste words. "You've got to talk him into it, though."

"Oh, Peach," I said in dismay. She knew I hated the selling part.

"No, no, it's all good, once he hears your voice it'll be fine, just let him know how sexy you are. It's Mario in Weston. If you can get him, you'll love him, guaranteed."

"He's the one who has a youth fetish."

"That's the one," she said briskly. "I told him you're twenty-five, but sweet and naturally sexy and new to the business. I told him to stop being so rigid and try something new. He's half-convinced."

"Great," I said gloomily. Another client who had to be talked into seeing me. "Give me the number."

He answered on the second ring. "Yeah?"

"Hi, is this Mario?"

"Yeah. Who's this?"

"My name is Tia. I'm a friend of Peach's." I paused, and he filled the gap. "Oh, yeah, right. You wear lingerie?"

This was okay so far. "Yes, I have –"

He cut me off. "Okay, wear something nice, not too cheap looking, you know what I mean? None of that garter belt bullshit, just something nice to look at. What brand of perfume you wear?"

It was all off-script, and I was a little off balance, but I recovered quickly. "Chanel Number Five," I said. "But if you don't like that, I also have –"

"No, no, that's good," he interrupted. "Peach says you're real smart, real educated. She bullshitting me? Tell me the truth, I won't hold it against you if she lied."

I cleared my throat and my mind. "No, she's right. I have an undergraduate degree in psychology from Harvard, and a master's in social anthropology from –"

I was becoming accustomed to the interruptions; in an odd sort of way they paced the conversation. "Yeah, okay. She said you wrote a book."

"I've published four books and a number of monographs," I started. "I've also co-authored –"

"Yeah, yeah. Okay. You wanna come over?"

"Yes, it sounds like we have a lot to –"

"All right," he said. "There's no room in the driveway; I got cars, you know, but don't park on the grass, all the girls they park on the grass, it's dying. They don't tow from in front of my house; you can park in the street, but be sure your wheels ain't on the grass, you get me?"

"Absolutely," I promised.

"Okay. Now, where are you coming from? Allston? Okay, here's how you get here . . ."

I put on lacy (but not revealing) white panties and a matching bra, then put on over them a loose camisole that I often wore on hot nights in lieu of pajamas. It covered my ass but stopped just below it, and outlined my breasts nicely because it was silk, and fell just right. I put on a gray little-nothing suit, trim at the waist, something I could (but didn't) wear to teach. He seemed to appreciate the academic side of me. I added black tights that shimmered a little (thanks to a high percentage of Lycra), moderate-heel shoes (he'd probably classify the fuck-me shoes as cheap), and added earrings, bracelet, and a slim chain holding a cross. If he was indeed Mafia, then he was also Catholic. I almost forgot the Chanel, sprayed it generously, tried to kiss Scuzzy goodnight (he was too busy trying to drink from the bathroom faucet to pay attention) and left.

The house in Weston was in a relatively nice neighborhood – relative for Weston, that is, which specializes in the mock-Tudor style mansions so beloved of the *nouveau riche*, the stone and stucco mansions favored by the inherited money, and a lot of simply really big houses. Mario's was modest by those standards, a sort of ranch that had expanded in several directions with several different choices of building materials. Charitably put, it was eclectic. I thought it was awful.

I hadn't, as the saying goes, seen nuthin' yet.

Mario answered the doorbell. He was probably in his very early fifties, with the tiniest suggestion of a potbelly, and hair everywhere. He was wearing a bathrobe and boxer shorts, the robe was open, and I didn't think I had ever seen anyone that hairy before. Maybe in a *National Geographic*. Maybe.

"Great, you're here," he said, shutting the door behind me and draping an arm casually across my shoulders. We were standing in his living room, graced by a replica of the statue of David, tremendous mirrors with black and gold borders, and a shag carpet. Really. I didn't know you could get one of those in the nineties.

Our immediate destination was the kitchen, where we stopped to pick up two bottles of champagne, then proceeded to a large bedroom that was on the same floor. "The bathroom," he informed me on the way, pointing. "This is the one you use."

"Okay." That was a nice touch, my own bathroom. If he lived alone, I sure as hell didn't want to use whichever one was his. Working for Peach, I'd seen enough bachelor bathrooms to last several lifetimes. Some of them I had actually been compelled to use. "This is a great house – everything is – so – convenient," I said.

"Yeah, I had to make it over to get it right," he agreed. I could believe that. He shut the bedroom door behind us.

In one corner was a big-screen television (can one say enormous-screen television?), tuned to a basketball game, with the sound turned off. Most of the room was dominated – dwarfed, even – by a tremendously large waterbed, one with a carved and elaborate headboard containing nooks and crannies for any conceivable accoutrement. Behind its myriad shelves was a mirror. Even the television was eclipsed by that bed.

"Did you wear something comfortable?" Mario wanted to know, and didn't wait for an answer. "Take off whatever you want to take off so you feel good. I'll get us some champagne."

I couldn't argue with that program. I had already seen the labels. Mario might have questionable taste in home furnishings, but his choice of champagne was impeccable. This was Cristal.

I slipped out of the shoes, blouse, and suit, and left the tights on for the moment. They looked good with the camisole, which was black and purple. I sat on the edge of the bed (not an easy task with it swaying beneath me in response to some internal current) and waited to see what might transpire.

Mario poured champagne into wineglasses and gave me one. Raising his glass, he said something rapid and incomprehensible in Italian, not one of my languages. I raised my own and said, in a hesitant foray into flirtation, "To you." We drank. It was really good.

We watched the game for a while, since apparently he had some serious money invested in its outcome. I inquired after his team and rooted for it, which seemed to amuse him no end. We drank more champagne. He brought out a gorgeous enamel tray, easily the most beautiful object in the house, on which he proceeded to generously pour white powder from an impressively large plastic bag. He smoothed it into lines, located a slim metal straw that looked like (and in all probability, was) gold, and offered me the tray.

I obviously didn't have a problem with that. It wasn't just the callgirls who did drugs: a surprisingly high percentage of clients under fifty used cocaine recreationally, and often wanted to party with their escorts. Peach was always keeping an eye on the girls, and if one of them had a problem with the stuff, she didn't get sent to any of the partying clients. The rest of us took our chances.

Sometimes there were other drugs. One client took a lot of different pills and insisted his guest do the same. I was warned about him (one girl nearly passed out on his *cocktail de maison*) so when I saw him, I palmed the pills and just followed his lead to see what I was supposed to be feeling.

But I was delighted any time anyone offered me coke, and tonight it might prove to be necessary, to counteract the champagne. I was currently on my third glass.

We did some lines and drank more champagne, and he talked a little about some unnamed illness he had. I wasn't really listening, I was trying to figure out what he might like in the way of activity; and I decided it was time for a little closeness. I crawled over to him and started a back massage, which turned into a front massage, which turned into my stroking his cock without a whole lot of expectations, not knowing how he was reacting to the coke.

A common side effect – a *really* common side effect – of doing cocaine is an inability to obtain or maintain an erection. Mario was slow, but surprising, and between my hands and my mouth he got excited, not even noticing when I slipped on the condom, and then, just as he was saying, "I don't think –," he came. Nice.

We retired to our respective bathrooms to freshen up, and then regrouped for another round of champagne and coke. He was talking nonstop now, about his family, his business, and the problems he was having with some recalcitrant (his word – he had an eclectic and fascinating vocabulary) business associates in Miami. He was planning a trip there, to let them know who they were dealing with. He looked at me appraisingly. "I'm taking one of Peach's girls down with me. Maybe you'd like a vacation?"

I agreed that it sounded like a terrific idea, but in the end he took someone else to Miami, which was just as well since I couldn't imagine how I'd explain an unscheduled vacation to the two colleges where I was teaching. But I'm sure that whoever ended up going had a marvelous time. Mario would have made sure of that.

I jumped when the phone rang. It was Peach, calling me out. "Can you stay?" Mario asked. "Sure," I said. I couldn't believe that an hour had already passed, which was definitely a first for me. Usually I couldn't wait for it to happen. He spoke into the receiver. "I'm going another two hours. Okay, sure, here she is."

I took the phone. "Hi, Peach."

"Jen? Is everything all right, honey? You want to stay?"

I shrugged. "Sure, Peach. He's nice. We're having a good time."

"Okay. I'll talk to you shortly."

Mario resumed chatting, asking my opinion on topics ranging from the creation of the solar system to the reasons that people get divorced. He asked a lot of questions on a plethora of topics. He talked about politics and ethics and the changes he observed in society. It was at a level I couldn't relate to, opinions formed during a life with little education and no exposure to abstract thinking. I was fascinated.

Yet he had clearly experienced financial success and had come to realize that he had a need for something more. He had tried the Church; of course he went to Mass every week, but it didn't answer his questions. We did more lines. He shyly told me I was pretty. I never took off my camisole.

He extended my stay yet another two hours. I finally left at four in the morning, my purse full of cash, a gift-wrapped package in my hands, an extra hundred-dollar bill pressed into my pocket at the last minute to "buy more stuff like that thing you was wearing tonight."

The package contained two bottles of Chanel No. 5. Perfume. Top of the line. I had spent a fascinating night, had enjoyed (more slowly than he thought appropriate, but I was driving) an incredible champagne, and had made over a thousand dollars. I was a little railed, but that would pass.

Two nights later, Mario requested me. New camisole, same tights. I arrived on time, was escorted to the bedroom. Same champagne. This time, a speech. "No one told you about me, I guess, so you don't know, but you was magic. See, I never can get it up, and if I ever get it up, I don't come. Not with nobody. But I did with you. And that makes you a really special girl – er – lady."

He was right, of course. It had happened because I didn't know, I thought that was part of the encounter, I was tender and enthused and expected success.

Now that I knew, the knowledge might prove a hindrance. I didn't have to worry about that for long. "I'm sayin' you shouldn't be doin' it every time, 'cause that one time will last me, you don't know, like someone took a curse off me. It was there, then it was gone. I'm old enough to enjoy somethin' like that and not want no more. Maybe sometimes you can touch me a little, I like that, but don't feel bad if nuthin' happens. It's what I was tellin' you about, back when I was sick, I never could do it since then . . ."

I hadn't been paying attention when he told me about his disease (in some graphic detail, as I recall, hence my tuning it out), and I resolved to get the particulars from Peach. "I like you," I said, and I was speaking the truth. "Sometimes that's all it takes, two people comfortable with each other."

Mario shook his head. "It's you," he said firmly, "You're blessed. It's like a miracle. I'll never forget you did that for me."

Then we talked about betting on horses, betting on dogs, and the problems in the two industries. As it turned out, Mario made a good portion of his money via gambling. "I'm not a flashy guy. I don't go to no casinos, that's for tourists. I bet on games, and I bet on fights, and once in a while I bet on how stupid the City Council is." There was a light in his eyes. "I always win when I bet on that one. They haven't failed me yet, them morons. They just get stupider and stupider."

He talked about his mother, but not about his father. His brother had been a fisherman out of Gloucester – they was all Sicilians up there, goombas, but getting out of the business, wasn't no future in it no more. "All them guys, they had their mortgages on their houses and on their boats, they thought it would go on forever. Then the feds come in and close the fishing grounds. Just like that. They never went to high school. Them guys, all they know is fish. They thought it would be there forever." He was concerned about his brother. "So what's a guy with a longline boat gonna do when he can't fish no more? Whaddya think? I'll tell you what he does. He finds other products to bring into port."

"What?" I was genuinely interested. My friend Irene had done her dissertation on the composition of fishing crews, so I knew a little about the industry. "What does he replace the cod with?"

He looked at the silent basketball game for a long moment, and when he spoke, he wasn't looking at me. "Heroin. They bring in heroin cause the money's good. But Gloucester – there's nuthin' there, not anymore. The fish factories are all gone, the quarries are all closed. People hanging out 'cause they don't know anyplace else to go, nuthin' to do, nuthin' to look forward to. So when the fleet comes in, their first customers are their goombas. You see them all the time outside the Crow's Nest an' Saint Peter's Club, just sittin' there, high, waitin' and waitin' for nuthin'." He roused himself and looked at me. "Joey, I've tried to get him outta there, I could get him a job here like that." He snapped his fingers by way of illustration, and I had no reason to doubt him. "Hell, I'd even just give him the money, I'd pay off his mortgages for him, ain't nuthin' to me. But he's too proud, he won't take nuthin' from me. And he can't leave Gloucester. It takes some people up there like that, they can't go over the bridge, anyplace that ain't Gloucester ain't home." He shrugged. "Joey, he respects the old ways, and the rules are the same now as they was then. Don't mess with the drugs. That ain't for us. We's above that. But he's got a boat, Joey does, and a family, and no fish to catch, and too much stubbornness in him to take what his brother wants to give him."

He paused. "So how does he make ends meet?" I asked, feeling pulled into this poignant and tragic tale. Anthropologists keep their distance; but this was no field study.

"He don't bring nuthin' in," Mario said finally. "He takes stuff out." He glanced at me, shrugged as though making a decision, and then spoke the damning words. "Guns," he said. "Guns to Northern Ireland. All them gung-ho paddy-boys here in Boston, they're always raisin' funds for the cause back home. They pays the money and gets the guns and whatever else the hell they need. And then at night they drives their trucks up to Magnolia Harbor, where there ain't no one watchin', and they loads up Joey's boat, and then he's off, same as the old days when he was settin' out for the banks. He stays out about the same time he used to, and when he comes home he stays drunk until it's time to go out again." He hesitated, then said, explosively, "Jesus Christ! It ain't fair. Just 'cause he loves his home. And there ain't nuthin' that nobody can do about it. What does the fuckin' government know about fishing? What do they know about my brother?"

I put my arms around him and held him. Anything that I could say at that point would be inadequate, meaningless, insulting. I knelt beside him and held him, rocking him gently.

I started seeing Mario at least once a week. I know that he was seeing other girls. I think Lori was right, he had someone in most nights, except of course for Saturdays, when he was in town with the goombas.

I thought that I was probably the only person who understood why he was such a steady client. I was the only one who knew of the great emptiness inside him, the aching love for his brother and his inability to make things all right for him, the infinite sadness that he sought to forget by filling his house and his life with women, champagne, gambling, drugs. I understood; but I never referred to it; and he never spoke of Joey to me again.

Interestingly, none of us was jealous of the others seeing him. There was enough of Mario to go around. Everyone drank his champagne and did his lines and listened to him; and by and large, they liked him.

But I remained the only one whose opinion he sought.

One night I awakened to the telephone. As soon as the answering machine picked up, the caller would disconnect, then start again. It was annoying: I lived in a studio apartment, and it was unbelievably loud.

Cursing fluently, I tried to pull the cord out of the socket, and instead picked up the receiver. It was Peach. Peach always closed the service by two o'clock (she has theories about the level of desperation and impairment in people who call services after two), and the clock at which I was squinting said three-thirty. "Peach. Are you all right?" Peach had had a history of dramatic suicide attempts. This sounded like it had some potential in that direction.

"I'm good. Is there any way you'd be willing to go see Mario?"

"Now?" I couldn't believe it. I didn't want to go to Weston.

"He just wants somebody around. Please go, I'll owe you one for this. He's lonely and depressed. He really needs us."

I had had another thought. "My car – I can't take my car, the battery died last night, remember?"

"Take a taxi. He'll pay for it. Please, Jen."

I went. Of course I went. The taxi driver was curious about me until I told him that I was going to sit with someone who had AIDS.

The driver was Haitian; that sobered him up, fast. My white lie was useful in that it circumvented the requisite invitation to share a quick sexual encounter, a highlight of most rides with Boston cabdrivers.

Mario was pleased to see me, and said so, repeatedly. We repaired to the back bedroom, where everything was the same as it had been on every other call, the rambling conversations about seemingly random topics, the gentle occasional kisses or caresses, the lines, the champagne. I left at seven; Mario said that he needed to get some sleep.

He never told me why he had needed company so badly that night. I never asked.

So life went on. Occasionally Mario would ask for two girls, but the pattern of the calls never varied. It was pleasant, lucrative, and regular.

* * * * * *

September brought a new school year for Boston's scores of universities and colleges – and new faces for Peach's business. That fall Zoe started working for the service. Peach talked about her a lot – the clients all loved her, she was tireless, she was glamorous, she was making Peach a lot of money.

Zoe went to see Mario for the first time that October, and everything changed.

We all talked about it, and nobody could understand what had happened between them. Whatever it was, suddenly Mario didn't want to see anyone but Zoe. He would have had her over there every night if she had been available and willing to go. He saw other girls only when he couldn't see her. He wasn't negative toward any of us; he just had decided that he wanted to see Zoe.

We didn't take it very well, of course. Losing Mario as a regular was going to mean working a whole lot more hours, a whole lot harder, and for a whole lot less money.

"It's a crap shoot," Peach used to say. "Sometimes you get lucky. Sometimes you don't."

I was really happy a few weeks down the line to hear that Mario wanted me out in Weston again. Usually girls were lined up for the nights Zoe couldn't go, and there had been one time when Mario wanted to see me and I had a not-to-be-missed-if-you-care-about-your-career faculty cocktail party, and I'd had to say no. Not many people said no to Mario.

I got to his house and found Zoe already there. It turned out that Mario had a friend over, and I was the entertainment for the friend. Mario saw it as a compliment. I was philosophical: any friend of Mario's . . .

So the friend and I went off to another bedroom. I don't know just what I expected, but he wasn't even remotely like Mario. I spent the next two hours truly doing hard labor. He had done a lot of cocaine prior to my arrival and some more while I was there, and was totally unwilling to admit its effect on his sexual abilities. "Work harder," he kept urging me, and so for two straight hours, with occasional pauses for the odd sip of champagne, my hands did everything they could to revive him.

I persuaded him to accept some other caresses ("It will relax you, you'll see"), and even got in a ten-minute backrub with some oil I had found in the bathroom; but he insisted immediately after that I continue to encourage his limp member. He wasn't helping things by sitting there doing lines even as I was working really really hard to get a response from him.

He wanted me to stay later, insisting that a full erection was just around the corner; but I said I couldn't. You get to a point where five more minutes of stimulation is *not* going to make a difference. He was irritated, mostly, because he had had a callgirl and hadn't had any sex with her.

I finally took refuge in the shower, after assuring him yet again that I had to be asleep early, and I really could not extend my visit for another two hours. I passed silently by the closed door to Mario's bedroom, and thought with some nostalgia and jealousy about what was going on there, while I was panting and sweating and getting nowhere.

I didn't go again. It simply wasn't worth it, and I did have my own regulars. For that kind of work, I didn't need that closed door reminding me of all the perks – and my genuine affection for Mario – that I was missing.

Later, long after I left the business, I heard that Mario had died. I heard it too late to do anything – the funeral was long over, the body buried. Once a few months after that, when I was up on Cape Ann, I went looking for the cemetery where Peach had told me he was buried. When I found it, there was not one grave, but two. Mario and his brother Joseph had, it appeared, died on the same day.

There was a lot of speculation surrounding his death. One girl said that he was shot, that there was a contract out on him, that it was some rival in the Mafia who had gotten to him.

I didn't tell what I knew. I wondered if one day the emptiness inside couldn't be filled anymore by alcohol or drugs or women – not even by Zoe. I wondered if that was what had driven him to confront his brother – and, perhaps, his brother's employers. I thought that there was a good chance that that was what had happened.

It wasn't something that I could talk about to anybody. But I thought in the end, the emptiness had been filled: with a love that gives up everything, even life itself.

It wasn't a bad epitaph.

Chapter Fifteen

I was spending Christmas Eve arguing with a client.

"Come on, doll," Freddie kept saying. "Just give me your number. I won't bother you, I'll just call to say Merry Christmas. You owe me that much."

"I owe you?" I was astonished. Peach had asked me to call Freddie, to set something up for the day after Christmas, Boxing Day. The agency was closed on Christmas Eve and Christmas itself; his was the last call she had taken before shutting down the phones. "Just set up a date, Jen," she said when she called me. "And then hang up and don't think about work for two days."

But now he was playing mind games, trying to get my number from me. It wasn't going to happen. He didn't even know my real name, and I was going to tell him how he could reach me?

Freddie changed tactics. "Peach won't mind," he assured me, even though we both knew that she would mind very much indeed. Commandment Number One: Thou Shalt Not Steal Any Clients. "It's just I'm not sure what time I'll be wanting to see you . . ."

"So I'll call you at noon, and you can decide then," I said. He couldn't trace my line, I'd had the caller-ID block installed on my telephone the second week I worked for Peach. "They'll think nothing of calling you back," she warned. "It gives them a sense of power."

Freddie was irritating me more than usual. I was tired and anxious to take a nap before getting dressed and heading out to Dedham for Christmas Eve dinner with Luis and his family.

"Nah, come on, Tia, I don't know where I'll be. Tell you what, I'll just use it this once and then I won't call you again, I'll even throw the number away."

Oh, good. You'll even throw the number away, what a gentleman. And if I fall for that one, I'll bet that you have some mighty fine swampland in Florida to sell me, too. "No," I said, crossly.

"Then fuck you!" His anger came out of the blue, taking me aback. "Fuck you, slut! See if I ever ask you for anything again!" He slammed the receiver down, and I immediately got a dial tone and called Peach. "What the hell was that about?"

"Oh, that's nothing, that's just Freddie," she said calmly. "He always tries to get girls' numbers. He'll probably try again. Don't take it too seriously."

"What's the point? He must know he's not going to get it."

I heard her light a cigarette, waited through the first inhale-exhale. "Well, once in a while someone will do it; that keeps his hope alive. Don't get hung up on this, Jen. He just wants to have a hooker's telephone number. He gets off on that."

It was the first time since Seth that I had heard that word in reference to what I was doing, and it was disconcerting. As if I were watching a film, I saw myself at the university, standing in front of a blackboard, lecturing. "We probably got the term hooker from the Union army's General Joseph Hooker, who during the civil war allowed prostitutes to follow his army in order to provide them with some of the comforts of home. They were known as Hooker's Division, and hence the modern adaptation of the name."

Peach's voice interrupted my mental lecture. "Jen? Jen, are you there?"

"Yeah, Peach, I'm fine," I said briskly. "Never mind. Merry Christmas."

"Merry Christmas, Jen."

Three hours later I was sitting around the family table with Luis and his parents, trying desperately to make reasonably scintillating small talk. I was exhausted, I had a headache, and Luis was annoying me with his attempts to present me to his parents as though he were a maître d' and I a succulent dish they had ordered.

"*Entonces,* Luis tells us that you are a university professor." His mother was beaming at me. She was one, too, or was in her native Ecuador. She left academia behind when she married Luis' father, a Venezuelan diplomat.

"Yes, just a lecturer at present, though. I hope to get tenured eventually."

"What is your field of study?" asked Luis' father, looking up for the first time from his plate of underdone beef.

I took a sip of wine before answering. "My doctorate is in anthropology. I teach –" Luis kicked me under the table. I coughed, none too convincingly.

His mother did not notice the exchange, or chose to ignore it. "So what classes are you teaching now?" she asked.

I glanced at Luis, helplessly, but he didn't say anything or otherwise come to my rescue, so I told the truth. "Three sociology electives, two of which I created." Leave it at that, I prayed silently, and then, because I didn't trust my prayers to work, I took the initiative and dove as smoothly as I could into another subject. "Luis tells me that you spend a great deal of your time traveling. Do you have any plans for the near future?"

Luis finally woke up, and answered for his parents. "They're going to Australia in February," he said. "Mama, this beef is excellent."

"What are the classes?" asks his father, a man with an unfortunate unswerving knack for staying on topic. I could have lived without it.

I blotted my mouth on the linen napkin and said, "There's a course called *On Death and Dying,* another titled *Life in the Asylum,* and a third called *History and Sociology of Prostitution,*" I said. "Luis is right, this is marvelous."

His mother was looking distressed. "Those seem – odd subjects," she said, uncertainly.

"They sound like a waste of time," said his father, not looking up from his plate.

And I was suddenly angry.

I was angry because of his easy dismissal, the same dismissal given these people for centuries on end. The people locked in mental institutions no better than prisons – but incarcerated without benefit of trial or hope of reprieve. The women forced into prostitution and then murdered for it, their sanctioned killers the very men who had used them for sex, obliterating traces of their first crime with their second. The children, abandoned, hurt, and frightened, who existed in the odd shadowy world left behind by these lost souls, nameless because their parents' existence was no longer acknowledged. The forgotten, whose voices echoed eerily through my syllabi, whose torture, death, and degradation had been created, sustained, and applauded before being dismissed by arrogant self-absorbed complacent men just like the one sitting across the table from me, examining his beef and avoiding any thought that might disrupt his comfortable narrow reality.

Well, I had decided to try to be their voice. I had designed the curricula for the classes; I passed on the truth of their existence to those I hoped would honor it. Those classes weren't about impressing the dean or getting tenure or being invited around as a guest lecturer. I had thought that they were, but that Christmas Eve I understood that they were not.

I was giving a history back to those from whom it had been taken. I was giving dignity to the memory of those who had been deprived of it in life. I was seeding outrage and pity for them in the hearts of young people who might actually use the information to help others – the homeless, the mentally ill, the forgotten, the abandoned.

The prostitutes.

I took a deep breath, and said, as evenly as I could, "You will excuse me, please. I need to leave now."

I wondered, as I let myself out the front door, how long it would be before Luis spoke to me again.

* * * * * *

Freddie and I didn't connect the day after Christmas, and the following days were slow for the service, too. Luis had gone with his parents to spend time with an elderly cousin who lived somewhere near New York City; there were no classes to prepare, no syllabi to write, and I got bored. I even had my nails done, I was that desperate.

Finally I called Peach, just to talk to somebody. "Isn't anything happening?" The truth was that I could use a call; I'd spent rather more on Luis' Patet Philippe Christmas watch than I had intended. Who knew, now, whether or not I'd have the opportunity to give it to him?

"Nothing, Jen. You know it's slow between Christmas and New Year's."

"You haven't put out *any* calls?" I sounded petulant. Well, fine, I was feeling petulant, too. It was a matched pair.

A sigh. "I put out a call for a client who wanted a twenty-year old Asian. Did you want me to send you on that one?"

"No, no, I know, Peach, I'm just being a pest. Let me know if there's anything."

I was halfway through re-reading *Midnight in the Garden of Good and Evil* when she called back. "Got somebody, but it's a new client, didn't know if you'd want him."

"Hmm," I said. "I – um . . ." There I was, always ready with the witty remark; I cracks myself up. But it was a good question. I had told Peach practically from the start: no new clients, just guys she knows, guys who aren't cops. I can only do this as long as nobody knows that I do it. It would only take one person to see one arrest report, and everything that was meaningful in my life would be gone. "What did you think of him?" I asked at length.

"He sounds okay. You can always leave if it feels funny."

So I went. The guy was taciturn on the phone, but I was used to all sorts of non-conversationalists, so I didn't think much of it, and went out on the call.

The setup was odd, to start with. I called him from my cell phone instead of ringing the doorbell, as he had requested; but I had assumed that it was because the doorbell was broken. Not so. I was met at the door by a very young, very thin man, who spoke in whispers and instructed me not to talk until we got upstairs.

Upstairs, it transpired, was simply his bedroom, nondescript and with a minimum of decoration, lit only by the dim bulb on the very high ceiling. We sat together on his single bed, and I took care of business. "Just to get it out of the way, since we don't know you yet, Peach wants me to be paid at the beginning."

He pulled a wallet out of his back pocket, but didn't open it. "Okay. It's one hundred sixty, right?"

I could feel myself tensing. "No, it's two hundred."

"Oh, the lady I talked to on the phone said one-sixty." Lady? How old was this guy, anyway?

"Okay," I said, "Let's just call her; she can straighten it out for us."

He opened the wallet but still didn't take any money out. "No, that's okay, I'll pay the two hundred. I just want to make sure – I want to get my money's worth. We'll be having sex, won't we?"

I froze. That was an oft-repeated passage in the World According to Peach: cops want you to say that it's sex for money. Or arms for hostages, I had thought fancifully at the time. It didn't seem so amusing, now. You have to spell it out before they can arrest you, Peach said. "We can do whatever we like," I responded slowly, wondering what the hell to do. "Let's just get this business part out of the way, and I'll call Peach and let her know that I got here safely, and then we can talk about it."

He wasn't looking at me; he was frowning at the floor. "I just want to be sure that's what's happening," he said. "I just want to know that actual sex will be included, for that price."

Oh, God. Please say that this isn't happening to me. I made one last effort. "You know, I hate to make plans. Why don't we just get comfortable with each other, and see what happens?"

His head jerked up, and he looked at me intently. "But we'll have sex, right?"

I stood up, and as calmly as I could, I asked, "Excuse me, sir, but are you a police officer?"

It was pretty dramatic, and incredibly anticlimactic. "No," he said, shaking his head and looking puzzled. "Are you?"

I had misread him, which, in my own defense, had been fairly easy to do under the circumstances. He was, as it turned out, an extremely awkward young man of marginal intelligence and limited social skills, who after that last conversational exchange paid me without another word, listened to me check in with Peach, and for all intents and purposes had sex with me without another word.

So I was wrong. But I could have been right, and I was more than happy to leave that call early.

I assume that had I ever in fact been arrested, Peach would have bailed me out, all that sort of thing. But the very thought was irrelevant. As I said, Peach always expected people to follow her plans for them.

In this case, I was happy to oblige.

I made New Year's resolutions that year. I'm not enthusiastic about them, usually. It seems such a contrived little list, and invariably, depressingly, the same as the one from the year before. Lose five pounds, read more edifying literature, join a fitness club, study a new language, stay more in touch with people, be more tidy.

That year, I had some time to think about things. The end of December and the beginning of January were a quiet time for me, punctuated only by one or two parties. There was the compulsory faculty New Years' cocktail get-together, a couple of Scrabble parties that Peach dragged me along to, and an oddly-timed costume party given by Irene. I went to them all and tried to be nice and have a good time.

But what I really did, mostly, was think a lot about what was happening to me. I thought about what I had discovered at Luis' house on Christmas Eve. I thought about where I had been, and where I might be going.

It seemed almost that I was at a crossroads of sorts. My career – my *real* career, my teaching – was starting to look as though it might actually come to pass. I had been promised as many classes as I cared to teach, and it seemed a logical assumption that after a year or two of that sort of thing, I might be considered eligible for one of the scarce tenure-track position openings. Certainly I was building good contacts – at my own school and at the ones where I was invited to guest lecture. It was looking more positive, more *possible* – than it ever had before.

On the other hand, it still wasn't enough money. Not to pay my rent, my accumulated credit card bills (many of which were the work of Peter the Rat Bastard, but I had signed the receipts, more fool me), my student loan payments, my private (and expensive) health insurance, and so on. That kind of security would come only with the professorship, the real job, the one with a regular salary and benefits attached to it.

So I still needed to work for Peach. The question was, how much, and how could I do it so that it wouldn't impact my work?

And all the while, the other question hovered over my thoughts, my lists, my plans. How could I do it so it wouldn't impact my life?

I had arrived where I was through no brilliance or extraordinary effort on my part. The class on prostitution, I realized, was what had really saved me. In the meantime, I wasn't doing such a good job of saving myself. My teaching was deteriorating from the lack of sleep, the lack of time, the inability to function without the drugs that woke me up and the drugs that put me to sleep. I hadn't done any cocaine since the end of the semester and had only drunk moderately at the holiday parties; but I was not deluding myself. Four classes a week, four calls a week, and I'd be back to my old ways. It seemed inevitable. And this time there wouldn't be any glitzy new addition to the curriculum to distract attention from my erratic teaching, my late arrivals, and my occasional zombie-like behavior. This time there would be no way to cover my ass. It could be the end of my career, without it having ever really started.

And Luis . . . I had no idea what to do about Luis. His own propensity for late nights had contributed to my problem. If I only worked for Peach on weekends, there would still be Luis during the week. I needed – I calculated rapidly on the edge of an envelope – I needed three, sometimes four calls a week.

My New Year's resolution was to figure out what to do. This was going to take more than an evening to think about. I watched the ball drop into Times Square, toasted Scuzzy with a glass of sparkling Vouvray, and went to bed.

As it turned out, I needn't have worried about Luis. He solved that problem all by himself.

Chapter Sixteen

Luis himself had seen it coming. "There are only two conclusions to a relationship," he said once. "Either you get married, or you break up." And it was fairly clear after a few months together that we weren't on the path to getting married.

I think that breaking up with Luis affected me more than I was willing to admit, or liked to think about. I got angry with him and with myself – I think that I was just plain angry, in general, for some time.

Classes started up at the beginning of February. I was doing calls on the weekends, trying to fit them as much as possible into that space, doing two calls on a Saturday night and one on a Sunday, so that I could keep the week fairly clear in preparation for teaching again. Peach didn't see the point, and I think that she was insulted when once or twice she asked me over after work for Scrabble and a drink, but I declined, saying that it would be uncomfortable seeing Luis there, and left it at that.

Still, it was hard to avoid getting swept back up into that whole glittering scene again. I think that Peach deliberately tried to pull me back in, even when I resisted, not through any nefarious purposes of her own but simply because she liked me and missed me when I wasn't around. She'd call me up and offer me dinner, saying that she'd arrange for me to meet a client afterward. I really didn't want Peach angry with me, a situation that could potentially translate into lost income, so I'd go.

There were at that time a fair amount of chefs and restauranteurs among our regular client base. When Peach suggested that we go out, that winter, it was almost always to the same place, her current favorite hang-out. It was an Asian fusion restaurant located in one of the major downtown hotels, very cutting-edge and chic, and Peach had somehow become friendly with the owner. He used her agency a lot: for himself, for friends, for visiting businessmen. He had some sort of arrangement with the hotel itself, and room keys seemed always to somehow magically appear in people's hands.

I saw clients in that hotel, waiters from the restaurant, sometimes visiting Japanese business connections or family members. They always brought up drinks from the restaurant, tidbits, appetizers. It was exceptionally good food. Once the owner told me that any night I wanted to stop by for a drink I'd be most welcome – and could more or less be assured of a client at the same time, if I wanted one. It was a sweet offer, but I never took him up on it.

One of the men I saw there, one of the chefs in fact, one night solemnly handed me a business card. "It's my new place." He was going off on his own, opening a sushi restaurant in the suburbs. I wished him well, took the card, promised to look him up and immediately forgot about it.. As it turned out, he must have seen some sort of writing on the wall, because the fusion restaurant closed a few months later. I think it's a steak joint now.

Sometimes my past comes back to – well, not exactly to haunt me, but just to remind me that it was there. Last summer I was attending a conference held at Wellesley College, and got into a conversation with a colleague about food. "Oh," she said, "you like sushi? Let me give you a tip: stay out of the city. Believe it or not, the best sushi restaurant in New England isn't far from here!" And she cited the restaurant whose distinctive name I remembered from the departing chef's new business card. So it's nice to know that somebody else got out and is doing well.

Odd little things like that crop up from time to time, reminders in the present of another life, one lived in the past. It's not such a bad thing, to be reminded of where we've been, where we come from. I smiled at the memory; for a moment I wasn't at a conference at all, but back in the hotel, with rich Japanese businessmen buying me cocktails, wearing a dress that had cost eight hundred dollars, feeling on top of the world. It wasn't such a bad memory. I won't go and have dinner at the restaurant, though. That chapter is over, and I love my life now.

Besides, my husband hates sushi.

But in the meantime it was February, I was teaching again, going out with Peach when I thought I could manage it without becoming too tired or doing too much cocaine, and working almost exclusively on the weekends.

I was a lot healthier. Maybe it was all the sushi I was eating. But there was something else new, an edge that even I could see in my teaching, something passionate and radical that hadn't been there before. I think that Luis' attitude had touched a nerve that was still pretty raw. Assumptions and stereotypes are the result of a lack of knowledge, a lack of critical thinking – I'd always liked Emma Goldman's phrase, "The most violent element in society is ignorance." And I was more and more determined to do something about it. The anger that I had been vaguely aware of since his departure was finding both direction and expression.

The first part of the prostitution course was strictly historical. "Vestal virgins, and all that," as my newly-appointed administrative assistant, Vicky, liked to say. I didn't qualify for a teaching assistant yet, but Vicky was really good about photocopying and putting books on reserve for me, that sort of thing. It was a pity, really, that I couldn't risk mixing my two worlds, because Vicky and Peach could have been great in business together. Vicky was gorgeous, ebullient, unflappable, single, and always short of money; Peach could have had her making a thousand or so a week.

I liked to include male prostitution as was appropriate in the course, since the need to purchase sex transcends gender, age, and ethnic/racial identity. It wasn't difficult to find examples in the ancient world, which for the most part was far more open and accepting of homosexuality than is our current culture. But, as is invariably the case in history, it didn't mean that everything stayed that tolerant forever.

I stood in front of my Tuesday morning class. I was preparing to shock them with information that they were not going to want to hear, that they could scarcely ignore, that might be the stuff of nightmares later. I've always marveled at people who see historians as meek, otherworldly innocents. They are clearly people with no knowledge of the cycles of violence and horror that make up the history of the human race. Historians, believe me, have seen it all.

"When I was in graduate school," I said to the class, "I had a friend who liked to say, 'Constantine converted to Christianity, and it was all downhill from there.'" The class was relaxed, smiling politely, even offering a courteous laugh or two. "My friend was right," I went on. "Constantine's successor, Theodosius, made it illegal, upon pain of death, to sell a boy into prostitution. Unfortunately, the people carrying out his edicts distorted them, and instead of punishing the slave-traders who sold prostitutes, it was the prostitutes themselves who were targeted. In Rome, prostitutes were dragged out of the male brothels and burned alive in the streets, while a cheering crowd looked on." Silence. No one was smiling anymore. "And," I went on gently, "hypocrisy and human nature being what they are I think that we can probably imagine one or two of their regular clients as being part of that crowd."

I waited a moment, then got them involved. "So why do you think that homosexual prostitution was such a problem under Theodosius, when both heterosexual and homosexual prostitution had been practiced fairly openly in the Empire up until then?"

There was another moment of silence, either to recover from the gruesome image I had summoned or to think about the answer; then a hand went up. "Because Christianity said it was wrong, and the Emperor was Christian?"

I nodded. "Was the problem homosexuality, or its practice by prostitutes?"

Another hand. "Both. Didn't the Church say that sex had to be procreative? Neither homosexuals nor prostitutes are planning on making babies."

A titter ran through the class, a release of nervous energy. "Right. Good. I see you've done your readings." I stood in front of the desk, leaning against it. I said, "There's another reason, too. As the authorities saw it, homosexuality was in essence using a man's body in the same way that a woman's body is used in sexual intercourse. Who had a problem with that?"

No hands this time. All right, so they'd done some of the assigned readings, better than nothing. "Remember Augustine, the poster child for misogyny? He said that – and I quote," as I pulled the text from behind me on the desk and read, "'the body of a man is as superior to that of a woman, as the soul is to the body.'"

Eyes were glittering now. I had them, and I had them in a place where they could listen, and hear, and think.

No hands were going up now, but that wasn't keeping them from talking. "You mean," said a very young man from the front row, "that homosexuality was bad because it made men seem like women? That it's all about being against women in the first place?"

I shrugged. "What do you think?"

I wasn't trying to convert anybody here. I just wanted them to look at facts and be able to draw their own conclusions in a thoughtful and informed manner. I wanted my contribution to the next generation to be that they would not all be sheep, following blindly whatever sound-byte of information was currently being offered up by network anchors or political pundits. To learn, to assess what one has learned, and to take a position armed with more than simply feelings or hearsay.

All right, so in my heart of hearts, I'm an idealist, and in that classroom, on that snowy morning, it felt as though anything could happen.

Chapter Seventeen

Teaching about the brothels of the Empire brought my thoughts back to how prostitution as a service is organized, and who benefits. Who makes the decisions about how a brothel, or an agency, or a service is run? How does that reflect on the well-being of its employees?

If I had ever questioned my great good fortune in having gotten involved with Peach's service first in my quest for employment with an escort agency, it hadn't taken me long to stop doing so. About the time it took, in fact, to meet and talk with some of Peach's other girls.

Some of the younger women were accustomed to, and in fact wanted, something significant in the way of volume. Some of them were spending a lot of money – so much sudden cash can take its toll on one's better judgment, especially if you're young and feel invincible, feel needy, feel that this will go on forever. But that meant that they needed more of it faster than people like me did. So in addition to working for Peach, they worked for other agencies, ones with higher volume, higher turnover. Higher risks, too, though that may not have been immediately apparent to them. Peach couldn't guarantee four or five calls a night; some of the other services could.

And as I did doubles with them and occasionally gave them rides and met them at bars and parties, some disturbing realities began to emerge.

I can tell these stories best as case studies, as individual vignettes:

There was Paula. She lived in New Hampshire, where she was attending college. Her part-time bartending job came with a hidden built-in expectation that she would be sexually available to certain customers, and she walked out, breaking a number of bottles as she went. So she decided to choose when and where and to whom she'd be available, and took the Greyhound bus down to Boston two nights a week to work for Peach. Paula's only requirement was that she had to be finished in time for the last bus up to Manchester.

We met each other when we did a double together in Quincy one night, and I drove her back to the South Station to get her bus. We were early, and I didn't have another call, so we went to get something to eat at the Blue Diner, and talked.

She had come to Peach, Paula told me, because of the way her first agency had treated her. "Lee, that's the owner, he doesn't let you use your own car or anything. So you're always at the mercy of the drivers, and they're all punks." She lit a cigarette. That was back in the days when you could still smoke in public places.

"What really did me in was last spring I was coming down to do some calls for him. So his driver meets me at the station and takes me to this place, this apartment, over in Dorchester somewhere. Lee had this new gig he was just starting; he was gonna start doing some of that Web sex stuff, you know, live video, and he was setting up this place as a studio for it. Only all he had so far was a bed, you know? So the driver left me there and they said they'd call me on my cell as soon as work came in."

I was horrified. "They left you alone to wait in an empty apartment?"

Paula shrugged. "Yeah, well, it was that or a bar somewhere, right? One place is as good as another. But I'm not so sure it was empty, either. I think he already had the cameras in place, you know? I had this creepy feeling that I was being watched, that if I turned around fast I'd catch somebody staring at me. And I didn't know who had the keys, so I didn't feel very comfortable falling asleep. Anybody could have come in."

It transpired that the deplorable Lee had left Paula in this empty apartment for three days. She couldn't leave, because she had no money, not for the bus, not even for a taxi to take her anywhere. She had counted on coming down to Boston to make money, not to spend it. She called in, and was assured that there would be work very soon, and so she sat waiting, sitting under the one naked bulb hanging from the ceiling, in a state of readiness. One hour passed, two, then three. She called and called, and was finally told that if she didn't stop bothering the service, they wouldn't get her work at all.

She fell into a fitful sleep, and in the morning got a call saying that there were no drivers available to take her to the station, but if she wanted to stay on, there would certainly be work for her that night. There was nothing to eat in the apartment, and the building appeared to be in a residential neighborhood. Paula was too afraid to leave, and in any case had no money with which to buy anything, and so ate nothing that day. She was sent on a call finally at four o'clock the next morning. According to the rules of this service, the driver collected the money, and this one did not give Paula any. Lee had specified that she was not to be paid until she went on another call for which she had been requested – the following night.

She was dropped off yet again at the apartment in Dorchester at five-thirty in the morning. She still hadn't eaten anything. She slept some during the day and was taken to the scheduled call at ten o'clock that night, after which she was duly paid – but had already missed the last bus to Manchester. She spent a third miserable night in Dorchester, called herself a taxi in the morning, and from the bus terminal called Lee and officially quit.

Unbelievable? One might have thought so.

Kimmie had worked for other services, too, before she and Peach found each other. Her past agency – also, I think not coincidentally, owned and run by a man – once sent her on a fishing trip out of Gloucester.

"It was supposed to be a birthday surprise for this guy," she explained to me when we met at one of Peach's bar gatherings, some new hip place in the financial district, built into an old bank vault. "Well, actually, I guess that *I* was supposed to be the birthday surprise for this guy. The driver took me up to Gloucester, because Howie wouldn't let me go on my own – they keep you on kind of a tight leash over there." She shivered, and I looked at her curiously. Kimmie was stunning – blonde and leggy and with odd beautiful emerald eyes. She was also very nice. She did favors for her elderly neighbors. She volunteered with an adult literacy program. At that time, she was also a graduate student in chemistry and a single mother. The thought of someone taking advantage of her was intolerable.

"It was this gorgeous day, and they had me get there early, and wait down in the bedroom that's in the bow – isn't that it? The pointy end? The bed there was in a point, anyway."

"The bow," I confirmed.

"Okay, and so eventually we got out there, wherever it was we were going, and they stopped the motor. They all were on about their third beer and they had fishing lines overboard and someone came down to get me. It was a surprise, all right. To me."

She didn't meet my eyes for the rest of the conversation. She looked at the bright sofas lining the wall across from the bar, where Peach sat giggling with one of the owners. Kimmie had agreed to the daylong call, was assured that the entire time was paid for by the buddies as a gift for the birthday boy, and that he would be her only partner unless she chose otherwise. The choice was made for her, though. "It wasn't rape," said Kimmie, staring off into the middle distance, her voice soft. "I had to agree, though. Or it probably would have been."

She *had* to agree, and that made it not rape? I still have problems with that one, even now, after all this time.

The kicker, though, came when the beers were gone and the boat finally got back to dock. She walked stiffly off, cold and sore and dazed. Her driver was waiting.

"Can you believe it, he interviewed each guy, found out if he'd done anything with me, and what, and he added up a fucking *bill*!" Kimmie bit her lip. "Howie knew all the time what was going to happen. He just hadn't bothered to tell me."

Angie did a double with me at a podiatrist's place, and afterward I dropped her off at a bar in South Boston to meet her boyfriend. She was working two agencies at once – she preferred Peach, she said, but Peach didn't always have as much work as some of the other services. Angie made it sound like show business, referring to Peach and the guy who ran the other service as "agents."

She signed on each night with both services, and then signed off from one if she got a call from the other, signing back on again when it was over. It all sounded very complicated to me. She juggled her cell phone, her beeper, and bits of scrap paper the whole time she was in my car, making arrangements for later that night.

The other service was the Lee outfit again. "Shit, they want me to see Jerome," she sighed.

"A difficult client?" I asked, sympathetically.

It wasn't, it transpired, that Jerome himself was difficult; it was just that Jerome had made additional arrangements with the agency. "All I have to do is bring in this stuff from the driver; Jerome pays me for it along with the call."

I wasn't naïve about what stuff she was referring to. "How much stuff?"

She shifted uneasily in her seat. "Twenty-eight."

I nearly went off the road. "Twenty-eight grams? Are you insane?"

She was examining her fingernails. They were long, fake, and blood red. "All I have to do is hand him the bag."

"Oh, that's all?" If Peter the Rat Bastard ex had taught me anything, it was about the various possible penalties for selling drugs. He talked about it incessantly. Didn't ever stop his dealing in pot, of course; he just liked to talk about it. "So he drops you off in front of the place and you walk in and walk out an hour later without your little package, while he sits outside waiting for you, and this seems like a smart thing to do, no one's going to wonder what's up?"

She squirmed again. "He drops me off down the street."

Better still. "Angie, you'll go away for fifteen years for that. It's called distribution, and Massachusetts is very big on getting distributors."

She turned in her seat to look at me. "Get off my case, Jen, okay? I have to do it, all right? I need the work. I've got two kids at home, I need the calls, and Lee isn't giving me any unless I do favors for him. So just back off."

I backed off.

Once I heard some of the stories out there, I realized that I wasn't just lucky to have found Peach. What I came to understand was that I wouldn't have lasted anywhere else.

I couldn't have imagined working for a service where not only the menu is open to negotiation, it is also the callgirl who is in charge of dealing, and can and will later be blamed if the deal does not live up to the driver or the dispatcher or the owner's expectations.

Elena, one of the many Russian girls that were active in Boston that winter, explained it to me. "It costs the client sixty dollars for you to walk in the door. That is all. He tells you what he wants, you add up the costs. To kiss and hug is forty dollars. A blowjob is another sixty. If he wants regular intercourse, that is one hundred. And so on."

And so on. A simple enough statement, but my imagination took hold of that one and positively ran with it. I imagined some of our more difficult clients, the ones who insisted on playing headgames, who wanted to continually assert their control over the callgirl. They were bad enough when one didn't need to quibble over the price. But I could just hear them spending ten minutes (during which time I presumably would not be being paid, for no specific service had been selected) asking me what it was that I was going to do to make my blowjob "worth" that kind of money. Yeah, I'd call that degrading. And he'd have no idea that it was at least as degrading to him as it was to me.

It takes a certain mentality to be able to shift from that kind of bickering, confrontational, and essentially oppositional stance to being instantly sexually intimate together.

So, all in all, I was glad that I had found Peach.

I have to admit to sometimes having a sense of smugness. One night I was out late on a "real" date – a setup arranged by Irene – and we went down to Chinatown for soup and dun-dun noodles.

Afterward, on the way home, we drove along Kneeland Street, with girls at every lamppost, every corner, tall and bright and a little scary. Instead of feeling grateful that I wasn't there with them, I felt safely superior because I didn't have to be. Peach's agency may not have attracted Boston's top politicians or Hollywood's sexiest actors or Silicon Valley's wealthiest CEOs, but being a rung or two below that was very nice indeed.

Well, I'm not proud of the feeling, but it was there.

The snow finally melted, sometime in late March. Everyone around here always says, "Well, don't be so sure, remember the time we had a snowstorm in April?" which is what New Englanders like to say, even though in point of fact that one snowstorm was an aberration that was years ago and hasn't repeated since. Midterms came and went, and I didn't go on calls that whole week, because I wanted to concentrate. Peach didn't have anything for me after that for three or four nights when I signed on, and I always wondered when that happened if it was deliberate or not.

I was at the health club, having swum twenty-five laps and spent another fifteen minutes with my eyes closed blissfully in the whirlpool, when Peach called me. The cell phone indicated one message when I took it out of my locker, and so I called her right back. "What's up?"

"Oh, Jen, I thought you'd want to hear it from me." Peach is nothing if not dramatic. "Bill Francis died."

I groped though my memory. "Bill Francis?" Then I had it: one of Peach's regular-regulars. I had seen him from time to time; he lived up on Beacon Hill in one of the houses that photographers made postcards out of. Nice man, I thought vaguely. Just another nondescript client. When it came down to it, most of them were. The really wonderful ones and the really awful ones were the exceptions.

Peach was going on. "I just didn't want you to get upset, that's all."

"How did he die?" I asked. She couldn't wait to tell me, that was clear.

"What I heard was, somebody broke into his place and he got hurt when he surprised them. I don't know how, I just know he's dead."

I didn't ask her how she had come by her information. "I'm sorry, Peach. You must feel awful." And not just because of the loss of regular revenue, either: Peach talked with these guys, often several times a week, often for a long time. She got to know them. Some of them came to mean something to her.

Bill Francis hadn't meant anything to me, though, and so I was surprised that night to wake up, crying and sweating, the dreams of death still wrapped around me like a shroud. The tears were running down my face, and even though I snapped on every light in the apartment, drank hot tea, and watched some late-night television, they were still there, waiting in the shadows around the edges of my consciousness, waiting for me to lie down again and become theirs.

I sat there, rocking rhythmically and unconsciously back and forth, as though rocking myself: the tears were running down my face and I couldn't stop them. I barely remembered this man. I hadn't been able to place his name at first. I had no anecdotes about him that I could remember, and nothing that he had ever said to me came to mind. *He was just a client.* And still the tears wouldn't stop.

I wasn't dreaming about Bill specifically: I was dreaming about loss, and grief, about everyone I had ever cared for who was no longer in my life, about my own fears of what was waiting for me.

The next day, naturally, I was doing *On Death and Dying.*

So I talked about my "friend" who had died, and about the nightmares I had experienced the night before, the bright and deadly images, and this segued naturally into a topic I had intended to do a little later but seized now instead, Death and Art. I did that because a great deal of art emanates from the subconscious, and the notion of death is so inextricably entwined with that of life; and from there I launched into a discussion of Goya, Dali, and Bosch.

I wondered, as I observed the class' eager participation in the topic, how Bill Francis might have felt, had he known that one of his "girls" had reached others through him. I like to think that he might have been pleased.

Chapter Eighteen

In May, as classes were inching toward finals and the liberation of summer vacation, it was more and more difficult to keep students focused on the topics at hand. For that matter, it was more and more difficult to get students to come to class at all. College, I have found, runs a poor second or third to summer plans and spring sports.

Maybe some day I'll go teach in China. Henry told me that students there honor their professors, feel privileged to be in class, and work their derrieres off. Not this year, however.

In *Life in the Asylum*, we talked about the use of restraints on patients. What was done in the nineteenth century, of course, was to simply tie or handcuff them to something immovable – a chair, a pillar, the wall. "So what have we learned?" asked a senior, rhetorically, sarcastically. "Now we use chemical restraints; we shoot them up with drugs so they just walk around like zombies."

"Yeah," agreed another. "Like that song – mirrors on the ceiling, pink champagne on ice."

"Excuse me?" I hadn't expected a reference to a song that was more from my generation than theirs, and certainly not one presented with a different interpretation than I'd always given it. "What are you talking about?"

"It's an Eagles song," he explained patiently.

"I *know* it's an Eagles song," I said. "But I always thought they were talking about using drugs."

"Sure they are, it's just the drugs are legal and prescribed," the student confirmed. "See, I used to work on a mental health unit, as an aide. It was for kids – for adolescents. All the rooms have these mirrors in the corner and on the ceiling, so that when you glance in when you're doing checks you can see what the kid is doing inside. And one of the drugs they used – I forget which one – the syringe had to be chilled, and the stuff in it was pink. So I'm figuring that the Hotel California was a psychiatric hospital."

It was a new and fascinating sidelight on the neo-classics. I encouraged him. "So you've actually worked in a modern asylum, a mental health unit. Can you talk about the use of restraints in your experience there?"

He looked around at his peers, self-conscious for the first time. "Well, I know it all sounds cruel and everything, but you know, it was like, sometimes it made sense."

A whisper of disapproval shimmered around the room, an unspoken criticism of his words. "When, exactly?" I asked gently.

"Well, you know, these were, like, kids, and kids can get out of control sometimes. Like scary out of control. And there's a point where you need somebody else to take control for you. Some of them, like, they calmed right down when they were put in restraints."

"Yeah," somebody muttered, "fascist tactics will do that for you."

He was undeterred. "It's not like that at all. It made them feel safe. Whatever scary things were going on inside their heads, they knew that we would keep them safe. The restraints told them that we wouldn't let them hurt themselves."

Another voice chimed in, and I let them go. I was drifting, going back in time to the night that I finally accepted that my mother was going to die, when I finally faced the stark reality of her cancer and what it was doing to her. I was with someone else then, it was before I met Peter. I remember us sitting in bed and me screaming and crying all at once, both enraged and in pain, and my boyfriend holding me down on the bed as I thrashed around. I don't know what I would have done, that night, without him there. I felt terrible, but I also felt safe, I knew that he would not let it go too far. I wouldn't go off the deep end, I remember thinking; he won't let me go. Alone, I might have. So I had my crisis and he held me down while I raged at him, my mother, the world, God . . . and I survived it. Yes, I could certainly understand the occasional need for external restraints.

I returned to my body and listened to what people were saying around me. "Look, it's a basic human right not to be imprisoned without due process. Putting people in restraints violates that law."

"People in hospitals are always having decisions made about them that are not necessarily what they might choose. What if —"

I broke into the conversation. "Okay, time," I called, making the appropriate signal with my hands, sports buff that I was. "For Wednesday's class, write a short argument on the use of restraints on mentally ill people in an inpatient environment. You can champion your own point of view, but you'd better back it up with something besides your own opinion. See you then."

They filed out, some of them still arguing. It felt good to have helped make that happen, to have been part of stimulating something inside their brains or hearts that caused them to care so passionately, and – oh wonder of wonders! – so near the end of term.

As for me, I was getting a headache.

I sat down at the desk and began shuffling papers, putting my notes away. Restraints, I thought . . . I may have been acquainted

Valid photo ID required for all returns, exchanges and to receive and redeem store credit. With a receipt, a full refund in the original form of payment will be issued for new and unread books and unopened music within 30 days from any Barnes & Noble store. Without an original receipt, a store credit will be issued at the lowest selling price. With a receipt, returns of new and unread books and unopened music from bn.com can be made for store credit. A gift receipt or exchange receipt serves as proof of purchase price only. An exchange or store credit will be offered for new and unread books and unopened music/DVDs/audio for the price paid.

Valid photo ID required for all returns, exchanges and to receive and redeem store credit. With a receipt, a full refund in the original form of payment will be issued for new and unread books and unopened music within 30 days from any Barnes & Noble store. Without an original receipt, a store credit will be issued at the lowest selling price. With a receipt, returns of new and unread books and unopened music from bn.com can be made for store credit. A gift receipt or exchange receipt serves as proof of purchase price only. An exchange or store credit will be offered for new and unread books and unopened music/DVDs/audio for the price paid.

Valid photo ID required for all returns, exchanges and to receive and redeem store credit. With a receipt, a full refund in the original form of payment will be issued for new and unread books and unopened music within 30 days from any Barnes & Noble store. Without an original receipt, a store credit will be issued at the lowest selling price. With a receipt, returns of new and unread books and unopened music from bn.com can be made for store

Calisiri: Confessions of	9.76
9780060736057	
DISCOUNT 13.95 - 4.19	
GOTHIC BEAUTY	3.46
0074470562320	
DISCOUNT 4.95 - 1.49	

SUB TOTAL	13.22
SALES TAX	.76
TOTAL	**13.98**
AMOUNT TENDERED	
CASH	20.00

TOTAL PAYMENT	20.00
CHANGE	6.02

with them only academically in mental health settings, but I knew a hell of a lot about them from my other line of work.

Being handcuffed on a call was always problematic for me. Restraints don't exactly fit into my definition of safe sex. In fact I refused, categorically, to be tied or handcuffed if I didn't know the client. Well. Extremely well.

I relaxed the rule for regulars, once I got to know them, once I got to trust that they would stop when I said stop, that they would stay within the agreed-upon boundaries.

I think that bondage plays a role in just about everybody's sex life, even if only in the form of fantasies; and these guys were no exception. The DoubleTree Suites Hotel on Storrow Drive has a foyer that reaches breathtakingly up to the top floor, and a glass-sided elevator that carries you transparently past all of the floors below your own. The elevator allows its passengers to see everything they pass – lounges, waiting areas, and the occasional open door to a private room.

But just as a passenger can see, so too can he or she be seen.

One client, one of my regulars, stayed at the DoubleTree once a month, during regular business trips to Boston. He was in the habit of meeting me in the lobby, and he would immediately put the cuffs on my wrists. That excited him, doing it in a public place, doing it without saying a word, just the silent mechanical act. He walked next to me across the lobby, my hands clasped demurely in front of me, the cuffs barely visible to the casual observer. His favorite moment, I think, was riding the glass elevator with me in handcuffs, potentially visible to anyone who cared to look. It certainly provoked a physical reaction. Once, he actually did come in his pants, just riding that elevator.

I sighed and rubbed my temples. It was a useless ritual; it never helped the headaches, but I felt a need to do it anyway. Thoughts of restraints led one down a particular thought path. Handcuffs, for those who practice bondage and discipline, were just the beginning.

There was a lot of spanking. As long as I wasn't tied up, that was fine with me, I could always get away from the situation if it became too intense or if the client wasn't listening to me. They always did it in the light, so they could see the imprint of their hand on my ass. I became adept at gauging what kind of reaction they were looking for, if they wanted me to cry out, if they wanted me to be stoic.

When I got to know a client, being tied up was fine – and to be perfectly honest about it, a little kinkiness sometimes made the hour pass more quickly. There were all sorts of ways it could be done: wrists together behind the back, wrists together above the head, sometimes attached to the top of a doorway or the headboard of a bed; wrists tied to a piece of furniture. Once a client had me bend at the waist, then tied my wrists to my ankles, which works well in theory but is really obnoxious to maintain. We used handcuffs, string, hairbands, scarves . . . It was a safe place to play out the kinds of fantasies that they didn't want to admit to, that they didn't want to tell their wives about. Things that people saw in skin flicks, things that they read about, this was their opportunity to try it. To taste the forbidden fruit.

I knew from what I was reading in the more popular press and on the Internet that people were curious about more than just the handcuffs. Okay, so I was, too. I had had some experience with bondage and discipline; the boyfriend before Peter was into it, and I liked what I was learning with him. I liked it a lot.

In that relationship, I was the submissive and Luke was the dominant. When I told my friend Irene about it, she wasn't impressed. "Why should you play out the roles that you're already forced into in the real world?" she demanded. "Sounds like you're just reinforcing negative stereotypes." I suspect that in certain situations, with certain couples, she would have been right. But for us, it was the right time and the right place for those roles.

Back then, I was in the process of applying to doctoral programs. I had to be beyond competent, incredibly on top of things, because of the volume and breadth of materials required for the various schools to which I was applying. I was going on interviews, which forced me to invent a persona, someone who thought originally, had the necessary stamina to stay the course, was a good candidate to fill one of very few spaces available. I had to go out and sell myself, again and again and again. I had to be organized, impressive, and in charge of everything. Everywhere in my life I was making decisions, taking charge, dealing with problems. When Luke and I started doing the bondage and discipline scenes, even within our somewhat timid first attempts, the utter relief I felt at finally being able to give up control was intensely overwhelming. Because I trusted Luke completely, I was free to go as deeply into the role as I wanted. I learned things about myself that I never would have dreamed of understanding. It taught me more about who I was, about my inner core, than had any of my past therapy sessions, any of my myriad psychology courses.

I was fortunate to have been with Luke, then. It takes a strong partnership to engage fully in a healthy B&D relationship. But that doesn't mean that parts of the experience cannot be separated from it and used independently. The handcuffs are a favorite object and I think that a lot of men really wanted to go a little further, to try out the forbidden toys and acts, but were too embarrassed to ask. Even to ask a callgirl.

As a point of fact, most of our clientele's sexual needs and desires fell within certain predictable parameters. By and large, what they wanted (or ended up getting, if they were unable to ask for something else) was very vanilla sex. Different positions, sure. Unusual venues: on kitchen tables, out of doors, standing in a doorway, on a piece of exercise equipment. Lots of verbal stuff, so many of them wanted you to talk dirty to them, to use words that perhaps they themselves didn't dare use.

I was ready for the unusual, the odd, the kinky. What I didn't know already, I read about. A lot of the stuff that I was reading about would have shocked the hell out of most of our clients.

Well, that's fine. A lot of what I was reading about shocked the hell out of me, too.

I shook myself out of my reverie, gathered up my books and briefcase, and walked down the college corridor. Empty, of course. Only a few more finals to take, and liberation was theirs; and if anyone was actually studying for the finals, they weren't doing it anywhere on campus.

"You *are* turning into a curmudgeon," I muttered to myself. "Just because you were an obsessive undergraduate doesn't mean that everyone else has to be. Live and let live. There's more than one way to skin a cat. Don't judge anyone until you've walked a mile in their moccasins." I was silent for a moment, contemplating my thoughts. "Use fewer trite expressions," I added.

There was Excedrin in the glove compartment of my car. I clutched it with the fervor of a worshipper touching a holy icon. I swallowed three of them, just to be sure.

Driving back to Allston, waiting impatiently for the Excedrin to kick in, I reflected again about how ironic it was that I was mildly disappointed in the lack of fetishes or unusual sexual practices among our clientele. What this means, I told myself sternly, is that you need some spice in your personal life. You can't expect the *clients* to give you what you need, for heaven's sake.

So what do the clients (gross generalization time here) like?

I'm clearer about what they don't like. They are phenomenally particular about girls' looks, and they don't like women who are outside a narrowly defined perception of beauty. Curiously enough, a majority of the clients specifically don't want to see girls who have any piercings at all, although in general I think that they were referring to belly buttons and eyebrows and lips, which I agree can be a bit off-putting. They were more open about nipple and labia piercings, though even there, opinion was divided. Which meant, of course, that they had a smaller group to choose from, because it seemed that around that time nearly every girl in Boston who was in her twenties had at least one unusual piercing. Some of them, to quote Harlan Coban's delicious phrase, looked very much as though they had fallen down a flight of stairs whilst carrying an open box of fishing tackle.

But piercing one's body is a fetish that is strictly for the young, and most of our clients were what the French describe as being "of a certain age," less likely than the callgirls' peers to appreciate their metallic embellishments.

Almost all of them were into control, which probably spoke volumes about their self-esteem and things like that; a lot of them enjoyed using any situation to get and keep the upper hand over the girl doing the call. If she was late, for example, he might make a show of it, exaggerating the inconvenience to which she had subjected him, letting her know that he was already not pleased with her performance. Most of the girls who worked for Peach took this kind of game in stride; but if the girl was new, insecure, or if she actually believed his act, it could be hurtful. They knew that, too.

There was a client who was famous among Peach's callgirls. When we could, we compared notes. He had, we all agreed, the control thing down to an art.

His need, clearly, was to insinuate himself into your life. He was severely handicapped – he had a heart condition, a number of ancillary diseases, and easily weighed well over four hundred pounds.

I'm not exaggerating; the only sex that ever happened with Abe was a furtive handjob, performed after locating his penis under folds and folds of flesh. He used that, of course. He started by preying on your sympathy, establishing himself as a victim. It worked; of course it worked—women are all suckers for a victim.

He got information from you, amazing information. You found yourself saying things to Abe that you would never have said to anyone else. He stored the information, kept it hidden, waiting, until he needed it.

One of Peach's callgirls, Estée, worked part-time at a Newbury Comics CD shop. She had mentioned to Abe, one night, in passing, that she worked in a music store; he called every one in Boston until he found her. After that, he'd call her at the shop, sometimes to arrange a call, sometimes just to talk. Estée wasn't supposed to take personal calls while she was on shift. Sometimes, when Abe called, she would have a line of impatient customers in front of her. "I can't talk now, it's busy here," she'd say to Abe; and he would become indignant, calling her back over and over again, telling her that if she didn't take his call then he'd tell Peach that she had seen him outside of the agency.

He knew that was Peach's one and only rule: Thou shalt not steal clients.

It was difficult not to "steal" Abe, however. He practically insisted on it. He refused any repeat visits through Peach, telling the callgirl that if she really cared she'd see him apart from the agency. It wasn't about the fee, either. It was about the time. It was about control.

Like many others before me, I accepted Abe's insistence and saw him without telling Peach. Boy, can I make bad decisions.

He asked me to spend the night. Just spend the night, he said, I'll pay four hundred dollars. We'll listen to music (he had hooked into my taste by dazzling me with his array of really good operatic recordings), we'll drink wine, we'll play, and we'll sleep. It would be relaxed, with no jangling telephone call to take me away.

Why not, I thought. Four hundred dollars, I'm gone in the morning, no problem.

I'd done overnights with clients before. You drink, you get high, you have sex, you go to sleep. Not a bad gig.

Abe, however, had different plans. Sleeping was, apparently, out of the question. I had to rub his back, his neck. I had to bring him things to drink. I had to kiss him, kiss him a lot, make him feel sexy. "I'm so sleepy," I protested at one point, it had to be after three in the morning. "I'm not," he said. "Play with my cock." I played with his cock, I massaged his legs; I kissed his mouth, his neck, his chest, his fingers. I brought him his medications. I brought him wine. I brought him food. I even – I swear to God that this is true – was roused from my semi-somnolent state at around five o'clock in the morning to feed his cat.

Clearly, if he was paying me, Abe expected *service*.

Morning finally dawned; I had fully experienced Alaistair McLean's *Night Without End*. I was expected to cook, serve breakfast, and to wash up after it. When I mentioned leaving, he became indignant: "Why are you in such a hurry? The money is all that matters to you! I need you to be here, I need you to hold me, so that I can face the world again."

Now, you're thinking, enough is enough, walk out, right? And that would be a great idea. Except for the fact that Abe still hadn't paid me, and apparently wasn't going to until he had sucked everything from me that he could.

I put away and took out CDs. I chatted. I cleaned his living room and sat on his bed next to him and dutifully listened while he sang along to *Don Giovanni*, *Rigoletto*, and *The Barber of Seville*. I put together lunch for him. I finally invented a one o'clock meeting that I had to attend, could not miss. He spent another twenty minutes trying to find out where the meeting was (he only asked, of course, so that he could tell me how long it would take me to get there), trying to find out what it was about, asking if I couldn't come back afterwards, complaining that I was in way too much of a hurry to leave and maybe he shouldn't pay me the full amount, after all.

As soon as I could, I got out of there. It wasn't easy. Up to the very end he hesitated about paying me, insisting that I should come back later, that he would pay me then for this and more. I refused, saying I had prior plans for the evening. Abe naturally pounced on that; any delaying tactic would do. What plans? With whom? What did I like to do? He only asked, of course, because he loved me so much, he wanted to be able to picture me moving through my day . . .

I took the four hundred and fled.

It didn't stop there. He invited me to his house for dinner – payment and extracurricular activities unclear – and I refused. Abe didn't like refusals. "You teach somewhere," he said abruptly.

I froze. There was a tight coldness in my stomach that hadn't been there before. No. This wasn't happening. "How do you know that?" I asked. Before I ever saw Abe, Peach had cautioned me about telling him too much. I had told him I was a freelance writer, that I worked from home.

"Someone else told me." Oh, great, thanks, ladies. I wasn't particularly surprised; Abe had a way of getting information from people without them realizing it. I probably at some point told him things I shouldn't have.

But it wasn't the end of the world; there really wasn't much he could do with that little information. I decided to go for indifference. "Well, I teach sometimes, yeah. Anyway, I'm sorry about dinner, but –"

He cut me off. "And I know that your real name is Jen, I know that you live in Allston, and I can find out the rest. I'm really doing a disservice to the school, you know, not telling them the truth about their faculty. They'd hate to know that you do drugs, you see. They'd hate to know that you work for an escort service. All I'm asking for is dinner, just one dinner. That's not so much, is it?"

He was brilliant. A brilliant detective, brilliant with people. He questioned callgirls about themselves and each other, pretending to already have the information he was trying to extract from them. "You know that Tia told me her real name, you can tell me yours . . ." He called up cab companies and bartered his famous store of Percocet – a drug that's always in demand; he had a virtually endless ongoing prescription for one of his many pain problems – for information on where girls had been dropped off after they left his place, and when. He sat in that little apartment like it was Information Central, and he learned, and used his knowledge.

Another of Peach's callgirls, Anne, was going through a hard time not long after that. She was working for Peach while spending all of her free time doing music gigs wherever she could get them, using her money for individual voice lessons. She had a goal she was working toward. But the Bogie Man had found her; her late nights and pressured career took their toll. She was drinking too much, doing too many drugs. She was seeing Abe through the service and seeing him outside of the service. Anne was young; she listened to his assurance that he cared about her, and she believed him. When her boyfriend beat her up, it was Abe that she turned to. And Abe welcomed her with open arms. No pressure, he assured her. She slept on his sofa and gave him sex, companionship, a sense of worth; and she talked to him a lot.

She should never have talked to him.

Anne got stronger, of course. That's what happens: either you get sucked in, or you get stronger. There aren't a lot of other alternatives. Anne finally saw her life clearly and she decided to make changes. She stopped drinking, stopped doing cocaine and taking Percocets, and focused on her music. She started going to AA. She still worked for Peach, but only took "early" clients. She was back at Abe's apartment and falling asleep on his sofa by ten. It was a fairytale with a happy ending.

For everyone, that is, but Abe. He needed people to need him. He needed Anne to be sick, to be addicted, to be shaking and coming down off a cocaine high while he held her, making her feel secure and safe. He would give her Percocet tablets and she would take the pills. They helped her down off the high, made the world prettier around the edges, as that particular drug usually does. She became soft, gentle, pliable, grateful. She would admit that she could not live without him. She would massage his back, massage his ego, give him what he wanted in return for his support so that she could finally go to sleep . . .

He was losing all that when she started getting stronger. She got an important break; somebody from the Royal Opera House in London was in town, heard her, had suggestions, showed interest. She was clean and she was feeling better about herself. She thanked Abe for his friendship, his help, and she prepared to move into an apartment by herself.

Abe couldn't handle it. Couldn't handle her not needing him, losing control over her. Couldn't handle her having a dream, a vision for her life that had nothing to do with him.

So he told her that he was going to call her parents and tell them that their daughter was working as a prostitute.

Abe needed, for whatever reasons, to control the women he took into his orbit. He lured us by preying on our sympathy ("Peach calls after an hour! She doesn't understand, with my disabilities, I'm not like everyone else."). He reinforced the illusional relationship by being flattering, pathetic, or helpful – whatever it took.

I had been feeling cynical about the level of general culture around me; he honed in on that, played operas for me, aspired to more intellectual capacity than he actually possessed. For Anne, he became a safe haven. For other callgirls he morphed into other things. Then he turned on us. He would blackmail us by threatening to tell Peach, or use information we had innocently given him to make us do what he wanted.

He did it with Peach, too, which floored me because I thought that she was impervious to that sort of thing. But the bottom line for Peach was always the money; and Abe was a very regular client, using all of his disability check to procure companionship. So she put up with Abe. He called her at all hours. If she needed to hang up or take another call, he was hurt, affronted, nearly indignant. She would call him back, later, to assuage his feelings . . . After she told me that, I felt less compelled to be courteous to Abe. His neediness may well have been real, but he used it to control and hurt – and feel that he had some sort of grasp on life. He was pathetic, and he was dangerous. He was not exactly, in this business, an exception.

After Abe, the guys who wanted to use ropes, cuffs, and harsh words were small potatoes.

Their attraction to minor B&D routines and accessories made perfect sense in the context that they all, to some extent or another, were like Abe. If the guy was already into controlling the escort, then any way that he could continue to keep her emotionally under his control, any way it could get played out sexually – well, that was icing on the cake.

Of course, no client was ever as controlling as he thought he was. A callgirl picks up on the clients' desires, and if she sees he wants to be controlling, then she'll play his game. It's his dime, after all. But in our little world, the one in this situation who was ultimately in control, all the time, was Peach. Anything else is illusion, a game in which the moves are secretly predetermined – in short, a visit from a callgirl.

Bondage and discipline, if played with at all, could only be of the most mild variety, a flavor only slightly more tangy than vanilla. If the relationship is only one hour in duration, and one knows nothing about one's partner going into it, it is hard to imagine a B&D scene being successful.

Or safe.

The trust was simply not there. The reality is that clients, taken as a whole, were difficult, self-centered, sometimes petulant, always demanding – not the ideal partners in a scenario that required trust. Clients played tricks, tried to make you feel bad, made up reasons to detain you, and tried to get between you and Peach.

There was a optician in Hull I saw sometimes who couldn't come, not even after a fifty-minute blowjob (I know, because I timed it by his bedside clock), and would yell at Peach on the phone when the time came for me to be called out. "She's no good, I should get another half-hour for free, I shouldn't have to pay for this one." From what I heard, no one could make him come, and he had this same yelling match with Peach after every call, no matter who the girl was.

There were regular clients, guys who should know better – who tried to give you less money than they were supposed to. "I'll make up for it next time; Peach knows I'm good for it." Uh-huh. One thing you learn in the business is that sex is like drugs: once it's over, ain't nobody gonna pay for it – they're too busy looking ahead, getting the cash together for the next fix. There were other clients who played games with the actual money itself, making you ask for it, ten-dollar bill by ten-dollar bill. For some men, I realize, these rituals were part of the transaction, just like spanking me or having me say I'm a whore or fucking me on their desks. That was a humiliation I really didn't like, and I avoided them whenever I could.

Peach helped, though. We always asked for the money up front if the client was new; but most of her clients were regulars, and they paid at the end of the hour. It seemed classier, somehow, to do it that way, to pretend that the call is a date and the money is just an afterthought tacked on at the end.

Her regulars expected it, but it was a courtesy that had to be earned. When Peach heard of someone playing games with the money, she withdrew the courtesy. Fast. "Walter," she would say, when she set up a subsequent call for someone like that, "I do have to tell you that you'll have to pay at the beginning of the hour. I'll tell the girl to leave. I don't let people take advantage of my girls like that, Walter." And Walter – or Fred, or Gary, or whomever it was –

would accept his punishment, grovel for a while, and maybe a month or two later she'd relent and let him pay at the end again.

That was how I got into that awful situation, that time that I spent the night with Abe. Because he was used to paying at the end, and took advantage of it, and that time there was no Peach to call, to make everything okay again. So one could say that I learned my lesson about going behind her back.

What was interesting about Abe, in the end, was that he really was all bluff. He never called any schools to track my employment down; he never called Anne's parents. Even Abe must have known that there was a line there: if he crossed it, he could never go back. He was childish and self-centered, but he wasn't evil.

So the control freaks were the worst, but they weren't our only source of income, thank God. One client, a guy named Martin who lived over in Malden, made up for a lot of the others. First of all, there weren't a lot of ethical dilemmas to deal with here: he had no wife, no girlfriend, and no real potential for either. He was mentally retarded, lived on Supplemental Security Income, got together enough money from his part-time work at a deli to see a girl once a month. He always called Peach; Peach was really good with men like him. There was another client, too, one I saw with some regularity, a quadriplegic in Dorchester, whose home health aide waited patiently in the kitchen while I was in the bedroom with him; Peach could not have been more accommodating than she was with that guy.

If she yelled and screeched at the clients who tried to cheat her or who were mean to her girls, there was also a maternal side to Peach that was very loving, patient, and kind to guys like the one in Dorchester . . . and Martin.

Martin had his own rituals, too. He usually had the television on in his small room – not to anything like a soft-porn station or an X-rated movie, but to whatever he had been watching when you arrived. You'd do a slow strip tease in front of him, then some minimal kissing and caressing, before proceeding to taking him into your mouth, then finally move up his body to straddle him. He'd come fairly quickly after that. Then he'd pay you, and add a tip, which would have been ludicrously insulting from anybody else, but was touching in view of his circumstances, usually amounting to something like three dollars and eighty-seven cents. Finally, he'd give you a magnet from the deli where he worked as an additional tip, with a whispered, "If you say you're a friend of mine, they'll take a dollar off a sandwich for you!" I still have a small collection of those magnets, somewhere. Even now, I don't want to throw them away. They meant too much to him.

So Martin was an exception. But for many, many of our clients, I knew that I couldn't trust them as far as I could throw them. And without that, there was no way in hell I was going to put myself in a position where I could get really physically hurt.

I know that some women do it. Hell, I know that some women specialize in it; I've seen their ads. I can appreciate the need: it must be difficult to tell one's wife, "Oh, honey, by the way, I'd like to spank you tonight." Much easier to go to a professional.

I just didn't want to be that particular professional. I'll keep that part of my sexuality in my Real Life, thank you very much.

* * * * * *

Scuzzy was waiting by the door when I got home, and the room's general ambience reminded me that it was time to clean his litter box. I made tea and sat down at my desk. The headache wasn't getting any better, and I had to prepare final exams for all four classes.

Two of the classes could potentially share one exam, of course; I was doing two sections of the prostitution class. But I wasn't so far removed from my own undergraduate days that I could delude myself that they could all take the same test, and that students in the first section wouldn't pass along the questions to the students in the second section. For a fee, of course.

What I've learned in life: Everything can be bought.

Maybe I'd just skirt the issue altogether by giving everybody a take-home exam instead.

I think that my conscious remembrance of my mother, earlier, had rattled me. For the first time, since I'd begun working for Peach, I allowed myself to wonder what my mother would think of what I was doing. She'd probably approve of neither of my jobs. My family was not academic: I was the first to earn a master's degree, much less a doctorate. I hadn't exactly dazzled any of them with either. I think that my mother would have been pleased to see me married, with children, maybe writing in my spare time . . . Not teaching college. And certainly not working as an escort.

Well, that's a little obvious, I told myself sourly. Like there are a whole lot of women out there whose mothers would be delighted to see them working as prostitutes. It's not that she'd be so very unusual in that regard. But . . . it was more than that. In the year and a half since she had died, I had come to terms with who my mother had been, what she thought and felt, and why she had done the things that she had, more than I had ever been able to do while she was alive.

My mother was all about appearances. She spent most of her life pretending that she was living in one world, even though she was actually living in another. What was real was bad, somehow, tainted. Only what we pretended was true was real.

I had embraced life in the real world, had turned my back on my mother's fictions, and in so doing had betrayed her.

I shook off the thoughts. I couldn't afford to go down this particular branch of memory lane, to indulge myself in a bout of guilt or feelings of inadequacy. I had work to do. And the damned headache wasn't going away.

In the Middle Ages, they believed that when you got an intense headache, it meant that a ghost was going to walk that night.

I reached for the Excedrin again. My mother was doing her utmost to haunt me at the best of times; I wasn't about to give her any encouragement.

Chapter Nineteen

That summer, I went on my first vacation in years.

Peach fretted, but I wasn't going for long, only two weeks. Two weeks between my two summer sessions, and I couldn't get out of town fast enough – freedom was calling me. Amazing how escape becomes possible when one has the financial means to access it.

Scuzzy went to stay with Vicky, my administrative assistant, yowling piteously all the way over to her apartment in the Fenway. Irene agreed to come in and water my plants.

There was nothing else keeping me in Boston.

I flew British Airways to London, as I had two years before, the summer when I went to lecture and started thinking about working for an escort service. I stayed in a modest hotel that was a big improvement over the student housing of my previous visit, I ate wonderful cholesterol-laden meals in pubs, and I played tourist. Big Ben. The changing of the guard at Buckingham Palace. Two whole luxurious days at the British Museum. Meat pies. Tea and clotted cream. Warm beer and cold toast.

This time, when I was on the Underground, the voice that told me to mind the gap didn't seem quite so bossy. Maybe it was because this time I knew that I was earning more then she was.

In London, callgirls (most of whom, it seems, are independent) advertise on the inside of telephone booths, with little colored cards that urge you to ring her for a good time. It's brilliant; I don't know why we haven't thought of that in the States. Then again, we have a lot more seriously disturbed people than they do in England; who knows who might call? England is marginally more civilized. At least little white boys haven't yet taken to decimating their entire school population with automatic weapons.

I went to see *Cats*, and it was when I was walking back to the hotel that I finally found a name for the malaise that had been following me around since spring. It was like the shadows of ghosts you encounter, sometimes, elusively staying just beyond your range of vision, and yet you know that they are there. They whisper in the empty hallway behind you, the presence that wasn't quite a presence when the wind twitched the curtains, the sure knowledge that there is something out there and the frustrating inability to name it.

That night I found its name.

I was lonely.

Oh, I had friends. I had people who would come over and sip wine and play board games and talk with me. I had friends who would invite me out on the town, keep me dancing until dawn. I spent time alone because I chose to be alone; there was never a time when I couldn't secure company if I wanted it.

But since Luis had left, there was no one for whom I was the most important other person in the world.

I hadn't thought that I wanted that, particularly. Apparently my subconscious disagreed. The city was filled with couples, touching each other, kissing each other, laughing together. Once I stared noticing them, they were all that I could see.

London is the ideal place for romantic fantasies about strangers, because British men's accents are so damned gorgeous – cultured and intelligent and sexy all at once. I loved their voices. You'd be walking along the street and hear this man behind you, and a shiver would run up your spine, and you'd turn around and – it would be a short chubby balding guy puffing away at a cigarette. The voice, I have found, has nothing to do with the persona.

Still, I went home to the hotel that night after *Cats*, imagining all the voices I had been hearing over the past week, lying in bed antouching myself and wishing with all of my heart that I was not alone.

* * * * * *

I arrived back in Boston on a blazing hot summer afternoon. The taxi in from Logan wasn't air-conditioned. What a surprise. In England, things *worked*. People fixed them when they were broken and made sure that they stayed functional.

Welcome home.

The feeling of loneliness had, if anything, intensified.

I stood on my bathroom scale, aghast at the three pounds that hadn't been there before vacation. I wondered about what it would be like to have a life where a temporary extra three pounds simply wouldn't matter, because the person that you were with would love you no matter what. Because your livelihood and your self-worth and your lifestyle wouldn't be hanging on what immature strangers thought of your looks. Because there was someplace where you belonged, and somebody with whom you belonged.

I was surprised to find tears, hot and unexpected, pressing against the back of my eyes. I was not going to cry about this. I was not going to be so pathetic that I burst into tears every time I felt a little lonely.

Besides, it was sensible, I thought, as I finally started the long unpacking process, sensible that I should stay single, at least for as long as I was working for Peach. After all, getting involved with someone while working this profession means that you're faced with making a choice between two unpleasant alternatives. You can either choose to not tell him about the escort work, and keep lying, keep covering up, keep living in fear that he'll discover your secret by himself. Or you can tell him, see how liberal he sounds, see how titillated he gets – at first. Then see how long the relationship takes to crash and burn after that.

I can't really say that I would blame him, to be completely honest. I know exactly where I stand with clients; having sex with them clearly constitutes a work-related undertaking. When I was sleeping with Luis and also seeing clients, I had no problems keeping the two activities separate. In a sense, Luis was having sex with Jen, the clients were having sex with Tia. I know, that's a little simplistic, but it's not an unreasonable way to look at it.

Anyway, it would be a tough thing to deal with at the beginning of a relationship. Far better to hold off until there aren't any skeletons halfway out of the closet.

The question was, of course, if I would ever reach a point where I *didn't* have skeletons in the closet. Probably not; but that shouldn't be such an obstacle, should it? Everyone has something in their life about which they are profoundly ashamed. Everyone had dirty little secrets, lies nurtured and guarded jealously. Everyone has skeletons.

Still, mine might be a little harder to swallow than others. It was really difficult to construct a happy ending coming out of that particular scenario. "Um, Honey, you asked about my part-time work . . ." How does one tell a lover that one has been a callgirl? Will he be turned on? Yeah, probably, at first. But not for long. In the age-old dichotomy of men's relationships with women, he'll want like hell to sleep with me. But I'm not the kind of girl he'd take home to meet Mom. Definitely not the kind of girl he'd marry.

He would end up eventually as all my clients do, fantasizing about me while he tiredly making love to his bored and indifferent wife.

Oh, yes, I was setting myself up to believe the worst. But even believing that, I wanted to find out, for real. I wanted somebody. I didn't want to be alone anymore.

In the end, I learned that the best planning in the world doesn't matter. When I met my husband, Tony, he knew that I had a friend who ran an escort service, he knew that I knew some women who were callgirls, and he didn't have much of a problem with it, or even much interest.

I had decided by then to live the lie, to keep the skeleton in the closet, to be sure the door was tightly sealed. I wanted a life with this man. And, anyway, why not? We were only talking about three years out of my past, after all – not such a big deal. I could do it.

There were a few verbal slips, of course. I said once something about, "back when I worked for Peach," but I covered that up reasonably adequately by saying that on occasion she had asked me to drive someone to a call when her own driver was busy or unavailable. Tony nodded; I had in fact once or twice performed that service for Peach in fairly recent memory, and he believed me.

It might have worked out. I might have kept the secret, maintained the story, denied the past. But in the end I wasn't given the option of keeping the closet door locked, the skeleton safely hidden. Because one night when I was not around, Tony opened the door himself.

By that time we were living together, though not yet married. I hadn't worked for Peach in over two years. I didn't think about it a lot, except for the fact that I was still teaching the prostitution class and was still amazed that people continued to cling stubbornly to those worn-out clichés about the business, amazed that the word "degrading" kept surfacing. I wondered if it might help things if I wrote a book on the real world of escort services.

I told Tony right away about the idea. "I've been friends with Peach for years, I've watched her work, she can give me anecdotes, and I'll write about it," I said. Tony was supportive – Tony has always been supportive. But I needed more than my husband's opinion, particularly when he was not in possession of all the facts.

I told a lie of omission earlier when I said that Seth was the only person who knew both sides of who I was back then, of what I did. Months after that awful night at the Ritz-Carlton, I went out drinking with my friend Roger, and decided to tell him. My decision probably was strongly influenced by the fact that Roger was gay, and unlikely to slap money down on the bar and unzip his pants for me. It wasn't a big deal. He had thought about doing it himself, he said, unimpressed, and we went on with our evening.

Roger had moved since then, and we had stayed vaguely in touch through e-mail. As I thought about the book I might write, I needed an opinion. Who should I ask? Not Peach; she would be appalled at the thought and would do everything in her power to dissuade me. Not Seth; he'd be too afraid that he might show up in its pages – as, in point of fact, he did.

So I wrote an e-mail to Roger in Key West, and asked him what he thought. He thought it was a great idea, he'd buy it when it came out, and he had met this fabulous guy just the night before that he was just dying to tell me about . . .

I went to bed, but Tony couldn't sleep later that night, and my e-mail was sitting open on the computer screen when he switched it on to play a hand or two of solitaire. Funny, isn't it: there was no psychic voice that awakened me as I lay sleeping a few rooms away, no omen that told me something momentous was happening in my life.

I never even heard the hinges on the closet door screech as he forced it open.

I probably should have opened it myself, long before that. I probably should have told him. It would have been the moral, the ethical thing to do. It would have been far kinder than what actually happened. I can only imagine his feelings as he read that e-mail; I can only imagine him wondering what other doors there were to open, what other secrets left undiscovered, what other lies had been told.

No, I take that back. I can't imagine. It must have been hell.

We survived it, in the end. We had each by then come to the conclusion that we were right for each other. It was . . . well, not to get too maudlin about it, but it was that we loved each other enough to get through it. And so my skeleton disappeared.

Still, I stand behind my earlier thoughts, there in Allston that day when I just got back from London and was feeling the ache for another person that wasn't really to be assuaged for some time to come.

It's an uneasy secret, one difficult to keep . . . and scary as hell to give away.

Chapter Twenty

And then it was fall again.

This time around, my spirits were perfectly in tune with the season. I'd always greeted autumn with an emotion approaching panic – another school year beginning, I still don't have a real job, etc., etc. But this year, if I didn't have a real job, I was getting close to it. I was invited to all the faculty parties. Professors with names I actually had heard of were calling me, writing me letters. The dean remembered who I was when he bumped into me one afternoon in the corridor outside his office.

The air felt cleaner, crisper. I had bought some new clothes and they felt soft and smart, as new clothes do. I had a plan, I was reaching my goals, I felt full of joy, full of anticipation. For the first time in years I, too, believed that this academic year would bring great things, great opportunities, great promises.

As though something marvelous just might be right around the corner.

I was working one evening a week now, sometimes two. Peach was not happy, but she was also fair: Peach never tried to coerce anyone into doing something that she didn't want to do. I promised myself I was only going to work Fridays and Saturdays this semester.

Three weeks into classes, she called on a Friday night. "Got work," she said, her voice brisk. "He's down in Milton, though: do you know where that is?"

"I'm sure I can find it. What did you tell him about me?" I'd gained three pounds in England (the clotted cream, I suspected, was the culprit), and they hadn't come off yet. This was by far the most nerve-wracking part of the job.

"Oh, relax, you're gonna love this. He asked for the oldest person I have. I told him that he could see Tia, she's thirty-nine, and he said are you sure you don't have anybody older than that? I said no, and that I'm sure he'll like Tia."

"That sounds weird, Peach." I'd never lied about my age in *that* direction before. In such an age-obsessed and age-biased profession, at thirty-six it was easy for me to always be the oldest person around. Maybe that wasn't good enough. Maybe he had some sort of wrinkle fetish.

"No, really, Jen, he sounds very cool. I got a good feeling from him. Why don't you call him and see what you think? I know you don't like new clients, it's your call, but I honestly think that this will work out fine."

I didn't get much feeling from him on the phone, one way or the other, but he seemed pleased enough about seeing me, and so I set off. "What would you like me to wear?" I asked, out of habit. He seemed surprised by the question. "Uh – whatever you want. That is, whatever you normally wear. That's fine."

I listened to Springsteen on the way down, the stereo turned as high as it would go, to hell with blowing out the speakers: *"Mister, I ain't a boy, no, I'm a man, and I believe in a promised land."* I sang along with him at the top of my lungs, and even as I sang, I wished I could enter even deeper into his words, into his pain, into his story.

It had been a long time since I had believed in a promised land.

Glenn met me at his apartment door. He was huge, and shaggy looking – unkempt hair, unkempt beard, a plaid flannel shirt over reasonably clean khakis. Lots of tattoos. I mean *lots*. "Hi, I'm Tia."

"Hi, come on in."

The place was filled with Harley Davidson – well, what do you call it? Equipment? Accessories? Paraphernalia? Stuff? Posters of motorcycles, framed photographs of people on motorcycles. Glenn was drinking a beer but didn't offer me one. I sat down next to him on the couch. We talked, and eventually I put my hand on his knee, and a few minutes later I began kissing him. When I was new at all of this, I used to let the client set the pace, and I still did now when he knew what he wanted – or what he was doing. But one night I'd talked and talked with a nervous Indian until we had to jump on each other for a few breathless minutes before Peach called me out. After that, if it seemed that he was unsure of himself, I took the lead.

Glenn and I made out on the couch for a while, and then he suggested that we move into the bedroom, a fairly suave move hampered only by his need to drain his beer can before following me in.

His nervousness was increasing. I began to hope rather strenuously that he wasn't doing drugs, or had a heart condition, or something that was going to cause him to come to grief here.

Then, in a rare moment of perfect clarity, I realized what was going on.

This Harley guy who owned his own business by day and raced motorcycles on the weekends was a virgin. Hence his request for an older (possibly more sympathetic?) escort. It was touching. It was sweet.

It was also a hell of a lot of work.

Although we experimented with various positions and rhythms, eventually Glenn found that what he really liked was the classic blowjob. And I'm reasonably good at it, even with a condom, and also unfortunately have some experience with lengthy oral encounters. But he was taking forever. I kept taking surreptitious glances at the neon Budweiser clock on his bedroom wall every time I came up for air, and I was astonished. And truly, truly tired.

We were approaching the forty-eight minute mark and I had about decided to give up at fifty and try my hand alone instead, when it finally happened. Given the fact that he was incredibly sweet afterwards, talking and cuddling with me, then adding an extra twenty dollars on to the fee, I was inclined to minimize in my mind the amount of work that he had required.

He called the following Friday, and asked for me again. A regular, which was a nice bonus going into the fall semester. Besides, I figured, surely it'll be quicker now. After all, last time was the first time, who knows what role his nervousness had played in his inability to ejaculate? This time will be fine.

This time wasn't. I did end up switching off between my hands and my mouth simply from fatigue. It was an odd little dilemma: he was one of the nicest clients I'd ever been with, and one of the most tedious.

Peach and I agreed that seeing Glenn every other Friday was probably a good idea for our collective sanity.

Most of that fall is a blur, to be honest, from the escort agency point of view. I was really becoming more and more focused on my professional life, on researching the classes I was teaching and others that I might teach someday. So the weekends sort of blended in to each other.

Certain clients stand out from that time. I remember the guy in Nahant who wanted to have sex on his home gym equipment while watching himself in the mirror. And then there were the students on Comm. Ave. who wanted to share me, just to see what a threesome was like (and were astonished to learn that they would have to pay double. "Price is on a per person basis," Peach said in her best no-nonsense voice; but her rule made sense. Two clients were, after all, more work than one).

There were a few decidedly jarring experiences. I went to see a new client up on the North Shore who could only have sex on the same sofa where his wife had died. He fortunately didn't tell me about that particular facet to our encounter until it was over. Just as well. I found in conversation with another client that he was a good friend of my dissertation advisor, and while he was just as likely to keep the secret of our time together as was I, it still made me a little nervous.

To be honest, I was starting to feel more and more as though there were a clock ticking somewhere in my brain, and that it was measuring the time that I had left. The late nights weren't as frequent anymore, and certainly not as much fun. I was getting up in time to do espresso instead of cocaine for my morning pick-me-up; and when I wasn't working for Peach, I wasn't even staying awake through the eleven o'clock news anymore.

It wasn't cerebral. It was emotional. More than anything, I was feeling the job, with all of its uncertainties and stresses, slowly slipping off my shoulders like an old, worn-out coat that has served its purpose well and is ready to be retired.

I went to Peach's place for a Halloween party. I hadn't been there in a long time, having finally gotten my act together enough to realize that I could not stay up and drink until five in the morning and then expect to function well the following day. It had taken me a few times and a few near-fiascoes to grasp that seemingly obvious fact, but I had done so at last. I had more or less forgotten what they were like, these all-night parties of hers.

Her big apartment – it was an architect's dream, that apartment – was filled with people, talking, laughing, drinking. I was doing the Morticia Addams thing – I had thought of going as Catwoman, but those three extra pounds were still between me and that catsuit, so I settled for Morticia.

I knew some of the people there, maybe about a third of them. I wandered around and talked and ate and drank, and eventually ended up on the roof deck, surrounded by glittering fairy lights, with someone putting lines of cocaine out on a slab of marble in front of me.

It just suddenly all felt really old. Not bad, not negative, not even sad – just old.

Or maybe it was me who was feeling old.

Whatever the reason, I knew as I sat on that deck that I didn't want to still be awake when the sun came up. I didn't want to bring somebody home with me that I'd later regret having to tiptoe around because he was sleeping until noon. I didn't want the hangover and the Excedrin and the immediate need to tell myself that it was all right to feel so sick, because, after all, I was cool.

What sounded *really* cool from where I was sitting was the thought of a bowl of Healthy Choice pecan praline ice cream, a comfortable sofa and my cat next to me, with the television tuned to something like Agatha Christie or Colin Dexter on *Mystery!*

I don't know if Peach saw me go. If she did, there was no reason for her to think that that night was the beginning of the end.

I'm not even sure that I knew, then, that it was.

Chapter Twenty-one

I was getting close to making a decision about leaving the business when the disaster happened. It hadn't looked like a disaster, not at first; but it became one all the same. At first, it was just a call.

It was cold; that's one of the things I remember about that night.

When I thought about it later – and I thought a lot about it later – I remembered the bitter sharp biting wind that cut through you, and the snow heaped everywhere that made driving and parking such an irritating process. It was really cold.

So I wasn't especially delighted when Peach called and said she had a client for me in Cambridge.

Parking in Cambridge can be rough at the best of times, and this wasn't the best of times. That's another thing I don't get about this city, by the way. Every winter, it snows, and everybody is taken by surprise when it does, as though they didn't really believe it was going to happen again.

And they drive like they've never seen the stuff before.

The parking situation was getting really ugly. After each significant snowfall, people would shovel the snow off their cars that were parked on the street, and then they figured that their effort had earned them ownership rights over that little piece of street. So they would bring out those old kitchen chairs, the ones made of aluminum with shiny plastic seats and backs, and they would put the chairs in the middle of the space they'd cleared, to reserve it for them.

I'd lived in Boston long enough to swear at the practice, but I also knew enough to respect it. You don't want to fuck with somebody who just risked a coronary to remove all that snow, somebody crazy enough to feel entitled to personal ownership of a section of public property. Besides, you'd be going off and leaving your car in the disputed space: do you really think that's such a good idea?

So I was less than thrilled about Cambridge.

"You'll like him," Peach said, her voice reassuring on the telephone. Easy for her to say; she was curled up in a very deep sofa in a well-heated room, no doubt reading an engrossing novel and drinking some exotic coffee drink. "You might be able to hook him as a regular. He said he wants someone smart."

"Flattery will get you everywhere," I grumbled, secretly pleased with the compliment; and then I bundled a big padded coat over my little black-nothing dress and set out. I parked about six blocks from the apartment building on Broadway and cursed the client as I walked back to his address, my Nine West shoes undoubtedly getting ruined in the snow, great piles of which I had to skirt periodically.

No one, of course, had bothered to clear the sidewalk. What for? Can't leave a kitchen chair there.

The temperature was in the twenties and the wind chill brought it way down into the single digits. Must be terrific, I muttered under my breath, to be able to stay in your nice warm apartment and put in an order for sex. The ultimate in take-out. That night, it was just me and the pizza delivery guy out there in the cold.

The client had sounded all right on the telephone. Young. Pakistani. Intelligent. He asked me what kind of brandy I preferred – not a question I get every day. I liked that.

His apartment, it has to be said, was gorgeous. Antique polished furniture, gilt-edged paintings on one wall, floor-to-ceiling books on another. A Persian rug in the living room with vibrant colors. A brass samovar on a sideboard. Indonesian ceremonial marionettes hanging over the desk. He had traveled, and traveled well.

He suggested that we sit, and he brought over the Hine Antique that he had already poured into snifters. He swirled his constantly while we talked.

His name was Kai. He read a lot; there was a whole shelf of Rushdie novels right beside us. I was forgetting that I was supposed to be seducing him. "What did you think of the death sentence they passed on Rushdie?" I asked, genuinely curious. The man was Pakistani, so he was supposed to be Muslim. But that didn't fit in with the brandy; and surely if he supported the edict he would not be reading the man's books.

He shook his head. "One should not try and make the Koran bend to one's will," he said, his voice gentle and troubled. "It is not the true way of Islam."

There was a pause. I sipped my brandy, and felt the warmth spreading physically through my chest and stomach. I was liking the feeling, and liking being next to him.

That was the first warning signal, of course. It appeared, sailed right by me, and continued unnoticed out into the ether. I should have caught the thought there, and re-adjusted my persona, my level of involvement. This was work.

But I was longing to touch him, to make love with him, to hold that dark beautiful head in my hands and taste his mouth. I was sure that something exciting and unique could happen between us; I could feel the excitement and anticipation building inside me, hot and seductive as the brandy.

My last remaining functioning brain cell roused itself then to remind me that this was a client and my thoughts should be more professional, but I had had time to prepare the other side of the argument. Yeah, yeah, so this is work, so what? There's nothing wrong with enjoying what you do for a living, is there?

The light of reason flickered a final time, and went out. The last wavering voice of rational thought gave up. It knew when it had lost.

"I don't have time to meet women," Kai was saying, explaining why he had called an escort service. A lot of clients do that, feel a need to rationalize why they have to – or choose to – pay for sex. But as Kai was telling me why he used a service for intimacy, instead of finding his explanations superficial or pathetic, the two conclusions I usually drew whenever other clients attempted to justify their use of the agency, I thought it was sort of endearing.

As if my opinion of him mattered.

He was still talking, making a segue from the subject of his busyness to its cause. "I'm at Harvard. I'm carrying a dual major, computer science and business. It's difficult, and I am doing it only because I have a limited amount of time to stay in this country. So I am always working, and to meet and court someone – well, I don't have that kind of time." He shrugged lightly. "I wish I could be close to a woman, but it is impossible at this stage of my life."

I bought it, of course. I didn't point out that if it was a relationship he wanted, LunchDates or match.com would probably suit his needs better than an escort service. I didn't say any of it. I wanted to think that I was the woman he was looking for.

"I understand," I said. Harvard was, of course, the clincher. I've always been sexually aroused by brilliance – well, everyone knows that competence is a turn-on – and the fact that he was at Harvard, combined with his very non-macho, non-Islamic respect for my opinions, my personhood . . .

It felt natural and mutual when he turned, pulled me gently toward him, and kissed me. It was a long kiss, deep, exploring the newness, the foreign taste of the other person.

When we did go into his darkened bedroom and embraced, when we pulled off each other's clothes, it was impossible to say who wanted to be there more. He was gentle and generous in bed, his long slender fingers in my hair, on my breasts, around my pussy; and when he entered me that, too, felt natural and right and perfect.

He paid me discreetly – an envelope slid into my hand as though it were not there at all – and he kissed me again at the door. I could have sworn I felt regret in his embrace. "We'll see each other again," he whispered, and I felt a thrill of unexpected sudden joy run up my spine.

So, okay, you could see it coming. Actually, everybody but the squirrels chattering in the tree outside my studio window could see it coming, and even they were getting suspicious. The only person who didn't see it coming was me.

I called Peach from my cell phone in the car, sitting with the engine running, waiting for the heater to kick in. There was a thin veneer of ice on the windshield. "Is everything okay?" she asked, just as she asked every night.

"Yes," I said, trying to sound casual. "He was nice, Peach. I liked him. Do me a favor, next time he calls, let me take it."

"He already called," she said. "He doesn't want to see anybody but you. You got yourself a new regular, babe."

And that's going to last until the first night that I'm not on and he calls. Peach's loyalties only go so far: they're never allowed to interfere with the bottom line. She'll talk him into seeing somebody else.

Peach's voice broke into my thoughts. "You want something else for tonight? It's only eleven-thirty. I can probably get you something if you want to hang out for a few minutes."

The thought of taking another call that night felt wrong – sacrilegious, almost. Normally I didn't mind going from one man to another, but tonight my usual callgirl sangfroid was missing. Tonight was different. Tonight I had left a call smiling and humming and not counting the money.

"Peach, I'm signing off. It's too cold. I want to go home and curl up with Scuzzy."

That was on Sunday night. On Thursday, just as I was taking my dinner out of the oven, the phone rang. It was Peach. "Got work. Your regular in Cambridge called. He wants to see you tonight."

"The Pakistani guy?" Casual, that's me.

"That's the one. Give him a call. 555-7483. And let me know when you're heading over there."

I scribbled the number on my paper napkin and felt a thrill of nervousness as I picked up the telephone receiver again. This is ridiculous, I told myself. He's just another call. One I like, but that's okay, he makes up for my other Cambridge regular, the one who wants me to keep saying how big he is, over and over again.

When I called, I couldn't detect any warmth in his voice. "Yes. Tia. What time can you be here?"

I craned my head to see the clock in the kitchenette. "Um, it's eight-fifteen now. Is nine o'clock good for you?"

"Yes, that is good. I will see you then."

"I'm looking forward to seeing you," I said. But he had already hung up.

I left my dinner on the coffee table, substituted a Pat Benatar CD for the television and opened the closet. Black velvet skirt. Didn't have to go too fancy with the underwear; he preferred the light off when we undressed. Black bra, black lace shirt, gray shawl. Chanel Number Five. Re-applying my makeup in front of the bathroom mirror, I suddenly felt like I was sixteen and getting ready for a date.

Scuzzy had jumped up onto the seat of the toilet and was watching me intently. "I'm going out," I said to him. "Should I leave my hair down or tie it back – what do you think?" His gaze was impassive. As usual, he was unimpressed. I left my hair down.

I put the car radio on really loud so I wouldn't have to think. Kai buzzed me in through the vestibule, and I took the elevator to the third floor. He was standing in the doorway, waiting.

He didn't say anything. I walked across the hallway, looking at his eyes, and I didn't say anything, either. Suddenly he grabbed me and pulled me against him, roughly, and I gasped as his mouth found mine. Then it wasn't gentle at all.

We made it as far as the entrance hall to the apartment. He managed to swing the front door shut behind me, but I was already on my knees on the Persian rug and fumbling with the snap on his jeans.

Later, he brought it up as though it had been weighing on him. He was showing me photographs, his parents in Karachi, his brother in Paris. "I love seeing you," he said, his eyes on the pictures. "I love having you here. I wish that I could afford more than an hour. I'd love to take you to dinner, to go to the Museum of Fine Arts."

I took a deep breath. "I'd like that." I hesitated, knowing that if Peach found out about this I'd be looking for a new madam and a new agency. "I could give you my phone number, at home."

He waited. Now I was the one who couldn't meet his eyes. "I'd like to see you outside of work," I said.

A smile lit up his face. "I would like that very much," he said gravely.

I felt daring. "Okay, then. And – I should tell you – my name isn't really Tia, it's Jen."

"I like Jen better. Is tomorrow night too soon? I can pick you up, we can have dinner at Biba."

"Yes – I mean no, it's not too soon, that sounds wonderful." Part of me was sifting through the conversation already, the illogic of his being able to afford Harvard, this apartment, Friday nights at Biba, but not being able to afford seeing me. Yet even as I thought it, I was glowing with delight; he liked me and wanted a real relationship with me. That was what I wanted to believe. That was what I believed.

We're known for that, of course. Women will always find a way of believing the unbelievable. Callgirls apparently aren't any different than the rest of the species.

And so we started seeing each other.

We left a lot out of our conversations, of course. Like the fact that I was still working for Peach. Like the fact that he only saw me at night, and never introduced me to any of the friends to whom he constantly referred. We ignored those spaces, talked around them, and sometimes they cast a shadow over my thoughts, but I got good at dodging the shadows.

It was fun . . . it was good. We went to ethnic restaurants and sampled the cuisines of the world, and over sole mornay or shish kebabs or sushi we talked about literature, politics, technology, ethics. We saw foreign films at Kendall Square and Coolidge Corner. We listened to new bands at the Middle East in Central Square and jazz at Scullers and blues at Wally's. We never went to my studio; Kai said he had an allergy to cats. So it seemed appropriate that we always went back after an evening out to his apartment on Broadway, where I often spent the night.

His manners were impeccable. His thoughts were obscure.

Peach knew that something was up. I finally told her the truth when I realized that what she was thinking was far worse – that I was seeing Kai professionally, without going through her.

She shrugged, not showing any surprise, just faint irritation at the apparent loss of a client. Faint, of course, because she knew her loss was temporary. She didn't share that thought with me. "I told you when you started that you'd fall in love with one of your clients," she said, dismissively. "It happens to everyone. There's always one, and you do what you need to do, and then you don't do it anymore."

Well, if you have any sense you don't. I knew one or two women who tried, and it doesn't work, not ever, no matter how much you want it to. The fact that the relationship began on such drastically uneven footing can never quite be erased. For one thing, the man assumes that the sex will always be the same as it was when it was professional. A prostitute's *job* is to make him feel good; her needs and desires and preferences are irrelevant. So she spends an hour intensely focused on him. Once they're in a relationship together, that intensity fades. She cannot fail to disappoint because she is now human, subject to headaches, mood swings, and her own wants and needs.

Peach knew all this, and she knew that it was healthier when it ended before it got to that point; but that knowledge meant that she wasn't exactly the best person in the world to go to for advice or sympathy. "It just happened," I said helplessly. "I really like him, Peach."

So I went on calls and told Kai there were nights I couldn't go out because I was working. I still carried the illusion that that was somehow normal, somehow all right. I convinced myself that this guy was the only man on earth who really did completely understand the differentiation that we draw between "working" sex and "personal" sex, and could see that my going on calls had nothing to do with my making love with him.

I didn't think about it having been me who had crossed the boundary, thereby taking away its safety, its protection.

One night after watching Catherine Deneuve, drinking brandy, and making love, I slept over at his apartment, and slept late. I was still in bed when he went to take his shower. Usually by then I had gone; we hadn't yet reached the stage where it was okay for me to leave any of my possessions at his place, and since I was usually still dressed appropriately for an evening out, a discreet early departure seemed the better part of valor.

I didn't want anybody seeing me and assuming that it was a pickup, a one-night stand. I wanted to protect his reputation. File that one under "ironic."

But I was tired and it was warm under the comforter, and cold outside. I wasn't really listening when the phone rang, when the answering machine picked up the call, when a man's voice began leaving the requisite message.

". . . and listen, dude, you never cease to amaze me. Dan just told me, it's all around campus. Getting a hooker for free, that's gotta be the best stunt anyone has pulled around here for a long time. Hall of Fame shit, man, that's pure Hall of Fame shit. When you gonna bring her over so we can all see what you're getting? That's too cool. You're a stud for sure. Talk to you later, man."

Click.

I don't remember getting up, or getting dressed, or leaving. I didn't wait for him to get out of the shower. I didn't leave him a note. I may have been too stunned. Or I may have realized that words, at that point, would have been redundant.

Remember those bad feelings I was supposed to have felt, back when I started doing this?

226

So do I.

Scuzzy was delighted with my depression. I called my department, pleaded a family emergency, and arranged for a teaching assistant to cover my classes, while the cat sat on my yet ungraded papers and seemed to nod approval. I stayed home with him, feeding movie after movie into the VCR and cat treat after cat treat into his mouth. I sent out for home delivery every night and over-ate and didn't bother cleaning up, so that within a few days there were empty take-out boxes scattered all over the studio, which Scuzzy assumed were exciting new toys obtained uniquely for his pleasure. I fell asleep on the couch without bothering to fold it out into a bed, and he slept contentedly on my chest. I didn't bathe, which he probably attributed to a new sensitivity on my part to his dislike of water and anything wet.

I knew that Peach was calling, even though I had turned off my ringer and my answering machine. I didn't care. Oh, I've been dumped before; haven't we all? But what had happened here . . . it was different. It was obscene, perverse, worse than any of the so-called degrading fantasies I had played out on calls. Those were experiments, sublimations: this was raw cruelty. He "got a hooker for free." I could be defined; I could be replaced; I was generic. I wasn't Jen; I wasn't even Tia. I was a hooker.

There may even have been a wager involved, and I could imagine his friends, laughing and swigging from their beer bottles. "No way. No hooker'll ever put out for free."

"Bet you I can have one begging to do me for free." It had to be some kind of ultimate ego-builder for him, the foreigner in an Anglo-Saxon country, the Muslim handling currency that said, "In God We Trust." Americans had to pay to have sex with me, but he could get back at them for their suspicious looks and their xenophobia. They had to pay, but he could have me for nothing, anytime and as often as he pleased. "Dude! That's Hall of Fame shit, man."

I'd watch television and after a while I wasn't hearing anything but those words in my head. It hurt more than anything I had ever felt before.

Eventually I started smelling myself, and almost mechanically I took a shower. After that it was a fairly small step to go to the grocery store, and the next day I did laundry and plugged my phone back in.

Peach was livid. "Where the hell have you been? What's wrong with your phone? I've been calling you every day! It was like you had disappeared off the face of the earth!" Her voice was a snarl.

Yes. Well. Something like that.

"You might have thought of someone besides yourself," she went on. "You might have thought about me. I've had problems, too, you know. I didn't know what to say to people."

Yes, that was my main concern, your social malaise. "I'm sorry, Peach," I said tiredly. "It's over now."

"So can you work tonight?"

I took a quick involuntary breath. I didn't know if I could trust the clients. I didn't know if I could trust myself. Given the right provocation, I could see myself taking all this out on some hapless inoffensive guy who had the misfortune to say the wrong thing, to refer to any of the places I had been with Kai, to listen to seductive music. On the other hand, if I didn't get out of the apartment I was going to go crazy. "Okay, Peach, sign me on when you turn on the phones."

"Good. Great. Then I'll be talking to you shortly."

I decided to make an effort to return to the land of the living. I shaped my nails and put on some dark red polish. I did my eyebrows. I rubbed moisturizer everywhere and brushed my hair the hundred strokes mandated by my grandmother. I watched *Jeopardy!* and blew through the European Literature category, but was moronic when they did the Table of Elements. I bet everything on Final Jeopardy and lost it all when I had absolutely no idea which president signed an act of which I had never heard, and then ate three cookies to compensate.

At my current rate of food consumption, if I didn't get to the gym soon I wouldn't be able to work for Peach at all anymore.

I tried to get interested in the latest Patricia Cornwell, and as usual got really irritated with her grammatical faux pas and resolved to compose a letter to her editor I knew I'd never actually write.

By the time it was nine o'clock I decided to see what was going on. Almost all of my regulars were early-evening kinds of guys, but I also hadn't been available for a while, and had no illusions about Peach's loyalty in those circumstances. If she could talk the client into seeing somebody else, she would. "Hey, it's Jen, haven't heard from you. What's up?"

"Slow night."

I was beyond tired of my four familiar walls. "I'll take whatever you've got, Peach, I just need to get out."

Silence. That either meant she was thinking or had become riveted to whatever was on her television screen. If it was *Ally McBeal*, I might never get her attention back. She'd been known to put her mother on hold when *Ally McBeal* was on. "It's slow, Jen. Give me another hour, okay? I'll try to get you something."

In another hour I would have gone back to thinking about what had happened and felt like an utter fool another – oh, let's say, thirty times. "No one called? Come on, Peach, it doesn't have to be Prince Charming."

She snapped, "Look, the only call I have right now is the Pakistani in Cambridge, okay?" She was exasperated, and maybe she really had been trying to shield me from something. I had to give her credit for that possibility.

I also didn't know when to let go. "What did he say? Did you tell him I'm on, tonight?"

"Oh, God, honey." Another small chunk of silence. "All right, yeah, I told him you're around tonight. And I told him who else is around. He said fine, you, whatever. I gave it to that new girl from Sudbury. I didn't think you'd want to go."

I didn't say anything. I was busy trying to assimilate the fact that, after whatever it was that had happened between us, he could agree to see me again professionally. That it really didn't matter. Whatever, that was what he had said. Good American colloquialism. Tia, the new girl from Sudbury, whoever. I was, in point of fact, only a hooker, one he had managed to get for free for a while but was willing to pay for when he couldn't.

I had thought that I couldn't possibly feel worse.

I had been wrong.

* * * * * *

I went to school the next day and sat in my new office meeting with an assortment of students whining about grades that shouldn't have come as such a surprise to them.

By seven o'clock I had worked out, showered, and eaten a Weight Watcher's pizza. I called Peach. "Checking in," I said, briefly. She called back within half an hour. "Work," she announced. "He's new, if you can handle that. But he checks out, he's staying at the Sheraton, the concierge says he's been there before. I had a good feeling about him. Let me know what you think."

I imagined that if the concierge had vetted him the client couldn't be too scary. And I really needed to get out of my apartment.

I didn't get any feeling at all about him on the telephone, but that probably wasn't his fault. I should have been excited. I always liked hotel calls, walking down a corridor in a classy place, feeling good, knowing I had just made one hundred fifty or two hundred dollars, knowing that I was attractive, desirable, feeling part of the expensive hush of the lobby, smiling at the doorman on my way out . . . I put on a loose skirt and sweater that covered up my bloating from my recent bingeing and drove to the Sheraton with the radio silent and my head, for once, the same.

Found the room. Found the guy. I felt a little rush of nervous energy when I went in the room, checking him out. New clients made me edgy. He was pleasant, poured me a drink from an opened bottle of white wine. "Can we talk for a few minutes first?"

"I'd like that," I said, the words rote and automatic, and watched him checking out my legs as I sat down on the edge of the bed. He didn't offer any help with my coat; I took it off, put it on the bed next to me, and sipped the wine.

"I just want to be clear," he was saying. "For the two hundred dollars, we can have sex, right? I mean, I can come? Maybe twice?"

Well, it wasn't exactly subtle, but I was used to that by now. "Let's just get comfortable with each other," I suggested, remembering to put the purr into my throat, "Then we'll see what feels good."

He brushed that suggestion aside. "But we'll be able to have sex, won't we?" He should have sounded anxious, but he didn't. He sounded like he was talking from a script. "I mean, for that kind of money, I expect to go all the way."

Odd expression, I thought, for a man in his forties. Something was off. The last time I had had this feeling, it was innocuous, the guy was just embarrassed. Maybe it was okay this time, too.

Or maybe it wasn't.

I put my wineglass on the floor and cleared my throat. If I was wrong about this, I was going to look foolish and I might lose the call, but this time I didn't think that I was wrong. Maybe I had finally been in the business long enough to have developed a feel, a sixth sense about this kind of thing. "Sir," I said, loudly and clearly, the purr a thing of the past. "Are you a police officer?"

He was. I could see it in his eyes even before he stiffened, glanced at the mirror on the closet door, cleared his throat. "I was given to believe that you came here expecting to be paid for sex," he said.

"You were misinformed," I said sweetly. "The dating service called me and said that you wanted to spend an hour with a young lady. You were visiting Boston, maybe I could show you around and we'd hit it off." I was glad I'd worn my loose sweater and not my black lace "uniform" shirt. "And I never go to bed with someone on the first date. Since that seems to be the only thing you're interested in, I guess this won't work out." I stood up and picked up my coat. "So I'll ask you again: are you a police officer, or just an asshole?"

The Gospel According to Peach says that if you ask that question, you're home free. If you ask and they say yes, then it's fine, there was a misunderstanding; Peach owns a dating service. If they don't answer the question, and they are a cop, then any subsequent arrest won't stick: it's entrapment or something like that. I was vague on the details, but I did remember the general idea.

He stood up with me and pulled a wallet out of his pocket. I thought for a moment he was going to try to get me to take money, but then I saw the badge. "I need to see some identification," he said.

The adrenaline that had fueled me until now was gone, and I suddenly felt scared and vulnerable. I couldn't be arrested; if I were, I'd never teach again. Not even evening classes in some community center. Never. Nowhere. "Why do you need ID?" I asked. He had pulled out a pad of paper.

"Routine questions," he said. "Your name?"

"I don't have to give you my name," I said. "You brought me to your room under false pretenses. Once here, I refused your advances and tried to leave. You tried to get personal details about me. What I'm thinking here is stalker, potential rapist, I don't know." He glanced again toward the mirror. I said, "Any video taken here will get thrown out of court, so don't try to scare me." Good thing I had a client who was a lawyer. Good thing my lawyer-client had wanted to impress me with his knowledge of the legal implications of my profession. Good thing I had found our conversations interesting, and had listened. Never knew I'd find them helpful.

He said again, "Your name and address, please. You're resisting an officer in the performance of his duty." He looked smug, and all of a sudden I had had enough. Enough of the smugness on men's faces, enough of playing to their fantasies, of making their pleasure my profession. Enough of the husbands who lied to their wives and fucked callgirls to make themselves feel superior to their poor faithful ball-and-chain. Enough of the pornography, the games, the role-playing. Enough of consorting with the enemy, the man who loves you and hates you all at once and can only resolve that conflict by blaming you for his unease, by taking away your humanity and making you into an object.

Madonna. Whore. Virgin. Slut. Tits. Ass. Womb. Feminist bitch. Medusa. Circe. Penelope. Wife. Prostitute.

This cop in front of me was just as into who I was (not Jen, not Tia, but a generic "hooker") as the clients who paid for their time with me. The only difference was he had managed to get a job where he could be a voyeur and get paid for it instead of paying someone else. Sweet.

I suddenly had had enough. Enough of putting up with bad behavior while condoning it with my participation. Enough of serving needs that should have been dealt with on mental health units. Enough of lying, of purring, of playing the game and feeling oh-so-superior just because I had a fistful of cash at the end of the night.

I took a deep breath. "I'm leaving now," I said to him. "If you try to stop me I'll start screaming attempted rape and I won't stop until you're back in uniform and your wife is asking for a divorce. I came to your room for a drink and a little socializing. You've done nothing but talk about sex since I got here."

The connecting door to the next room opened and another man, older, walked into the room. He opened the closet and turned off the video camera that was mounted on a tripod inside. He looked tired. "How did you know?" he asked, simply. "How did you know he wasn't a trick?"

I stared at him. "You're out of date, I think," I said. I wondered if it was only me to whom my voice sounded on the edge of hysteria. "I've never heard anyone actually say that, before tonight. But maybe I don't move in the right circles." I slid into my coat. "Go down to Kneeland Street," I said. "I've seen women there, if you slow down in your car, they'll come over and talk to you. I'll bet some of them turn tricks, and work for pimps, and talk about their johns. I'll bet you can find your stereotype there if you look hard enough." I turned up my collar. "What if I *had* been a callgirl, Officer? What would you look like, taking me in? I'm not wearing any makeup, my body is pretty much covered up, and I am obviously educated and intelligent. Just like your wife, you're thinking. Or your sister. Or your daughter." I thought he was going to say something; he made a sudden movement that he checked. I was exhausted, and nothing was going to change. Not here, not anywhere.

I called Peach on my way out of the lobby. "Watch your back, girlfriend, I almost got arrested."

"What happened?" She thought I meant I had gotten pulled over, or something.

"Your new client with the good vibes was a cop, babe. Video behind the mirror and everything."

"What? What happened? How did he pick us?" Usually the police went after the "big services, the ones in the Yellow Pages, the ones that could make a splash.

"I don't know. I told him it's a dating service. It's fine, everything's fine, but I'd watch out for a while if I were you."

"Are you all right?" She was a little late in saying it, but I knew that she was sincere. She was doing her best. No; she thought she was doing her best. She really believed that she could make anything all right by her voice, her laughter, her concern. I had fallen for that for three years. I was starting to see through it.

Besides, I was in no mood for an argument. "I don't know, Peach. I'm going home, I'm taking a shower, and I'm throwing out all my work clothes. I'm going back to being poor for a while. I need to be teaching. I need to – God, I don't know. I don't know what I need. All I know is that this isn't it."

She tried to get me to change my mind, of course. I had made a lot of money for her; in the end, I was requested more frequently than the twenty-year old blondes. A lot more frequently. I was helping to define who Peach was, to help her settle into her niche. I wasn't going to be easy to replace.

She had helped me make a lot of money, too. I won't say that it wasn't tempting to do it, to ignore my inner voices and my pride and my feelings and just do it. Spread my legs, say yes, baby, baby, yes, and then go home and pay the bills. But I was troubled by an active intellect. And it wasn't making sense in my head anymore.

I've always made the assumption that life is easier if one is stupid. I stand by that assessment.

Chapter Twenty-two

I don't know, in the end, exactly why I left.

I'm not even sure that it matters. Take your pick: I left because I got scared, or because I got hurt, or even because I grew up, grew out of it. Or for a whole lot of other reasons that I may not even be aware of myself.

In the end, I think that I left because it was simply time to leave. The business had given me what I needed. It gave me financial security while I prepared myself for my career. It gave me an opportunity to feel beautiful and desirable just at the point in my life when Madison Avenue was telling me that I was over the hill. And maybe, too, it gave me the thrill of having lived on the edge for a while, of having done something illegal and glamorous and gotten away with it.

I know that a lot of women leave and come back, because they miss it. They miss whatever it was that it did for them, or because there isn't a lot of work out there that pays as well. A lifestyle becomes a habit if you don't watch out.

I was lucky, because I had known from the beginning that it wasn't forever. I knew that my tenure was finite, that time and gravity were going to take their toll on my body, that I would eventually encounter a situation that my beleaguered ethics couldn't justify away. I had known, from the beginning, that it wasn't my real life. It was wonderful in part, I think, precisely because I knew that it was temporary, ephemeral, impermanent. Knowing that, I could leave it without destroying myself in the process.

I had my own strengths. I had been alone for a long time, alone for years in fact, except for the months I had lived with the rat bastard.

No: come to think of it, I had never been so alone as I had been when I was with him. So even that didn't count.

I knew how to fill my own empty spaces. I didn't ignore them, or deny that they existed; I accepted them and did not allow them to make my decisions for me. By the time I left the escort business, I was teaching full-time, I was learning t'ai chi, I had stopped doing cocaine, and I was beginning to write another book.

I won't say that there were no regrets. Sometimes, even now, when it's around seven o'clock, I'll stop and wonder what's going on tonight. Who's working, what clients will call, that sort of thing. It won't be anybody that I know, not anymore: time has moved on, in this business faster than anywhere else.

But the names don't matter: the needs will always be the same. I know that telephones will ring, drivers will be pulling up to suburban houses, girls will fix their makeup in the vanity mirrors. I remember – with no regrets – the clients posturing, demanding, angry or pathetic or ordinary. I know that tonight, as every night, money will change hands. Slim lines of cocaine will be laid out in somebody's bathroom. Callgirls will give pleasure, excitement, mystery, hope, enchantment. And the clock will be ticking all the time.

I stop and I think if it; then I shrug and head out to the bike path for a ride, or I load the kids into the car for a visit to a bookstore, or I'll remember how seductive I used to be and I'll entice my husband into our bedroom to make sure that I still have the touch. He assures me that I do.

Living your own real life, I have found, is one hell of a lot more interesting than being a professional enacter of somebody else's fantasies.

I still live and work in the Boston area. I have changed my name, have gotten married. I am happily working as a writer now, and find myself challenged and fulfilled by the work that I do. Scuzzy has a microscopic backyard in which to pursue his never-ending fantasy of catching a squirrel.

My husband continues to deal with his knowledge of my former profession. Once, I asked him how he would feel if ever any of his friends found out about my having worked as an escort. "You know those commercials where they say, 'trained professional, do not attempt this at home'?" he asked. "I'll just tell them, well, *we* attempt this at home!"

In those months after he read the e-mail I had written to Roger, I think that it took Tony a long time to rid himself of the myths, of the stereotypes. He thought he was pretty liberated. I put all of his notions to the test. He is a better man than most for being willing to go through it with me.

* * * * * *

Peach is doing well, these days, too. She is married, owns a house. She is no longer the center of a glittering circle of admirers, and she frequents the gym more often than she does the city's newest clubs and restaurants. She travels. She has cook-outs.

I don't think that either of us can remember the last time that we stayed up, still dressed and jazzed and a little railed, drinking and partying, to meet the dawn. I don't think that either of us regrets it.

I can't really tell you anything about the rest of the people I've talked about here. While I am not ashamed of this part of my past, neither am I attached to it, and any connections that I formed then are no longer particularly relevant to my life. I feel some sadness for some of them. I don't think that that will ever go away.

I do expect that some of the women went on, as I did, to claim their career and family choices, enabled by the experience. I also expect that many others did not know when to quit, mismanaged their money, left themselves minimal options and no exit strategies. It is a world that encourages that kind of thinking.

But I still, sometimes, find myself with the same Secret Smile playing with the corners of my mouth, when I'm having a bad day and the kids are being difficult and I have a stack of papers to grade . . . I remember, then, the glamour of those days. And it does, still, make me smile.

Epilogue

As I am writing this book, a number of years after the events I describe occurred, I have to issue a caveat. This morning I listened to a report on the BBC about girls from poverty-stricken countries in eastern Europe being trafficked as prostitutes to serve the "needs" of the peacekeeping troops in Kosovo, and I found myself feeling slightly nauseous.

I am appalled, even now, at the ideas and misconceptions concerning prostitution and women's participation in it. I remain baffled by and angry at the common assertion that the men who employ prostitutes are normal, but that the women who engage in the trade somehow are not.

I have here told one story – mine. I willingly and in fact deliberately entered the employment of an escort agency. At no time, then or now, do I regret having made that decision, or having held that employment.

Because agencies like Peach's exist, agencies that do not exploit or injure or corrupt their employees, a number of women like myself were and continue to be able to attain some measure of financial security in a society where it is statistically difficult for a woman to do so.

I am aware, however, and most urgently want you to be aware, that many women are not in this profession because they hold doctorates and need to pay off student loans. Many women are in fact forced, raped, lied to, torn from their homes and lives and given nothing in return . . . and, to top it off, treated then as morally inferior beings because they have been used to satisfy both the sexual and monetary appetites of supposedly morally superior beings.

Many females, a whole lot of them children, never had the luxury of my choice. And that has not changed. Only the faces, only the names change. There is, it seems, a never-ending supply of young beautiful bodies to satisfy the varied requirements of the predators of our world.

Many women experience what I describe briefly in this book: the slavery of drugs that was imposed on them deliberately so that they in turn could serve as slaves in a business that regards their lives as cheap. Addiction is a horrifying illness. To see its seeds sown and nurtured on purpose, to see life after life ruined for the profit of others, is in my mind beyond criminal. I hope that Dante has a very special ring of Hell reserved for the people that do this.

The only way to stop this trafficking in and profiting from

the use of women's bodies is for prostitution to be legalized. Legalization will open it up to regulation; and regulation means safety.

I have a positive story to tell.

I'm not at all sure that my experience is that of the majority of the women involved in this business.

I started to write this book to answer some of the questions that you might have about the business of mid-level escort services. I am ending it with a request that your interest not stop here. Please refer to the short bibliography and the Web sites that are listed in the Appendix (for what academic can write a book without inserting at least one Appendix?!), and read more about the business.

And please don't be so quick to call us hookers, to dismiss us, to judge us.

We could be your mother, your sister, your girlfriend, your daughter. Even your college professor.

No, I take that back. It's not a matter of saying that we could be. Statistically, we already are.

Appendix

The Web, as you know, is in a constant state of change, so these sites may or may not work for you; but if you go to any search engine and query "prostitution," you'll be able to access these and other sites, some informational, some less so.

In the same way, new books and articles on the subject are always appearing in print. I've arranged the ones that I've encountered into three sections: books on prostitution for a general audience, books for a more academic and/or activist audience, and fiction.

I hope that you'll find something here of use to you

Web sites that might be useful include:

www.prostitutionresearch.com. This site, run by the nonprofit San Francisco Women's Centers, includes pages on Basic Information, Quick Facts, The Law, trafficking, Prostitution and Violence Research, and a number of other articles.

www.bostonphoenix.com/archive/features/97/10/23/prostitution_theory_101.html. Sarah McNaught's brilliant introduction to prostitution.

www.bayswav.org/NTFP.html. National Task Force on Prostitution Web Site.

www.worldsexguide.org. Archives from the Usenet newsgroup. alt.sex.prostitution

www.usa-poll.com. Survey on the possible decriminalization of prostitution.

www.capcat.ksc.net. Childwatch International's Web Site on child prostitution.

www.realm-of-shade.com/meretrix/museum. I cannot comment on the factual reliability of anything in this very personal museum about prostitution, but it's an interesting site.

Books that might be useful (general interest) include:

Bushnell, Candace: *Sex and the City,* c. 2000, Time-Warner, audiobook. Derived from the author's New York Observer column (and made into a television series), chronicles society parties, including presence of prostitutes.

Chapkis, Wendy et. al: *Live Sex Acts: Women Performing Erotic Labor*, c. 1997, Routledge, hardcover & 2nd edition paper

Delacoste, Frederique (ed.): *Sex Work: Writings by Women in the Sex Industry*, c. 1987, 1998, Cleis Press, 2nd edition is in paper. A collection of short stories, essays, poetry written by street prostitutes, exotic dancers, nude models, porn stars and massage parlor workers.

French, Dolores: *Working: My Life as a Prostitute*, c. 1998, Gollanc, Victor (publishers), paperback. First-person account of the life of a street prostitute.

Godwin, Rebecca: *Keeper of the House*, c. 1995, St. Martin's Press, trade paperback. Story of a famous South Carolina house of prostitution from its inception during the Depression to the end of its 40-year life. Unclear to me whether this is fiction or non-fiction or a mixture of the two.

Goodall, Richard: *The Comfort of Sin: Prostitutes and Prostitution in the 1990s*, c. 1996, Renaissance Books, trade paper. Overview of prostitution, its history, causes, arguments for and against legalization, homosexuality in prostitution, brothels, and case histories.

Hensen, Maria Rosa: *Comfort Woman: A Filipina's Story of Prostitution and Slavery Under the Japanese Military*, c. 1999, Rowman & Littlefield, trade paper. Autobiography of a Filipina woman who was abducted in 1943 at age fifteen and forced into prostitution.

Howard, Keith (ed.): *True Stories of Korean Comfort Women*, publishing information unavailable, hardcover.

Jeffreys, Sheila: *The Idea of Prostitution*, c. 1998, SpiniFex Press, paperback. Analysis challenging the ides of prostitution as sexual liberation.

Jenness, Valerie: *Making It Work: The Prostitutes' Rights Movement in Perspective*, c. 1993, Aldine de Gruyter, hardcover. A chronicle of the COYOTE movement.

Louis, Lisa: *Butterflies of the Night: Mama-Sans, Geisha, Strippers, and the Japanese Men They Serve*, c. 1992, Weatherhill, hardcover. Explores what is called in Japan the "ejaculation industry."

Seabrook, Jeremy: *Travels in the Skin Trade: Tourism and the Sex Industry*, c. 1997, Pluto Press, paperback. Centers on the sex industry in Thailand.

Seagraves, Anne: *Soiled Doves: Prostitution in the Early West*, c. 1994, Wesanne Productions, paperback.

Shaner, Lora: *Madam: Chronicles of a Nevada Cathouse*, c. 1998, Huntington Press, hardcover. Anecdotal stories written from the perspective of a former Defense Department employee who was a madam at Sheri's Ranch for five years.

Sisters of the Heart: *The Brothel Bible: The Cathouse Experience*, c. 1997, Sisters of the Heart Publications, trade paperback. Feminist perspective.

Sprinkle, Annie: *Annie Sprinkle: Post Porn Modernist: My Twenty-Five Years as a Multimedia Whore*, c. 1998, Cleis Press, 2nd edition paperback. Scrapbook of the author's life as the self-proclaimed "High Priestess of Porn."

Tattersall, Clare: *Drugs, Runaways, and Teen Prostitution*, c. 1999, Rosen Publishing Group, hardcover. Explores the path from runaway to teen prostitute.

Washburn, Josie: *The Underworld Sewer: A Prostitute Reflects on Life in the Trade, 1871-1909*, c. 1909, 1997, University of Nebraska Press, 2nd ed. paper. Reprint of the reflections of a former prostitute and madam talking about her career in a brothel in Lincoln, Nebraska.

Williams, Miriam: *Heaven's Harlots: My Fifteen Years as a Sacred Prostitute in the Children of God Cult*, c. 1998, William Morrow & Co., hardcover. An account of a woman's life in and escape from a cult where she was used by the leader to provide sex to further the cult's cause.

Wiltz, Christine: *The Last Madam: A Life in the New Orleans Underworld*, c. 2000, Faber and Faber, hardcover, subsequently in paperback. Account of the life of Norma Wallace, who ran the last famous bordello in Storyville, New Orleans.

Books more academic in nature include:

Anderson, Amanda: *Tainted Souls and Painted Faces: The Rhetoric of Fallenness in Victorian Culture*, c. 1994, Cornell University Press, trade paperback. Examines the conceptions of prostitutes, adulteresses, and other "sexually illicit" women in mid-19th century England.

Bales, Kevin: *Disposable People: New Slavery in the Global Economy*, c. 2000, University of California Press, trade paperback. Bales' study is of what he calls the "new slavery" which he documents in Thailand, Mauritania, Brazil, Pakistan, India, the United States and France. Prostitution appears to be a minor part of the industry that he is documenting.

Bernheimer, Charles: *Figures of Ill Repute: Representing Prostitution in Nineteenth-Century France*, c. 1989, Harvard University Press, hardcover. Discusses prostitution as a social phenomenon and as a subject in literature and art.

Best, Joel and David R. Johnson, eds.: *Controlling Vice: Regulating Brothel Prostitution in Saint Paul, 1865-1883*, c. 1999, Ohio State University Press, trade paperback. Interesting approach: the criminal justice system in Minnesota regulated rather than attempted to eradicate prostitution.

Bishop, Ryan and Lillian S. Robinson: *Night Market: Sexual Cultures and the Thai Economic Miracle*, c. 1998, Routledge, hardcover. Detailed account of sex industry in Thailand that is the centerpiece of the country's tourism industry.

Brock, Rita: *Casting Stones: Prostitution and Liberation in Asia and the United States*, c. 1996, Augsburg Fortress, trade paper. Analysis by feminist theologians of the role of religion in prostitution.

Butler, Anne: *Daughters of Joy, Sisters of Misery: Prostitutes in the American West, 1965-90*, reprint 19990, University of Illinois Press, paperback/textbook. Delineates the role played by prostitutes as workers in the development of the West's institutions, especially the legal order.

Connelly, Mark Thomas: *The Response to Prostitution in the Progressive Era*, c.1980, University of North Carolina Press, hardcover.

Corbin, Alain: *Women For Hire: Prostitution and Sexuality in France after 1850*, translation c. 1996, Harvard University Press, trade paper. First systematic study of the commercial and political aspects of the sex trade with a special focus on brothel-based prostitution as an enterprise integral to capitalism.

Davidson, Julia O'Connell: *Prostitution, Power and Freedom*, c. 1999, University of Michigan Press, trade paperback. The author is a sociologist whose study includes a number of very brief interviews with people from all corners of the international sex trade.

Gibson, Mary: *Prostitution and the State in Italy,* 1860-1915, c. 2000, 2nd ed. trade paper. Traces the history of prostitution during the period delineated, when all prostitutes were required to register with the police, live in licensed brothels, undergo health examinations, and be treated in a special hospital if infected with venereal disease.

Gilfoye, Timothy: *City of Eros: New York City, Prostitution, and the Commercialization of Sex, 1790-1920*, c. 1994, WW Norton, trade paper. Examines the role of sex in forming New York's neighborhoods, social roles, and politics.

Goldman, Marion: *Gold Diggers and Silver Miners: Prostitution and Social Life on the Comstock Lode*, c. 1981, University of Michigan Press, trade paper/textbook.

Gronewold, Sue: *Beautiful Merchandise: Prostitution in China, 1860-1936*, c.1982, Harrington Park Press, trade paper.

Guy, Donna: *Sex and Danger in Buenos Aires: Prostitution, Family and Nation in Argentina*, c. 1995, University of Nebraska

Press, trade paper. A study of prostitution in the Argentine capital from the 1860s to 1954.

Hall, Bruce Edward: *Diamond Street: The Story of the Little Town with the Big Red Light District*, c. 1994, Black Dome Press, trade paperback. Until 1950, Hudson, New York, was "the place to go for a good time," where prostitution fairly flourished. Straightforward narrative.

Hart, Angie: *Buying and Selling Power: Prostitution in Spain*, c. 1997, Westview Press, hardcover. Examines the identities of both clients and prostitutes with an emphasis on gender-specific power.

Hershatter, Gail: *Dangerous Pleasures: Prostitution and Modernity in Twentieth-Century Shanghai*, c. 1998, University of California Press, trade paperback.

Hicks, George: *The Comfort Women: Japan's Brutal Regime of Enforced Prostitution in the Second World War*, c. 1997, WW Norton, hardcover. Narrates story of officially sanctioned brothels set up across Asia to service the needs of Japanese forces.

Hill, Marilyn Wood: *Their Sisters' Keepers: Prostitution in New York City, 1830-1870*, c. 1993, University of California Press. Argues that prostitution was more positive than negative, releasing women from gender constraints and granting them economic opportunity.

Hoigard, Cecilie and Liv Finstad: *Backstreets: Prostitution, Money and Love*, c. 1992 Pennsylvania State University Press, trade paperback.

International Labour Office: *The Sex Sector: The Economic and Social Bases of Prostitution in Southeast Asia*, c. 1998, International Labour Office, trade paper. Case studies prepared by a number of different researchers.

Karras, Ruth Mazo: *Common Women: Prostitution and Sexuality in Medieval England*. c. 1998, Oxford University Press, trade paperback. Issue at stake is not sexuality but women's independence. In my opinion, *should* be rewritten for a general audience, too fascinating to keep cloistered in academia.

Kempadoo, Kamala (ed.): *Global Sex Workers: Rights, Resistance, and Redefinition*, c. 1998, Routledge, hardcover. A collection of essays by scholars, journalists, and sex workers with a focus on developing countries.

Kim, Elaine (ed.): *The Comfort Women: Colonialism, War, and Sex, Vol. 5*, c. 1997, Duke University Press, trade paper.

Kim-Gibson, Dai Sil: *Silence Broken: Korean Comfort Woman*, c.2000, Mid-Prairie Books, trade paper.

Langum, David: *Crossing over the Line: Legislating Morality and the Mann Act*, c. 1994, University of Chicago Press, hardcover. Discussion of the underlying basis for the Mann Act (1910) that made it illegal to transport women across state lines for "immoral purposes."

Lowry, Thomas: *The Civil War Bawdy Houses of Washington D.C.*, c.1997, Sergeant Kirkland's Press, hardcover.

Moon, Katherine H.S.: *Sex Among Allies: Military Prostitution in U.S.-Korea Relations*, c. 1997, Columbia University Press, trade paperback/textbook. An exploration of how Korean prostitutes were used by the U.S. and Korean governments in their security agreements.

Mumford, Kevin: *Interzones: Black/White Sex Districts in Chicago and New York in the Early Twentieth Century*, c. 1997, Columbia University Press, hardcover. A reconstruction of the mixed-race underworld of the Great Migration and the Progressive era to reveal how these subcultures transformed American culture.

Nagle, Jill (ed.): *Whores and Other Feminists*, c. 1996, Routledge, trade paper. Uses essay and personal narrative to discuss sex practices and their interface with feminist thought.

Pettiway, Leon: *Honey, Honey, Miss Thang*, c. 1996, Temple University Press, trade paper. This study, done by a professor of criminal justice, explores the life of five African-American "drug-using, street-walking, cross-dressing gay hustlers."

Pettiway, Leon: *Workin' It: Women Living Through Drugs and Crime*, c. 1997, Temple University Press, hardcover. Anecdotal study of five female drug users involved in a number of crimes, including prostitution.

Rosen, Ruth: *The Lost Sisterhood: Prostitution in America, 1900-1918*, c. 1990, Johns Hopkins University Press, textbook-paperback. Covers a period in which one of the most vigorous campaigns against prostitution took place.

Schellstede, Sangmie Choi (ed.): *Comfort Women Speak: Testimony by Sex Slaves of the Japanese Military*, c. 2000, Holmes and Meier, hardcover. Accompanied by photographs.

Selcer, Richard: *Hell's Half Acre: The Life and Legend of a Red-Light District*, c. 1991, Texas Christian University Press, trade paperback. Details the "Paris of the Plains" existence of Fort Worth, Texas, beginning with the cattle drives of the 1870s and ending after World War One.

Sleightholme, Carolyn: *Guilty Without Trial: Women in the Sex Trade in Calcutta*, c. 1997, Rutgers University Press, hardcover. Examines the double standards of the Indian sex-trade industry.

Stange, Margit: *Personal Property: Wives, White Slaves, and the Market in Women*, c. 1998, Johns Hopkins University Press, hardcover. An analysis of white slavery literature between 1909 and 1914 in relation to other key American writings of the time.

Statz, Margaret et. al., eds., *The Legacies of the Comfort Women of World War II*, c. 2000, ME Sharpe, hardcover & mass market paper.

Walkowitz, Judith: *City of Dreadful Delight: Narratives of Sexual Danger in Late-Victorian London*, c.1992, University of Chicago Press, trade paperback.

Walkowitz, Judith: Prostitution and Victorian Society: Woman, Class, and the State, c. 1982, Cambridge University Press, trade paper/textbook. Examines the state regulation of prostitution in mid-Victorian England as established by the Contagious Diseases Acts of 1864, 1866 and 1869.

Finally a small sampling of novels written about prostitution:

Benderson, Bruce: *User*

Chua, Lawrence: *Gold By The Inch*

Cleland, Jamesa: *Fanny Hill*

Corbett, Jack: *Death on the Wild Side*

Crane, Stephen: *Maggie, A Girl of the Streets*

Flanagan, Mary: *Adele*

Friedman, Josh Alan: *Tales of Times Square*

Gash, Jonathan: *Prey Dancing*

Guyotat, Pierre: *Prostitution*

Hall, Patricia: *Perils of the Night*

Hamilton, Fritz: *Love, Debra*

Harvey, James Neal: *Painted Ladies*

Holman, Sheri: *The Dress Lodger*

Hugo, Victor: *Les Misérables*

Jennings, James: *The Autobiography of a Flea and Other Tart Tales*

Kunin, Vladimir: *Intergirl*

McCabe, Patrick: *Breakfast on Pluto*

O'Brien, John: *Leaving Las Vegas*

Rechy, John: *City of Night*

Robinson, Spider: *Lady Slings the Booze*

Vollmann, William: *Whores for Gloria*